Against Cognitivism
Alternative Foundations for Cognitive Psychology

edited by
Arthur Still and **Alan Costall**

New York London Toronto Sydney Tokyo

First published 1991 by
Harvester Wheatsheaf,
66 Wood Lane End, Hemel Hempstead,
Hertfordshire, HP2 4RG
A division of
Simon & Schuster International Group

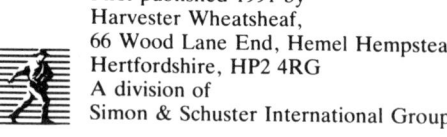

© Editors' Introductions, preparation and Chapter One,
   Arthur Still and Alan Costall
© Chapter Two, Arthur Still 1991
© Chapter Three, Don Mixon 1991
© Chapter Four, Alan Costall 1991
© Chapter Five, John Shotter 1991
© Chapter Six, Ivana Marková 1991
© Chapter Seven, Neil Bolton 1991
© Chapter Eight, Edward K. Morris 1991
© Chapter Nine, Alan Costall 1991
© Chapter Ten, Edward Reed 1991
© Chapter Eleven, William Noble 1991
© Chapter Twelve, Arthur Still and Alan Costall 1991
© Chapter Thirteen, Benny Shanon 1991

All rights reserved. No part of this publication may be
reproduced, stored in a retrieval system, or transmitted,
in any form, or by any means, electronic, mechanical,
photocopying, recording or otherwise, without the
prior permission, in writing, from the publisher.

Typeset in 10/12 pt Times by Photoprint, Torquay

Printed and bound in Great Britain by
BPCC Wheatons Ltd, Exeter

British Library Cataloguing in Publication Data

Against cognitivism: Alternative foundations for
cognitive psychology.
   I. Still, Arthur II. Costall, Alan
   153

ISBN 0-7450-1025-3

1 2 3 4 5   95 94 93 92 91

Contents

Contributors   vii

1. Introduction: Cognitivism as an approach to cognition   1
   Alan Costall and Arthur Still

2. Mechanism and Romanticism: A selective history   7
   Arthur Still

3. On not-doing and on trying and failing   27
   Don Mixon

4. Frederic Bartlett and the rise of prehistoric psychology   39
   Alan Costall

5. The rhetorical-responsive nature of mind: A social constructionist account   55
   John Shotter

6. The concepts of the universal in the Cartesian and Hegelian frameworks   81
   Ivana Marková

7. Cognitivism: A phenomenological critique   103
   Neil Bolton

8. The contextualism that is behaviour analysis: An alternative to cognitive psychology   123
   Edward K. Morris

9. 'Graceful degradation': Cognitivism and the metaphors of the computer   151
   Alan Costall

10. James Gibson's ecological approach to cognition   171
    Edward Reed

11. Ecological realism and the fallacy of 'objectification'   199
    William Noble

12. The mutual elimination of dualism in Vygotsky and Gibson   225
    Arthur Still and Alan Costall

13. Alternative theoretical frameworks for psychology: A synopsis   237
    Benny Shanon

Index   265

Contributors

Neil Bolton is Professor of Education at the University of Sheffield. During the 1970s he published detailed critiques of the empiricist and Piagetian theories of cognition, and began the phenomenological approach to education which he has developed over the last ten years. His most recent publication in this area is 'Educational psychology and the politics and practice of education', in N. Jones and N. Frederickson (eds), *Refocussing Educational Psychology*, (London: Falmer Press, 1990).

Alan Costall is Senior Lecturer at Southampton University. He is co-author of *Michotte's Experimental Phenomenology of Perception* (Hillsdale, NJ: Erlbaum, 1991). His work explores the implications of an ecological approach to psychology. He is currently working on a book on children's drawings that examines the assumptions – about pictures, vision and children – that structure existing theories.

Don Mixon is Associate Professor of Psychology at the University of Wollongong, Australia. He is well known for his critical studies of the use of deception in social psychology, and Milgram's research on conformity. He has recently published *Obedience and Civilization: Authorized crime and the normality of evil* (London: Pluto Press, 1989), and is currently working on a new book, *Psychology of Freedom*.

Ivana Marková is Professor of Psychology at Stirling University. In her books (especially *Paradigms, Thought, and Language*, Wiley, 1982) she has made powerful use of her Hegelian background in developing alternatives to the Cartesian and empiricist assumptions that

Anglo-American psychologies of development and language are still struggling to overcome. She is at present concerned with biological approaches to language and mind, and is studying dialogues and conversations in people with impaired speech and learning difficulties. She is co-editing a series of books for Harvester Wheatsheaf on the dynamics of dialogue; the first of these, *Dynamics of Dialogue* (edited by herself and K. Foppa), has already appeared.

Edward K. Morris is Professor in the Department of Human Development and Family Life at the University of Kansas. His research and many publications promote a contextualist approach to psychological problems, in contrast to the mechanistic emphasis of cognitive psychology. He has recently co-edited a book with J.T. Todd reassessing the status and history of behaviourism (*Modern Perspectives on Classical and Contemporary Behaviorism*, Westport, CT: Greenwood Press, 1990).

William Noble is Associate Professor of Psychology at the University of New England, Armidale. His publications include *The Assessment of Impaired Hearing* (New York: Academic Press, 1978) and a series of papers on auditory spatial perception, and auditory disabilities and handicaps. His recent work (in association with Iain Davidson) has concerned the evolutionary emergence of modern human behaviour.

Edward Reed is Professor of Philosophy at Drexel University, and also a Research Associate at Moss Rehabilitation Hospital. He has published extensively on the history and theory of perception and action, and has brought together a wide range of resources (from history, philosophy and biology, as well as psychology) to develop an ecological alternative to cognitivist theory. He has published a biography of James Gibson (*James J. Gibson and the Psychology of Perception*, New Haven, CT: Yale University Press, 1988) and is writing a book on the degradation of intellectual labour in the twentieth century.

Benny Shanon is a Professor in the Psychology Department at the Hebrew University, Jerusalem. He has been Visiting Professor and Fellow Scientist at Cornell, Princeton, Swarthmore, Bielefeld, and the Centre for the Study of Epistemology and Autonomy in Paris. His research interests range from the semantics and pragmatics of natural language to the phenomenology of creative thought, but the main topic of his current work concerns the conceptual foundations of cognitive science. The prime focus of this work is the criticism of the representational theory of mind and the search for alternatives; this research is summarized in a forthcoming monograph, *Representations and Presentations* (1992).

John Shotter is at present Cornell Visiting Professor at Swarthmore College. With the publication of a collection of his papers in *Social Accountability and Selfhood* (Oxford: Blackwell, 1984) he has established himself as a prominent critic of the mechanistic assumptions of academic psychology, and as a pioneer in exploring alternatives based upon a social conception of human beings. He and Kenneth Gergen co-edited *Texts of Identity* (London: Sage, 1989), a volume in their series 'Inquiries in Social Construction'.

Arthur Still is a retired Senior Lecturer in Psychology at Durham University. He is joint editor, with Irving Velody, of *History of the Human Sciences*, and is co-editing a book on English reactions to Michel Foucault's *Madness and Civilization*. He is trying to spell out the history and philosophy of a mutualist approach to psychology and, with Jim Good, is attempting a synthesis of ecological and Vygotskyan approaches in their studies of infant–caretaker interactions during meal times.

1
Introduction
Cognitivism as an approach to cognition
Alan Costall and Arthur Still

> The human is an animate organism, with a biological basis and an evolutionary and cultural history. Moreover, the human is a social animal, interacting with others, with the environment, and with itself. The core disciplines of cognitive science have tended to ignore these aspects of behavior. The results have been considerable progress on some fronts, but sterility overall, for the organism we are analyzing is conceived as pure intellect, communicating with one another in logical dialogue, perceiving, remembering, thinking when appropriate, reasoning its way through well-formed problems that are encountered in the day. Alas, that description does not fit actual behavior.
>
> (NORMAN, 1981, p. 266)

Over the last twenty-five years, psychology has become preoccupied with a particular concern. Psychology has become *cognitive* psychology. This emphasis is reflected in the content of research, with a widespread proliferation of work on many of the topics described in Neisser's *Cognitive Psychology* (1967). Yet processes one would most directly identify as 'cognitive' – creative thinking and consciousness – have been surprisingly neglected. The real change within psychology concerns an approach – cogniti*vism* – and what is claimed for it. Thus, although cognition is taken to be the primary object of study, the claims of cognitive theory go well beyond this, and the theory is being used to integrate many of the previously diverse areas of psychology: perception, social psychology, emotion, development and psychopathology.

When did these new expansions in cognitive psychology begin? Gardner (1987) has suggested the Hixon symposium of 1948, whereas George Miller (cited in Baars, 1986, p. 211) proposes a meeting on information theory held at Harvard in 1956 – where he read a paper – as a more significant starting point. Then there were the definitive textbooks, such as *Cognitive Psychology*, and the founding of institutions such as the Center for Cognitive Studies at Harvard in 1960. Some, however, would regard these earlier developments more as preparations for 'cognitive science', the coalition of several disciplines that occurred sometime during the 1970s.

This cognitivist turn in psychology has attracted sustained criticism from many directions: from marginalized groups within psychology (ecological psychology, radical behaviourism; sociohistorical psychology); from philosophy and sociology (ethnomethodology, linguistic philosophy and phenomenology); from computer science; and from a number of writers on ideological rather than academic grounds. (See, for example, Bickhard and Richie, 1983; Bruner, 1990; Coulter, 1983, 1989; de Gelder, 1985; Dietrich, 1990; Dreyfus, 1972; Gibson, 1979; Hamlyn, 1990; Heil, 1981; Heritage, 1984; Lakoff, 1987; Lave, 1988; Malcolm, 1971; Middleton and Edwards, 1990; Prilleltensky, 1990; Russell, 1984; Sampson, 1981; Searle, 1988; Shanon, 1988; Skinner, 1977, 1985; Varela, 1988; Williams, 1985; Winograd and Flores, 1986; and Woolgar, 1987.)

Cognitivism involves an appeal to 'internal cognitive processes' (Haugeland, 1978) and these processes are usually envisaged in terms of rules and representations defined in symbolic or propositional form (Newell, Shaw and Simon, 1958). Many of the criticisms levelled against cognitivism have therefore been aimed at this particular version of cognitive theory, even when the argument has had a more general force. The impact of such criticisms has been softened by the fact that serious limitations of 'rules and representations' as an explanatory scheme have been recognized within cognitive psychology itself. There is the problem of *solipsism*: how can the knower ever reach beyond internal representations to the reality they are supposed to represent? There is the problem of *development*: how can a system of formal rules ever be flexible enough to capture the mutuality between a growing organism and its richly structured and changing environment? And there is the related problem of *relevance*: how does anyone following a rule know when to apply that rule? (The so-called 'frame' problem.) Most generally, there is the problem of *meaning*: how do symbolic representations attain their semantic status?

These problems, however, have not provoked any noticeable anxiety within cognitivism. Of the possible defensive options available, the main one chosen has been the 'no alternative' option, the insistence that cognitivism is the only game in town. With this goes an airy optimism, a confidence that these problems will eventually be solved, and hence are not *really* problems at all (e.g. Johnson-Laird, 1988, p. 34). Less common has been the 'Fodor option' where one tries to keep a reasonably straight face while presenting the absurd consequences of the scheme as exciting theoretical revelations (Fodor, 1975, 1980, 1981). Finally, and more positively, there is the recent attempt by neo-connectionism to reformulate representationalism in order to address some, if not all, of these problems.

In spite of fundamental difficulties, the 'cognitive revolution' is now well established, and several books have recently appeared which attempt to assess its achievements (Baars, 1986; Gardner, 1987; Knapp and Robertson, 1986; Schlecter and Toglia, 1986). Although the authors and editors of these books were by no means intent upon mere celebration, they largely accept cognitivism as the basis for any future developments.

In 1985 we first started to prepare a edited collection of criticisms of current cognitive psychology, from several different viewpoints – historical, philosophical, phenomenological and political, as well as psychological. The point was to question cognitive psychology, but not to deny it altogether. Even less did we intend to deny the existence of cognition, or its validity as a concept. The questioning implied by the title was of the dominant modern approach to cognitive psychology – namely, cognitivism. This book, *Cognitive Psychology in Question*, was published in January 1987. The present version is not a completely new book, since four of the chapters (by Don Mixon, Ivana Marková, Neil Bolton and Edward Reed) are the same, apart from minor revisions and updating, and two (by John Shotter and William Noble) address themes these authors had raised in their earlier chapters. But neither is the present book simply a revision, since the bulk of the material is new and seven chapters have been omitted. Why then this rather anomalous publication, neither revision nor an entirely new book, but a redoing of the old?

Part of the reason lies in the reactions to the earlier book, by publishers' readers and by reviewers of the finished product:

Basically the authors are against the study of psychology as such and set up straw 'cognitivism' men to represent what they don't like about psychology. . . . Some dislike the experimental method as such, some dislike a mechanistic approach to man, some don't think human behaviour is lawful, some are opposed to rules, most seem to be against the rather innocuous idea that we have mental representations of ideas in our heads. (Publisher's review)

[The] editors do their best to stitch a theme together with short introductions to each section containing often irrelevant attacks against cognitivists. . . . [The tone of their commentaries suggests that] the editors must have both been bitten by rabid cognitivists in their early childhood. (*Current Psychological Research and Reviews*)

4 Against Cognitivism

The insidious part of this book is that (at the editorial level) it variously refers to 'cognitivism', cognitive psychology, and cognitive science as though they were synonymous, and as though they were homogeneous. This is wrong, and the book does not do justice to the variety of activity, breadth of thought, and differences in interest which make up the community of individuals to which one or more of these labels might apply. (*British Journal of Psychology*)

The most extreme reaction was by a reviewer for *The Quarterly Journal of Experimental Psychology*, the house journal of the Experimental Psychology Society. The reviewer began: 'This book almost makes one envy the illiterate. Rarely has a work of such wooliness of thought, meandering prose, and gross self-congratulation appeared'; the reviewer continued, after pointing out copious errors, 'I have tried long and hard, but I cannot think of anything complementary [*sic*] to say about this book'; and ended: 'cognitive psychology is never put in question, but the business sense of Harvester Press who published this appalling work is.' Reading between the lines, we could not help feeling that this reviewer did not really like the book (or us) very much at all. Our spirits were raised, therefore, by Robert Sternberg's review in *Contemporary Psychology*, where he wrote: 'A truly attractive feature of this book is that it not only questions the assumptions and practices of cognitive psychology but also provides constructive alternatives to the cognitive enterprise.' This captures nicely what we ourselves had in mind for the book.

Several things seem clear from these and other reactions to *Cognitive Psychology in Question*. First, evaluations were diverse and sometimes extreme, suggesting to us that the topics of the book reflected an important focus of intellectual change. It seemed worthwhile, therefore, to try to take it further, and to include some relevant recent developments, especially in connectionism (Chapter 9), social constructionism (Chapter 5) and contextualism (Chapter 8). Second, our attempts to understand cognitivism and its alternatives *in historical and political context*, did not have as much impact as we had hoped. Accordingly, we have placed a greater emphasis on these aspects (Chapters 2, 4 and 5). Finally – and most striking – there was a frequent assumption that *Cognitive Psychology in Question* was launching an attack on cognitive psychology in itself, and on cognition as a concept and as a topic for scientific study. Reed's chapter on the ecological approach to cognition (Chapter 10 of the present book) should have made it clear that this was not the case, but the misunderstanding remained. As the title of the present book indicates, our purpose is to challenge cognitivism as a basis for the psychology of cognition. The concern, therefore, of the following chapters is to explain what cognitivism really means, and why alternative approaches are required. The chapters are introduced by brief editorial commentaries to help underscore their common theme. If *Against Cognitivism* still appears to be 'against the study of psychology as such', then this may be a reflection of the problem we seek to address – the domination of psychology by cognitive psychology, and of cognitive psychology by cognitivism.

References

Baars, B.J. (ed.) (1986), *The Cognitive Revolution in Psychology*, New York: Guilford Press.
Bickhard, M.H. and Richie, D.M. (1983), *On the Nature of Representation*, New York: Praeger.
Bruner, J. (1990), *Acts of Meaning*, Cambridge, MA: Harvard University Press.
Costall, A.P. and Still, A.W. (eds) (1987), *Cognitive Psychology in Question*, Hemel Hempstead: Harvester Wheatsheaf.
Coulter, J. (1983), *Rethinking Cognitive Theory*, London: Macmillan.
Coulter, J. (1989), *Mind in Action*, Cambridge: Polity Press.
de Gelder, B. (1985), 'The cognitivist conjuring trick or how development vanished', in C.J. Bailey and R. Harris (eds), *Developmental Mechanisms of Language*, London: Pergamon Press, pp. 149–66.
Dietrich, E. (1990), 'Programs in the search for intelligent machines: The mistaken foundations of AI', in D. Partridge and Y. Wilks (eds), *The Foundations of Artificial Intelligence: A Sourcebook*, Cambridge: Cambridge University Press, pp. 223–9.
Dreyfus, H. (1972), *What Computers Can't Do*, New York: Harper & Row.
Fodor, J.A. (1975), *The Language of Thought*, New York: Crowell.
Fodor, J.A. (1980), 'Methodological solipsism considered as a research strategy in cognitive psychology', *Behavioral and Brain Sciences*, 3, 63–110.
Fodor, J.A. (1981), *Representations*, Cambridge, MA: MIT.
Gardner, H. (1987), *The Mind's New Science: A history of the cognitive revolution* (paperback edn), New York: Basic Books.
Gibson, J.J. (1979), *The Ecological Approach to Visual Perception*, Boston, MA: Houghton Mifflin.
Hamlyn, D.W. (1990), *In and Out of the Black Box: On the philosophy of cognition*, Oxford: Blackwell.
Haugeland, J. (1978), 'The nature and plausibility of cognitivism', *Behavioral and Brain Sciences*, 2, 215–60.
Heil, J. (1981), 'Does cognitive psychology rest on a mistake?' *Mind*, 90, 321–42.
Heritage, J. (1984), *Garfinkel and Ethnomethodology*, Cambridge: Polity Press.
Johnson-Laird, P.N. (1988), *The Computer and the Mind*, Cambridge, MA: Harvard University Press.
Knapp, T.J. and Robertson, L.C. (eds) (1986), *Approaches to Cognition: Contrasts and controversies*, Hillsdale, NJ: Erlbaum.
Lakoff, G. (1987), *Women, Fire, and Dangerous Things: What categories reveal about the mind*, Chicago: University of Chicago Press.
Lave, J. (1988), *Cognition in Practice: Mind, mathematics and culture in everyday life*, Cambridge: Cambridge University Press.
Malcolm, N. (1971), 'The myth of cognitive processes and structures', in T.

Mischel (ed.), *Cognitive Development and Epistemology*, New York: Academic Press, pp. 385–92.

Middleton, D. and Edwards, D. (eds) (1990), *Collective Remembering*, London: Sage.

Neisser, U. (1967), *Cognitive Psychology*, New York: Appleton-Century-Crofts.

Newell, A., Shaw, J.C. and Simon, H. (1958), 'Elements of a theory of human problem solving', *Psychological Review*, 65, 151–66.

Norman, D.A. (1981), 'Twelve issues in cognitive science,' in D.A. Norman (ed.), *Perspectives on Cognitive Science*, Hillsdale, NJ: Erlbaum, pp. 265–95.

Prilleltensky, I. (1990), 'On the social and political implications of cognitive psychology', *Journal of Mind and Behavior*, 11, 127–36.

Russell, J. (1984), *Explaining Mental Life: Some philosophical issues in psychology*, London: Macmillan.

Sampson, E.E. (1981), 'Cognitive psychology as ideology', *American Psychologist*, 36, 730–43.

Schlecter, T.M. and Toglia, M.P. (1986), *New Directions in Cognitive Science*, Norwood, NJ: Ablex.

Searle, J. (1989), *Mind, Brains and Science: The 1984 Reith lectures*, Harmondsworth: Penguin.

Shanon, B. (1988), 'Semantic representation of meaning: A critique', *Psychological Bulletin*, 104, 70–83.

Skinner, B.F. (1977), 'Why I am not a cognitive psychologist', *Behaviorism*, 5, 1–10.

Skinner, B.F. (1985), 'Cognitive science and behaviourism', *British Journal of Psychology*, 76, 291–301.

Varela, F.J. (1988), *Connaître – Les sciences cognitives: Tendances et perspectives*, Paris: Editions du Seuil.

Velichovskii, B.M. (1986), 'Methodological problems in cognitive psychology', *Soviet Psychology*, 25, 29–77.

Williams, M. (1985), 'Wittgenstein's rejection of scientific psychology', *Journal for the Theory of Social Behaviour*, 15, 203–23.

Winograd, T. and Flores, F. (1986), *Understanding Computers and Cognition*, New York: Ablex.

Woolgar, S. (1987), 'Reconstructing man and machine: A note on sociological critiques of cognitivism', in W.E. Bijke, T.P. Hughes and T.J. Pinch (eds), *The Social Construction of Technological Systems: New directions in the sociology and history of technology*, Cambridge, MA: MIT, pp. 311–28.

2
Mechanism and Romanticism: A selective history

Arthur Still

Editors' introduction

The seventeenth-century philosopher Descartes, with his dualisms of body and mind, organism and environment, and his mechanistic account of the physical universe, is commonly taken as a starting point for cognitivism. The following chapter is no exception, but the focus is less on dualism as such than on Descartes's carefully elaborated method for acquiring scientific knowledge, and his insistence that one should rely only upon 'clear and distinct' ideas of a kind he found in mathematics. On this view, the proper function of language is to describe the world by attaching labels to ideas, and its ultimate achievement is to represent the reality uncovered by science. An inevitable development of this thinking leads to the cognitivist account of experience as based upon mental representations of the world, and the rules governing their manipulation.

The result has been an attitude towards modern science that elevates physics and the exact sciences at the expense of the social sciences, leading to the familiar partitions of academic disciplines. Partitions have been especially divisive for those caught in the middle, like psychologists. Cognitive psychology has identified with the hard sciences by drawing its methods from the laboratory and its vocabulary from computer engineering, and neglecting vital areas of human experience that cannot be assimilated to this mechanistic approach. This one-sidedness is not new. It was part of the tradition of associationism in the eighteenth and nineteenth centuries, which was made possible by Cartesian dualism and opposed by the philosophers of the Romantic movement, such as Coleridge.

The greatest challenge, however, came from William James. His description of the 'stream of thought' contained a thoroughgoing recognition that consciousness is not made up of discrete, static

8 Against Cognitivism

ideas, but is primarily a flow of vague, fleeting feelings of relation. This effectively undermined the concept of the mind as a repository of representations, and opened the way to the critiques of dualism and alternatives to cognitivism that have been a feature of twentieth-century thought.

*   *   *

Cognitivism is a complex of interrelated methods, arguments and assumptions. Especially important are two dualisms – of mind and body, and of organism and environment – though nowadays they tend to be stated less starkly – as hardware and software, for instance (see this volume, Chapter 9). Together these make possible the abstractions from everyday activity embodied in laboratory research on cognition.[1] To be against cognitivism is generally to be against dualism, to support a mutualism of organism and environment, and to be suspicious of abstract generalizations established under the constraints of laboratory psychology. But questioning of isolated parts may have only a limited impact, if the vitality of the whole complex remains strong. Like capitalism, cognitivism has proved able to assimilate criticism, and to accommodate without genuine compromise. It is necessary to delve wider and deeper, and to examine principles that seem even more self-evident and unquestionable than those commonly exposed.

One such is the priority that has been given to the referential function of language. In science, for instance, language seems to be geared to providing an unambiguous and precise description of reality, whether at the level of theory or observation. Once the true account is given there should be no room for disagreement, and persisting arguments can in principle be settled by looking more closely in order to arrive at a consensus. When this is done there is perfect transparency through words to the reality they articulate. All trace of vagueness will then be eliminated. Science, on this account, aims for a truth that is essentially incontestable. And if the possibility of human error cannot be entirely eliminated as a source of disruption, human observers can always in principle be replaced by machines that receive inputs and carry out computations according to rules. This mechanical ideal was used by Winston Churchill in his proof of the reality of physical objects. Churchill is better known as a warlord and politician than as a philosopher, but in his autobiography he had occasion to argue that the reality of the sun (for instance) is guaranteed by confirmation of astronomical predictions. To the imagined objection that this depends upon the fallible evidence of the senses, he replied that they might be 'obtained by automatic calculating-machines set in motion by the light falling upon them without admixture of the senses at any stage' (quoted in Popper, 1972, p. 43). Correspondingly, the human scientist implied by cognitivism is an unreliable substitute for Churchill's automatic calculating-machines.

If this view of science correctly characterizes the true function of language, then everyday language is quite unsatisfactory. Disagreement is rife, and it is rare that arguments are settled by focusing more closely upon disputed topics. This is because much of our experience is vague and impossible to articulate, and it seems natural to treat scientific method as a way of dispelling the fog that normally surrounds our activities. The vagueness in everyday experience and language is thus seen as an unfortunate obstacle to be left behind by expert practitioners of science. As automatic calculating-machines most people are imperfect, but they can be improved by training.

But it is not only ordinary language that falls short of the ideal of a mechanized science. The social sciences are also imprecise and subject to unresolvable disputes, and it would generally be impossible to imagine their procedures being carried out by automatic calculating-machines. As a result there have been many attempts to distance them from the exact or hard sciences of physics, chemistry and biology. Unsympathetic critics have wanted to deny them the title 'science' altogether; Sir Karl Popper (1959), for instance, believed that their theories are often unfalsifiable, and therefore, according to his own criteria, unscientific; and recently Sir Keith Joseph insisted that the word 'Sciences' be eliminated from the name of the Social Sciences Research Council. Such views are not new, and they have led to an invidious partition, with the 'hard' sciences on one side, sociology, history, and the other 'soft' sciences on the other.

Writers sympathetic to the social sciences, concerned to maintain their integrity as intellectual disciplines, have tried to develop a more suitable ideal than that of automatic calculating-machines. Dilthey's (1976) division of *Geisteswissenschaften* and *Naturwissenschaften* implied a different, but equally commendable mode of knowledge for the social sciences, based on interpretation and understanding [*Verstehen*]. More recently, Gallie (1964) has suggested that propositions of the social sciences should be celebrated as 'essentially contestable', and Gergen (1973) has argued that social psychology is essentially historical, and should not be modelled upon the physical sciences. But these well-meaning attempts to restore the self-esteem of the social sciences have served, if anything, to reinforce the partition, which is now embedded in all institutions of higher learning in the Western world. As an academic recipe it has been remarkably successful, but like all political partitions imposed from without it has proved disastrous for communities, like psychology, perched in the middle of the sectarian divide. Such communities tend to suffer destructive divisions as members identify with one side or the other.

Cognitivism involves a thoroughgoing and lucrative identification with the hard side of the partition, which places psychology firmly within the causal nexus of the physical sciences. Social psychology is left to fend for itself – to take on the trappings of cognitivism or to redefine itself as defiantly and irreducibly social. Confronted with such a dilemma, a radical solution is called for, and in this chapter we re-examine the origin of the partition in the bias towards the referential function of language. One consequence of this bias is, as we have seen, that vagueness is an obstacle to be overcome. But why, in that case, should experience and ordinary language be so vague? Why, if we are automatic calculating-machines, should we be such bad ones most of the time? Is vagueness really just an obstacle, or does it have a function in its own right? One psychologist who has addressed this question and answered decisively in the affirmative is William James. The unique importance of his answer can be understood only as the culmination of a long history, which began in the seventeenth century with Descartes.

Descartes is famous for the dualist thinking that led to the study of mental processes in isolation from a mechanistic universe (Burtt, 1955; Rorty, 1980). But there is a more subtle Cartesian legacy, one that presupposes both dualism and a mechanistic view of the world. This is Descartes' method, especially the doctrine of clear and distinct ideas, which expressed a confidence in the human potential for a true representation of the world that lay behind the development of many Renaissance achievements.

But Descartes' was not simply the voice of the new replacing an outworn tradition. For by the seventeenth century the old confidence was already waning, and needed shoring up against scepticism. This change was general, and not true just of philosophy. In painting, for instance, there had been a distinctness of line and contrast and a bold simplicity of theme which mirrored Descartes' account of the power lying in the clarity of reason. Perspective representations were dominated by the exact and mechanical constructions of Euclidean geometry, and there was little or no place for the vaguer subtleties of aerial perspective. But by Descartes' time, sixteenth-century Mannerism had begun to undermine faith in clarity of vision, and the dark ambiguities of Rembrandt and others followed in the seventeenth century. In literature too there were sceptics, mockers of human pretension, of whom the greatest were Montaigne and Shakespeare. Descartes set out to re-establish confidence in human reason in the name of mathematics and science. In *Discourse on Method* and the *Meditations* he affected extreme scepticism in order to demonstrate its limitations (Curley, 1978) and thus to clear the way for the application of method.

The most comprehensive statement of the method was in *Rules for the Direction of the Mind* (the *Regulae*). Rule V, which was said by its author to contain 'the sum of all human endeavour', states that:

> Method consists entirely in the order and arrangement of those things upon which the power of the mind is to be concentrated in order to discover some truth. And we will follow this method exactly if we reduce complex and obscure propositions step by step to simpler ones and then try to advance by the same gradual process from the intuitive understanding of the very simplest to the knowledge of all the rest. (Descartes, 1961, p. 19)

This, Descartes believed, is the way to attain the 'consummation' of knowledge. To characterize this method for uncovering empirical truth he used the metaphor of a chain, which is like both a mechanical causal chain (Descartes, 1960, p. 95) and a chain of deductive reasoning exemplified by mathematics. Each link in the chain has the certainty of a clear and simple idea, whose truth is guaranteed by the *lumen naturale*, the natural light which for Descartes was the source of reason. In this way we can be assured of the truth of a complex idea, even though 'the capacity of our intellect is not great enough to comprehend all of it in a single act of intuition' (Descartes, 1961, p. 26; this is a corollary of Rule VII). The important thing is to avoid impatient speculation, and when we reach a step where there is no clarity, we should stop until it is restored (Rule VIII). These are recommendations for a trained mind, and much of the *Regulae* contains advice on training. Rule IX, for instance, states:

> We should bring the whole force of our minds to bear upon the most minute and simple details and to dwell upon them for a long time so that we become accustomed to perceive the truth clearly and distinctly. (Descartes, 1961, p. 35)

This was directed against 'the sublime and profound reasoning of philosophers', reasoning which 'depends upon principles which have never been sufficiently examined by anyone. How foolish they are who prefer darkness to light' (Descartes, 1961, p. 36). As Beck put it in his study of the *Regulae*:

> Just as a man who tried to take in with a single glance all the pictures hanging, for instance, in one of the rooms of the National Gallery would have no more than a vague and confused vision of the pictures, so a man

who in his study disperses his mind over a variety of problems would achieve little or nothing in the way of solid knowledge. He would merely obtain a few confused ideas, a few vague opinions on diverse topics. (Beck, 1952, p. 57)

This, and the method in general, may easily seem to be a matter of common sense, or 'a rather pedestrian and obvious set of maxims' (Cottingham, 1986, p. 26). Why, then, has the method seemed so important to some philosophers? Why did Heidegger, for instance, recommend close reading of the *Regulae* as a 'prerequisite for getting an inkling of what is going on in modern science' (Heidegger, 1967, p. 101)? Part of the answer, perhaps, lies in the apparent obviousness noted by Cottingham. It is because they seem obvious that the maxims are not questioned. Their important and restrictive implications for our model of ourselves and our world tend to be ignored, and they continue to hold sway as an ideal for attaining scientific knowledge.

Descartes' recommendations were psychological, not logical, since the marks of truth are given in the mind rather than the outside world. They implied a psychology of science, but one which is far from neutral about the nature of reality. For the method requires that the world is organized like a machine, each of whose parts can be studied independently of the rest, and in a cumulative fashion which will eventually give us the workings of the whole. Only if this is the case will the method work, and this indeed is how Descartes and classical physicists following Newton have conceived the subject matter of the physical sciences. A natural way of describing a machine is to describe how it was put together, and this is the fiction Descartes deliberately adopted in the treatises containing his Physics and his Physiology, *The World* and *Treatise on Man*. To avoid conflict with the 'accepted opinions of the learned . . . I decided . . . to speak solely of what would happen in a new world. I therefore supposed that God now created . . . enough matter to compose such a world' and then lent 'his regular concurrence to nature, leaving it to act according to the laws he established' (Descartes, 1985, p. 132). This conveniently obliged Descartes to describe physical and physiological mechanisms step by step in a manner that exemplifies the method.

Thus a consequence of adopting the method is that only if your account can be couched as a mechanism can it be a true representation of the world, and the method can be applied to check each link to confirm the mechanical feasibility of the whole – to check, in other words, that it will work. Nowadays the checks themselves have sometimes become mechanical. Wittgenstein's (1922) development of truth tables in the *Tractatus* was a mechanical way of determining the truth value of complex propositions, and the mathematical notion of an effective procedure has been claimed as a requirement for theory in cognitive psychology (Johnson-Laird, 1983) – a psychology worthy of an honoured place within the sharp clarity of the Cartesian universe.

And who would want to deny the advantages of clarity and distinctness? There is a rhetorical trap in Descartes' advocacy. As a writer he was admirably clear and distinct, unlike many other philosophers. He also espoused a method for reaching the 'consummation of knowledge' by following the way of clear and distinct ideas, and this depended upon the psychology of science embedded in his method. But there are separate points here. A critic may deny the universal validity of the method, both as normative procedure and as psychology of science, without denying the value of clear and distinct writing. The danger is that in denying the method one may seem to deny clarity and distinctness themselves, and be open to the charge of tolerating a mystifying vagueness – of returning, in the words of John Locke, who anglicized the Cartesian revolution and launched the 'way of ideas', to those 'Vague and insignificant Forms of Speech, and Abuse of Language, [which] have so long passed for Mysteries of Science' (Locke, 1975, p. 10).

So what are the limitations of the method, why should it be necessary to risk censure by exposing oneself to this rhetorical trap? The problem lies in what seems to be left out altogether, the humanities, and what gets too limited a share of the epistemological cake, the social sciences and psychology, especially social psychology.[2] Descartes recognized the problem but did not think it important. He believed that the achievements of literature, art, theology, and other humanities are at best the inspired products of talented individuals, 'gifts of mind rather than fruits of study' (Descartes, 1985, p. 114), and therefore not part of knowledge, which requires method.

Not all commentators have accepted Descartes's relegation of the humanities and the social sciences to a pleasant relaxation from the serious business of science. An early critic – and one of the most radical – was Vico, who rejected the method altogether (Vico, 1948). He wrote during the early eighteenth century, and argued against the fashion of the time (the 'Age of Enlightenment') that mathematics, far from being the paradigm of knowledge assumed by the method, is not a case of knowledge at all. Instead history, what human beings have created through their actions, is the true paradigm of attainable knowledge.[3] Later the so-called Romantics,[4] possibly building upon Vico, refused to comply meekly with the secondary role assigned to sensibility.

For the historian of psychology, the most interesting philosopher of the Romantic movement was Coleridge. He is best known for his literary criticism and his poetry, especially *The Ancient Mariner*, but he was an intellectual genius of broad scope, able to draw on exceptionally wide reading in the interests of his anti-mechanistic psychology. His contributions to psychology tend to be forgotten nowadays, probably because he left no systematic statement of his views, which are scattered throughout essays, letters, notebooks and even the marginalia in the books he owned.

In 1801 Coleridge wrote four long letters to his patron Josiah Wedgwood, giving a detailed textual comparison of Descartes and Locke. Locke is generally accepted as one of the great founders of British Empiricist philosophy and of Associationist Psychology, but Coleridge had a low opinion of him. He claimed that Locke's debt to Descartes had been grossly underestimated, especially by Locke himself. Locke had taken the framework offered by Descartes and distorted it without adding anything original. In particular his preface to *An Essay Concerning Human Understanding* (the 'Epistle to the Reader') explains rather laboriously that he will use 'determinate' or 'determin'd' rather than 'clear and distinct' ideas, and it is these ideas that are, or *should* be, '*determined* to a name or articulate sound' (Locke, 1975, p. 13). 'Should' be because we are careless, and failure to use words for their corresponding determined ideas 'is the cause of no small obscurity and confusion'. In other words, 'clear and distinct' (or 'determined') ideas are to be sought as an intermediary in the proper use of language, and thus Locke launched the nominalist, empiricist version of the Cartesian method. With such 'idly chosen' words which mean 'too many things to mean anything *determinately*' (Coleridge, 1956, p. 690), and with his ponderous style, Locke distances himself from Descartes – but the apparent originality is an illusion and Locke managed, according to Coleridge, to combine superficiality and error about subjects that Descartes 'has treated in a manner worthy of the Predecessor of Hartley' (*ibid.*, p. 689).

So much for Locke, one of the darlings of the eighteenth-century Enlightenment whose impetus Coleridge tried so hard to resist. Descartes' worthy successor, Hartley, fared little better.[5] Hartley's *Observations on Man* (1749) described a mechanistic associationism based on physical 'vibrations' in the brain, and it had a wide following. Coleridge started as an enthusiastic disciple (he named his first son Hartley), but even by 1801 he was beginning to react against the passivity entailed by the dualist structure described by Descartes. The system of *Observations on Man* was based on this structure, and bore the brunt of Coleridge's critical reaction. He welcomed the philosophies of Kant and Schelling as emphasizing the mind's active contribution to experience of the world, thereby breaking down the separation of subject and object and therefore, more generally, the dualism of organism and environment. The *Biographia Literaria* (1815) contains a lengthy refutation of Associationism; and the contrast between Hartley and Kant, and Kant's distinction between reason and understanding, fuelled Coleridge's own distinction between 'imagination' and 'fancy'. Fancy is mechanical, a product of lawful associationism, and is the origin of poetic simile; imagination is the origin of metaphor, the product of an active or interactive mind, which 'reveals itself in the balance or reconciliation of opposite or discordant qualities' (Coleridge, 1965, p. 174).[6]

Like Descartes, Coleridge believed in method, but it was a method which took Shakespeare as an ideal as well as geometry. In his uncompleted *Treatise on Method* he wrote:

> The Idea may exist in a clear, distinct, definite form, as that of a circle in the Mind of an accurate Geometrician; or it may be a mere *instinct*, a vague appetancy towards something which the Mind incessantly hunts for, but cannot find, like a name which has escaped our recollection. . . . In the infancy of the Human Mind all our ideas are instincts; and Language is happily contrived to lead us from the vague to the distinct, from the imperfect to the full and finished form . . . this distinction between the instinctive approach towards an Idea, and the Idea itself, is of high importance in Methodizing Art and Science. (Coleridge, 1934, p. 6)

Descartes had recognized that ideas may be vague, but had seen this as a regrettable and temporary state to be eliminated by method, which would transform a passively receptive mind that is 'imperfect and confused' into one that is 'clear and distinct' (Descartes, 1960, p. 114). For Coleridge the active mind necessarily starts in a state of 'vague appetancy' which leads us, through language, 'from the vague to the distinct'. Vagueness is not a kind of unfocused state to be corrected as one would a microscope. It is an essential part of experience, the source material acted upon by the restless mind of the Romantic imagination.

Coleridge's reaction against associationism set the terms of a persistent concern about its limitations in Britain and the States. This concern formed an anxious background to the successes of James Mill, John Stuart Mill, Bain, and Herbert Spencer. Those who owed most to Coleridge – Carlyle in Britain and the Transcendentalists in New England – formed an outspoken opposition to the mechanistic antireligious implications of associationism. But John Stuart Mill himself, in his essay on Coleridge (Mill, 1950), recognized limitations in mechanism, and attempted to overcome them through the social sciences of Book VI of his *Logic*.[7] And Herbert Spencer – who attempted to provide, in William James's words, 'a purely mechanical explanation of nature' (James, 1978, p. 117) – tried to justify these limitations by claiming that they accord with reality – for outside them lies *The Unknowable!*[8] By the 1870s, with the rise of Darwinism,[9] mechanism was in the ascendancy, but there were hopes for a swing of the pendulum towards a reconciliation between the hard virtues of science and the more human values supported by religion. William James shared in these hopes and was struggling to fulfil them, as his letters of the time make clear.[10]

James's immediate struggle was with Herbert Spencer, the famous apostle of evolution as well as The Unknowable and a nineteenth-century inheritor of the mechanistic and associationist tradition stemming from Descartes through Locke and the British Empiricists. Spencer was to James what Hartley was to Coleridge – a favourite whom he outgrew, but who continued to serve him as 'a punching bag . . . in his intellectual gymnasium' (Perry, 1935, I, p. 475).[11] It was through sparring with Spencer that James discovered that vagueness is not just a fault to be eliminated from scientific discourse, but also an indispensable part of experience – the beginning of his greatest insight.

At the beginning of *The Principles* James recommended some degree of vagueness 'at a certain stage of the development of every science', and praised Spencer's formula 'the adjustment of inner to outer relations' (James, 1890, p. 6). Although this is 'vagueness incarnate' (*ibid.*), it is also useful and fertile because it 'takes into account the fact that minds inhabit environments which act on them and on which they in turn react' (*ibid.*).[12] James had first read Spencer's *First Principles* when he was about twenty and 'was carried away with enthusiasm by the intellectual perspectives which it seemed to open' (quoted in Perry, 1934, I, p. 474). Later he used Spencer extensively in his teaching, but increasingly as a source of difference rather than agreement – his first two major published papers, in 1878, were directed against Spencer's doctrines. His final verdict on *First Principles* was: 'almost a museum of blundering reason' (James, 1911, p. 128). He was scornful of Spencer's 'The Unknowable' as a way of reconciling science and religion. James approved of the sense of mystery, through which Spencer found common ground between science and religion, but only as 'the sense of *more-to-be-known*, not [as entailed by The Unknowable] the sense of a More, *not* to be known' (*ibid.*). In 1904, reviewing Spencer's *Autobiography*, he had nothing good to say about the vagueness in Spencer's definition of evolution as the 'passage . . . from a state of indefinite incoherent homogeneity to a definite coherent heterogeneity' (James, 1911, p. 131). It was not, for James, that the words used by Spencer (words such as 'homogeneity', 'definite', 'coherent' and 'indeterminateness') were inherently vague, and therefore intolerable. They were intolerable because they were used out of place, to characterize nature rather than the mind. After rewording Spencer's definition to his own satisfaction, James concluded:

The human use of Spencer's adjectives 'integrated', 'definite', 'coherent' here no longer shocks one. We are frankly on teleological ground, and metaphor and vagueness are permissible. (*ibid.*, p. 136)

'Indeterminateness', he wrote elsewhere, is a mental state, and the attribute of things had better be called by some other name (Perry, 1935, I, p. 483).

How can we characterize these two senses of vagueness, one positive, the other negative, sometimes both present in the same usage? The bad sense is straightforwardly logical or conceptual; the good sense refers to an essential part of experience, including scientific investigation. It conveys possibilities that cannot as yet be spelt out and applies to mind and mystery, with its sense of more-to-be-known. In painting the virtues of a suggestive vagueness of this kind were fully appreciated at the time James wrote, and it is possible that this was one of his sources. Many of his most compelling metaphors were visual, and several writers have commented on the lasting impact of James's early training as a painter, and of the paintings he studied in his youth.[13] He was to call on some of the most intense of his painterly imagery to convey exasperation at the pedantic rectitude of Spencer's writing. In the *Autobiography*, 'Every smallest thing is either right or wrong, and if wrong, can be articulately proved so by reasoning. Life grows too dry and literal, and loses all aerial perspective at such a rate' (James, 1911, p. 113). ' . . . one finds no twilight region in his mind. . . . All parts of it are filled with the same noonday glare, like a dry desert where every grain of sand shows singly, and there are no mysteries or shadows' (*ibid.*, p. 112). Spencer's mind was incomplete, even crippled, because it was lacking in an essential part, what James called 'the vague'.[14]

William James gave 'the vague' an important role in one of the key passages of his *Principles of Psychology*, where he made explicit for the first time the essential part played by vagueness in thinking. In the stream-of-thought chapter he wrote:

> . . . what I contend for, and accumulate examples to show, is that 'tendencies' are not only descriptions from without, but that they are among the *objects* of the stream, which is thus aware of them from within, and must be described as in very large measure constituted of *feelings* of *tendency*, often so vague that we are unable to name them at all. It is, in short, the reinstatement of the vague to its proper place in our mental life which I am so anxious to press on the attention. (James, 1890, p. 254; James's emphasis)

This passage, together with most of that chapter, was written in 1883, seven years earlier than the appearance of the book. It sums up what many commentators[15] have considered James's greatest insight – into the flowing, stream-like temporality of consciousness, whose *transitive* parts and fringes (the 'feelings of tendency') are as real as the *substantive* parts of traditional association theory. Associationism had ignored the transitive parts, and James was correcting this by the 'reinstatement of the vague'. The contrast between his theory and what preceded it in associationist psychology is brought out in a famous passage where James's sedate figures of 'substantive' and 'transitive', taken from logic or grammar, are replaced with a vivid sensuous metaphor, mostly visual but also tangible and alive with movement and sound:

> The traditional psychology talks like one who should say a river consists of nothing but pailsful, spoonsful, quartpotsful, barrelsful, and other moulded forms of water. Even were the pails and the pots all actually standing in the stream, still between them the free water would continue to flow. It is just this free water of consciousness that psychologists resolutely overlook. Every definite image in the mind is steeped and dyed in the free water that flows round it. With it goes the sense of its relations, near and remote, the dying echo of whence it came to us, the dawning sense of whither it is to lead. The significance, the value, of the image is all in this halo or penumbra that surrounds or escorts it, – or rather that is fused into one with it and has become bone of its bone and flesh of its flesh; leaving it, it is true, an image of the same *thing* it was before, but making it an image of that thing newly taken and freshly understood. (James, 1890, p. 255; James's emphasis)

Thus 'the vague', consisting of the transitive parts or, more generally, the 'fringes' of consciousness, is no less than the source of significance and value. The mechanistic psychology of associationism, having no place for 'the vague', must be abandoned. Significance cannot simply be added by taking the substantive parts of traditional associationism and injecting a dose of 'the vague', as though the two were distinct. Taken out of context, the metaphor of the clear and distinct pails and pots with the free water between certainly allows this interpretation, but James's meaning was deeper. Each substantive part or definite image is *steeped and dyed* in the free water that flows round it; thus the transitive parts that make up 'the vague' are not like links or chains that are separable from the substantive parts they connect together. He made this explicit in a footnote added for the book chapter. Correcting a misunderstanding by 'the late Prof. Thos. Maguire of Dublin', James wrote:

> This author considers that by the 'fringe' I mean some sort of psychic material by which sensations in themselves separate are made to cohere together, and wittily says that I ought to 'see that uniting sensations by their "fringes" is more vague than to construct the universe out of oysters by platting their beards'. . . . But the fringe, as I use the word, means nothing like this; it is part of the *object cognized*, – substantive *qualities* and *things* appearing to the mind in a *fringe of relations*. Some parts – the transitive

parts – of our stream of thought cognize the relations rather than the things; but both the transitive and the substantive parts form one continuous stream, with no discrete 'sensations' in it such as Prof. Maguire supposes, and supposes me suppose, to be there. (James, 1890, p. 258; James's emphasis)

'The vague' is not just a rejection of associationism, it is also a rejection of its traditional antithesis, the intellectualism that relies upon an organizing principle to supply meaning and significance to experience, but is not itself experienced. James objected to calling upon any such 'transcendent' principle and substituted 'the vague', which was both directly experienced *and* a vehicle of meaning. It is thus a middle way between the philosphical positions of what he calls in one place Sensationalism and Intellectualism (James, 1890, pp. 244–5) and in another Associationist and Spiritualist theories (*ibid.*, p. vi).

In this way James made mock of the rhetorical trap set by Descartes. Coleridge had given vagueness a more positive role, but only with James did 'the vague' come into its own as a source of meaning that is itself a part of experience, and coexists (inseparably) with the clear and distinct substantive parts. But 'the vague' remained unpersuasive as a scientific term and was doomed to oblivion – in spite of James's effort, a few pages later in *The Principles*, to show how readily it can be anchored to physiological processes. The stream of consciousness has had influence, to be sure. Phenomenologists acknowledge it as one of the cornerstones of their research (see Note 15), and it has become a standard part of literary technique. But psychic fringes and transitive parts and all that constitutes 'the vague' have failed to appeal to the scientific imagination, and they play little part in modern cognitive psychology. The most interesting impact has been on Wittgenstein, who used James time and again as his exemplar of the view that meaning can be conveyed by a 'feeling of tendency' added to a word. A dubious fame, to be remembered as Wittgenstein's straw man, and later we shall have reason to question whether James was really so naive about meaning as to deserve it.

Thus William James's 'reinstatement of the vague' was the product of a long history and a short past. It undermined the Cartesian (and more generally Renaissance) precedence given to 'clear and distinct ideas' which, by fostering the illusion that vagueness can be eliminated from experience, had provided an undercover support for associationism and a mechanistic psychology. Closer in time, 'the vague' was a residue from the Romantic resistance to mechanistic thinking, and it captured, for James, a reconciliation of that resistance with a scientific psychology. Finally, reacting to the immediate past, 'the vague' supplied what was lacking in a nineteenth-century *reductio ad absurdum* of Cartesian thinking, the philosophy of Herbert Spencer.

But 'the vague' pointed forwards as well as backwards. The future development of James's thought lay in a further tension concealed within 'the reinstatement of the vague'. Even if clarity and distinctness could no longer be taken as the ideal for representation, the Jamesian stream of thought remained a dualist concept – a mirror reflecting the outside world, just as nineteenth-century painting, for all its use of suggestive vagueness, remained representational. However, it was never for James a dogmatic dualism, but one that he accepted provisionally in *The Principles* for its convenience in exposition. Elsewhere, even before 1890, in his lectures to students and his letters, he was already undermining that dualism in favour of the later doctrine of pure experience.[16] Like painting itself, James was poised on the brink of an intellectual revolution. This is signalled by the ambivalence of the following passage, which asserts the apparent consequences of deriving meaning from the transitive parts of consciousness:

> We ought to say a feeling of *and*, a feeling of *if*, a feeling of *but*, and a feeling of *by*, quite as readily as we say a feeling of *blue* or a feeling of *cold*. (James, 1890, pp. 245–6; James's emphasis)

This is famous as the psychologistic theory that made James the butt of many of Wittgenstein's philosophical investigations – for treating the words 'and', 'but', etc., as though they acquire meaning by referring to invariant 'objects of the stream'. James appears in this role in *Philosophical Investigations*, *Zettel*, and *Remarks on the Philosophy of Psychology*. Thus, from the latter:

> 264. James might perhaps say: 'I read each word with the feeling appropriate to it. "But" with the but-feeling,' and so on. – And even if that is true – what does it really signify? What is the grammar of the concept 'but-feeling'? – It certainly isn't a feeling just because I call it 'a feeling'. (Wittgenstein, 1980, II-267)

This serves Wittgenstein's purpose, which is to expose the muddles that result when we extend a referential theory of language to apply to mental 'objects', but he takes James too literally, missing the boisterous irony with which James often undermines his own position. The 'ought' in the above passage from James is used less to recommend than to draw out an unacceptable conclusion in order to disprove the premiss. The feelings of tendency are *in principle* unnameable, as James made clear by the addition of the word 'inarticulate' when he came to reassert the 'reinstatement of the vague' in the *Briefer Course* (1892) ('It is . . . the reinstatement of the vague and inarticulate to its proper place in our mental life which I am so anxious to press on the attention': James, 1892, p. 165). 'Ought' conveys the *reductio ad absurdum* of a dualism that purports to *represent* meaning within a consciousness (*if* dualism is true, we ought to say a feeling of 'and', 'if', etc.; but we cannot say this, *ergo* dualism is false). The 'reinstatement of the vague' thus makes dualism untenable and was, so to speak, the final absurd and repressive act that ushered in James's revolutionary phase. After 1890 James developed his theory of pure experience, which is neither in an outside world nor in the mind, but is more fundamental than either as a source of knowledge:

> As 'subjective' we say that the experience represents; as 'objective' it is represented. What represents and is represented is here numerically the same; but we must remember that no dualism of being represented and representing resides in the experience *per se*. (James, 1912, p. 23)

James made no attempt to define pure experience except in relational terms, but that was sufficient to fulfil his aims – to provide a basis for the verbal construction of the dual poles of mind and matter, of subjectivity and objectivity.

Descartes, Coleridge and James agreed that the development of thought was a movement from vagueness to clarity and distinctness. But for Descartes the mechanist, vagueness was 'imperfect and confused', and the task of method was to eliminate distortion in the mirror of reality. For Coleridge the Romantic, 'the vague' was a necessary starting point, and the movement towards clarity was part of the restless mind's incessant hunt for its own truth. Finally, for James, 'the vague' was an essential part of all experience, and he therefore reified it as part of the structure of dualist consciousness – reified it ironically, since he half-recognized the absurdity, and anticipated his own rejection of dualism in favour of the doctrine of pure experience. This in turn has opened the way to new accounts of the origin of knowledge – pragmatist, social constructionist and perceptual realist accounts that have provided psychology with some of the most important alternatives to cognitivism.[17] If there is a single event that should be celebrated by the opposition to cognitivism, it is William James's reversal of Cartesian priorities by his 'reinstatement of the vague'.

Notes

1. But by no means all research on cognition is cognitivist. See, for example, Jean Lave's (1988) *Cognition in Practice*.
2. Descartes had plenty to say about psychology, but it was not social. He developed three psychologies, the perceptual psychology of the *Optics* and elsewhere; the implicit psychology contained in *Regulae*; and the psychology of emotion of *Passions of the Soul*. The first was developed by applying the method to the new discoveries about the dioptrics of the eye, especially the recent demonstrations of the retinal image, and led to his thoroughgoing dualism and an early version of cognitivism (Reed, 1980). It was a

psychology to mirror the method, tracing the course of light through the lens of the eye to form sharp images on the retina, which act upon the nerves to produce corporeal ideas in the brain, which eventually emerge as clear and distinct ideas through the exercise of the *lumen naturale*. The method itself was his second psychology, a psychology of science as an individual rather than a social achievement. The third psychology was part of his attempt to give a coherent account of the interaction of mind and body, as well as to develop a practical psychology. These were individual psychologies, which took little account of social life or culture.

3. Isaiah Berlin (1976) gives an excellent account of Vico's rejection of Cartesianism. Recently Shotter (1986) has convincingly claimed Vico for a non-mechanistic psychology.

4. 'The Romantics' refers here to both a period – about 1780 to 1830 – and a doctrine: the rejection of mechanistic views of the world, based on reason, and the demotion of reason in favour of a more intuitive faculty, sometimes called imagination. One of the best-known and characteristic substitutes for Cartesian reason is Keats's 'negative capability' – 'that is when a man is capable of being in uncertainties, Mysteries, doubts, without any irritable reaching after fact and reason' (Bloom and Trilling, 1973, p. 768). Or Shelley's 'Reason is to the imagination as the instrument to the agent, as the body to the spirit, as the shadow to the substance' (*Ibid.*, p. 746). Coleridge, the most learned of the English Romantics, was careful to redefine reason rather than to undermine it.

The Romantics were not in general 'anti-science' (Cunningham and Jardine, 1990; see especially the introductory essay by David Knight). They were against the assumption that scientific truth is necessarily mechanistic truth, and the successful Romantic scientists working within this assumption include Humphry Davy and Oersted. Vitalism was a Romantic concept, and played an essential part in the development of sensory physiology (Danziger, 1984) by insisting that sensory stimulation was not a mechanical, billiard-ball process – there was, instead, an active contribution on the part of the organism. It is part of the triumph of mechanism that this active process itself became seen in mechanical terms, and vitalism was thrown on to the historical rubbish heap. What can one conclude from this? That mechanism is true and we should stick to it, or that we should be warned by this example of the dangers of obstinately adhering to mechanistic thinking? One possibility is that vitalism's success in this instance was due to its approach to a mutualist language, in which organism and environment are treated as inseparable. Vitalism ultimately failed because it invoked an alternative and mysterious internal principle to explain this.

5. Unlike Locke, both Hartley and Descartes retained Coleridge's respect and admiration, even when his views were clearly incompatible with theirs.

6. Imagination is a product of Coleridge's version of 'method', which 'becomes natural to the mind which has become accustomed to contemplate not *things* only, or for their sake alone, but likewise and chiefly the *relations* of things, whether their relations to each other, or to the observer, or to the state and apprehension of the hearers' (quoted in Holmes, 1982, p. 62). William James's (1890, p. 221) distinction between 'knowledge by acquaintence' and 'knowledge about' is based on a similar contrast. The distinction was later defined in terms of the stream of thought and 'the vague' (see below): ' . . . we may feel assured that the difference between those [states of mind] that are mere "acquaintance," and those that are "knowledges-*about*" . . . is

reducible almost entirely to the absence or presence of psychic fringes or overtones' (James, 1890, p. 259; James's emphasis).
7. Adding a social dimension to a mechanistic psychology as a way of softening the hard determinism of this approach has become encapsulated in the structure of psychology as an academic discipline – in textbooks, chapters on social psychology are kept distinct from those on basic perceptual and cognitive processes. This solution was impossible for William James (see below), since he was unwilling to divide up experience into compartments. Ironically, this has sometimes led to James being criticized for ignoring the social, in spite of the frequency with which he appeals to social factors, most obviously in his discussion of the material and social selves in *Principles of Psychology* (James, 1890).
8. In *First Principles*, which first appeared in instalments between 1870 and 1872. The attempt to keep science and religious experience separate while valuing both is a common theme in British positivism. Mystics are respected as long as they keep quiet; 'Whereof one cannot speak, thereof one must be silent' (Wittgenstein, 1922, p. 189) expresses the same sentiment as Spencer's and found an equally appreciative British and American audience. William James would not have agreed – see below.
9. The impact on psychology can be traced in the mechanization of the concept of 'trial and error' in successive editions of the textbooks of Alexander Bain (Still, 1988).
10. For instance, in a letter to Renouvier in 1872, he wrote: 'With us it is the philosophy of Mill, Bain, and Spencer which just now carried everything before it. This philosophy has done good work in psychology, but from the practical point of view it is deterministic and materialistic; and already, I think, I can discern in England the symptoms of a revival of religious thought' (Perry, 1935, I, p. 662).
11. 'James followed poor Spencer relentlessly into every bypath of his thought with a criticism that was the more devastating because of the earnestness with which he sought to do the author full justice' (Perry, 1935, I, p. 482). In 1878 James published his first two major articles, both criticisms of Herbert Spencer. According to Bjork (1988, p. 108), 'These essays established James' reputation as Spencer's major American opponent. They cast him in the role of a psychologist-philosopher who defended the mind's creative potential against a determined destiny. They outlined foundational positions . . . that James spent the next thirty years elaborating.'
12. He gives an alternative justification for vagueness on the same page – 'let a science be as vague as its subject', having in mind psychology. The most telling justification, since it contains an implicit reference to Cartesian method, was in a letter to Pillon written in 1909: 'I believe that philosophy stands at present at the beginning of a new sort of activity . . . which will end by defining . . . the limits of what the conceptual or logical method can accomplish. . . . But it gives me very little anxiety, for I think the final . . . result will be a greater distinctness and clearness than philosophy has ever seen'. (Perry, 1935, II, p. 662).
13. The influence of painting and paintings on William James's thinking has been discussed most recently in McDermott (1968), Feinstein (1984) and Bjork (1983, 1988).
14. Several recent writers have stressed the importance of 'the vague' for James; see especially Gavin (1976) and Siegfried (1982). Coleridge's use (quoted above) was still the adjectival use of 'vague', with the qualified

noun understood. But both this usage and the later substantive form 'the vague' suggest a very unCartesian psychological or spiritual realm whose contents are the reverse of clear and distinct. The substantive form was current during the nineteenth century amongst those intellectuals most sensitive to the tensions engendered by the limitations of mechanistic accounts of the mind. Judging from the illustrative quotations in the *Oxford English Dictionary*, it was used in the circles centring around Thomas Carlyle and John Stuart Mill. The first example given is from Carlyle himself in 1851, writing of John Sterling, an ardent disciple of Coleridge: 'John Mill . . . spoke of him . . . as a gifted amiable being, . . . in danger of dissipating himself into the vague', and examples are given from Jane Carlyle's letters and one from Alexander Bain's *Life of J. S. Mill*. The intellectual milieu picked out by these scattered indications was international, and included members of the James family – first Henry James senior, and then his sons: William, the psychologist and philosopher, and Henry, the novelist.

15. Perry's assessment was that 'Except possibly for the dependence of knowledge on will, this was James's most important insight' (Perry, 1935, II, p. 77). Aron Gurwitsch claimed it as more than an insight. Speaking for phenomenologists, he described it as William James's fundamental *discovery* about consciousness: '*What underlies the doctrine of the "transitive states" is a new conception of consciousness, the definition of consciousness in terms of temporality* . . . James may be said to have discovered temporality as the fundamental structure of conscious life' (Gurwitsch, 1966, p. 326; Gurwitsch's emphasis).

16. On 11 September 1884 he wrote to Renouvier: ' . . . before it is reflected on, consciousness is felt, and as such is continuous, that is, it potentially allows us to make sections anywhere in it, and treat the included portion as a unit . . . our divisions of consciousness are arbitrary results of conceptual handling on our part' (Perry, 1935, I, p. 698). On 15 November of the same year, he wrote to Stumpf ' . . . you speak as if the sensation to be judged were an unvarying and permanent bit of content, no matter what its concomitants. In *Mind*, for January last, I gave some reasons for thinking that we never have the same subjective modification twice' (Perry, 1935, II, p. 63). These letters were in reply to criticisms of James (1884), where the stream-of-thought material (and 'the vague') first appeared.

17. For Dewey's pragmatism, see this volume, Chapter 3. For Mead's pragmatism, see Chapter 11; for social constructionism, see Chapter 5. For J.J. Gibson's perceptual realism, see Chapters 10 and 11. Gibson's Jamesian heritage is brought out in Tighe and Tighe (1966).

References

Beck, L.J. (1952), *The Method of Descartes: A study of the Regulae*, Oxford: Oxford University Press.

Berlin, I. (1980), *Vico and Herder: The studies in the history of ideas*, London: Chatto & Windus.

Bjork, D.W. (1983), *The Compromised Scientist: William James in the development of American psychology*, New York: Columbia University Press.

Bjork, D.W. (1988), *William James: The center of his vision*, New York: Columbia University Press.

Bloom, H. and Trilling, L. (1973), *Romantic Poetry and Prose*, New York: Oxford University Press.
Burtt, E.A. (1955), *Metaphysical Foundations of Modern Physical Science*, Garden City, NY: Doubleday.
Coleridge, S.T. (1934), *S.T. Coleridge's Treatise on Method*, ed. A.D. Snyder, London: Constable.
Coleridge, S.T. (1956), *Letters of Samuel Taylor Coleridge*, vol. 2, ed. E.L. Griggs, Oxford: Oxford University Press.
Coleridge, S.T. (1965), *Biographia Literaria*, London: Dent.
Cottingham, J. (1986), *Descartes*, Oxford: Blackwell.
Cunningham, A. and Jardine, N. (eds) (1990), *Romanticism and the Sciences*, Cambridge: Cambridge University Press.
Curley, E.M. (1978), *Descartes against the Sceptics*, Oxford: Blackwell.
Danziger, K. (1984), 'Origins of the schema of stimulated motion: Towards a prehistory of modern psychology', *History of Science*, 21, 183–210.
Descartes, R. (1960), *Discourse on Method and Other Writings*, Harmondsworth: Penguin.
Descartes, R. (1961), *Rules for the Direction of the Mind*, Indianapolis, IN: Bobbs-Merrill.
Descartes, R. (1985), *The Philosophical Writings of Descartes*, vol. 1, Cambridge: Cambridge University Press.
Dilthey, W. (1976) *Selected Writings*, ed. H.P. Rickman, Cambridge: Cambridge University Press.
Feinstein, H.W. (1984), *Becoming William James*, Ithaca, NY: Cornell University Press.
Gallie, W.B. (1964), *Philosophy and Historical Understanding*, New York: Schocken.
Gavin, W.J. (1976), 'William James and the importance of "The Vague"' *Cultural Hermeneutics*, 3, 245–65.
Gergen, K.J. (1973), 'Social Psychology as history', *Journal of Personality and Social Psychology*, 26, 309–20.
Gurwitsch, A. (1966), *Studies in Phenomenology and Psychology*, Evanston, IL: Northwestern University Press.
Heidegger, M. (1967), *What is a Thing?*, South Bend, IN: Regnery/Gateway.
Holmes, R. (1982), *Coleridge*, Oxford University Press.
James, W. (1884), 'On some omissions of introspective psychology', *Mind*, 9, 1–26.
James, W. (1890), *Principles of Psychology*, vol. 1, New York: Holt.
James, W. (1892), *Psychology: Briefer course*, New York: Holt.
James, W. (1911), *Memories and Studies*, New York: Longmans, Green.
James, W. (1912), *Essays in Radical Empiricism*, London: Longmans.
James, W. (1978), *Essays in Philosophy*, Cambridge, MA: Harvard University Press.
Johnson-Laird, P.N. (1983), *Mental Models*, Cambridge: Cambridge University Press.
Lave, J. (1988), *Cognition in Practice*, Cambridge: Cambridge University Press.
Locke, J. (1975), *An Essay Concerning Human Understanding*, Oxford: Oxford University Press.
McDermott, J.J. (1968), 'To be human is to humanize', in M. Novak (ed.), *American Philosophy and the Future*, New York: Scribner's.
Mill, J.S. (1950), *Mill on Bentham and Coleridge*, London: Chatto & Windus.

Perry, R.B. (1935), *The Thought and Character of William James*, 2 vols, Boston, MA: Little, Brown.
Popper, K.R. (1959), *The Logic of Scientific Discovery*, London: Hutchinson.
Popper, K.R. (1972), *Objective Knowledge*, Oxford: Oxford University Press.
Reed, E.S. (1980), 'Descartes' corporeal ideas hypothesis and the origin of scientific psychology', *Review of Metaphysics*, **35**, 731–52.
Rorty, R. (1980), *Philosophy and the Mirror of Nature*, Oxford: Blackwell.
Shotter, J. (1986), 'A sense of place: Vico and the social production of social identities', paper read to the Research Group for the History of Human Sciences, Durham, UK.
Siegfried, C.H. (1982), 'Vagueness and the adequacy of concepts', *Philosophy Today*, **25**, 357–67.
Still, A.W. (1988), 'Word meaning and historical change: The case of "trial and error"', in *Proceedings of the Seventh European Cheiron Conference*, Budapest.
Tighe, L.S. and Tighe, T.J. (1966), 'Discrimination learning: Two views in historical perspective', *Psychological Bulletin*, **66**, 353–70.
Vico, G. (1948), *The New Science of Giambattista Vico*, Ithaca, NY: Cornell University Press.
Wittgenstein, L. (1922), *Tractatus Logico-Philosophicus*, London: Routledge & Kegan Paul.
Wittgenstein, L. (1980), *Remarks on the Philosophy of Psychology*, vol. 2, Oxford: Basil Blackwell.

3
On not-doing and on trying and failing

Don Mixon

Editors' introduction

Explanations in terms of underlying rules that 'generate' behaviour have been an important feature of modern cognitive theory. Critics, however, have insisted that a distinction needs to be respected between activities that are actually governed by explicit rules, and performance that is merely describable in terms of rules. For, ultimately, practice is primary, and theory derivative:

> Efficient practice precedes the theory of it. . . . The consideration of propositions is itself an operation the execution of which can be more or less intelligently executed, or less or more stupid. But if, for any operation to be intelligently executed, a prior theoretical operation had first to be performed and performed intelligently, it would be a logical impossibility for anyone ever to break the circle. (Ryle, 1949, p. 30)

In the following chapter, Don Mixon describes an important episode in the life of the American philosopher John Dewey that concerns the insufficiency of rule-based explanation even when rules are actually employed in the process of instruction (see also Sudnow, 1978). What Dewey realized as he tried to carry out simple everyday activities in novel ways was that skilled actions are more than a matter of following rules. He knew exactly what the rules were, yet he was unable to execute them.

John Dewey had been a resolute critic of both mechanism and intellectualism in psychological theory throughout his very long career. Even before S–R theory achieved its importance in American psychology, he had identified its commitment to the older dualism of body and soul. The reflex arc is, he argued, 'not a comprehensive, or organic, unity, but a patchwork of disjointed parts, a mechanical conjunction of unallied processes' (Dewey, 1896, p. 358). He believed that a radical change was required – it was no use trying to repair the S–R formula by adding mediating processes between stimulus and response (as happens in much modern theory). His subsequent attempts to describe an alternative led him to emphasize

27

the mutuality of organism and environment. Dewey's insight was more than that organisms and environments 'interact': the environment is not fixed but develops and evolves along with the organism (Dewey, 1898/1976, p. 284). To consider the interdependence of organism and environment as a transformative relation is to take the critical step beyond a conception of knowledge as mere representation or correspondence (Rorty, 1977).

References

Dewey, J. (1896), 'The reflex arc concept in psychology', *Psychological Review*, 3, 357–70.
Dewey, J. (1898/1976), *Lectures on Psychological and Political Ethics: 1898*, ed. D. F. Koch, New York: Hafner.
Rorty, R. (1977), 'Dewey's metaphysics', in S.M. Cahn (ed.), *New Studies in the Philosophy of John Dewey*, Hanover, NH: University Press of New England, pp. 45–75.
Ryle, G. (1949), *The Concept of Mind*, London: Hutchinson.
Sudnow, J. (1978), *Ways of the Hand: The organization of improvised conduct*, London: Routledge & Kegan Paul.
Wittgenstein, L. (1953), *Philosophical Investigations*, Oxford: Blackwell.

* * *

All of us experience times when, like Hamlet, with 'every motive and cue for passion', we are unable to do the deed. Why can't we? Why the inaction? For inaction and action as complex, as psychologically central as Hamlet's, nothing short of Shakespeare's play will begin to give a satisfactory answer.

But I can make it simpler. Much simpler. Most of the things we are unable to do, or try to do and fail, are less complicated than sorting out the rottenness in Denmark.

Take, for example, sitting down in a chair. Ordinarily I pay little attention to how I get in and out of chairs. Suppose that I form the wish to sit down in a particular manner and find, no matter how hard I try, that I cannot. Why can't I? Given current fashion, should you ask a psychologist any of the above questions, the answer you are most likely to hear is a cognitive one. Not that cognitivists ordinarily address themselves to not-doings. But I assume that those who believe cognitions are acceptable explanations for doings must believe they can account for not-doings as well. Or they should, if they wish their theories to be taken seriously.

One problem with cognitivism is that it feeds on the illusion that people are organized hierarchically, that something – an information-processor, a mind – is at the top and is responsible for what goes on in the ranks below. This illusion is particularly dangerous because, when examples are selected carefully enough, cognitivism can appear somewhat plausible. The plausibility is gained by seeming to come close to common experience. When we, for example, tell our legs to propel us forward and they do, an information-processor may seem to be in command. But this is a special case, is it not? Ordinarily we needn't tell them. Our legs, without command, simply take us forward. Even the special case is only fairly close to common experience because, though we may be comfortable saying, 'I tell my legs to propel me . . . ', we are less likely to say, 'My mind (or my information-processor) tells my legs to propel me . . . '

Whatever plausibility cognitive explanations have when the information-processor seems to be in control is lost when the ghost in the machine is not even seemingly in control: when, like Hamlet, we cannot. I shall explore examples of not-doing and of trying and failing.

Given our training and occupation, the grip of cognitivism on psychologists is not surprising. We live our lives, at least metaphorically, in our heads. Most of us are scholars and if we no longer as lecturers dispense knowledge, we as students have spent a considerable portion of our lives imbibing knowledge. For a scholar, knowledge, the mind's product, is at the centre of experience. It liberates, it leads to advancement, to action. Coming up with the right words, the right bits of knowledge, at the right time on tests and examinations is what it's all about: ' "Cognitive" belongs to the vocabulary of examination papers' (Ryle, 1949, p. 258).

The importance of knowledge to the lives of academics is clear. What may not be obvious to scholars is that, for most of *social* behaviour, knowledge, while important, takes one only part of the way towards action. To give a broad example (to which I shall return) – Liza Doolittle in Bernard Shaw's *Pygmalion* quite rapidly could have absorbed with her quick mind all the knowledge necessary to pass as a duchess at the Embassy reception. But this knowledge (which could be verified by an exam or an objective test) would not have enabled her to succeed in passing for a duchess or even emboldened her to try.

Another example involving a common, everyday behaviour comes from the life of the philosopher and psychologist John Dewey. My choice of Dewey is not accidental. As early as 1922 he wrote an *Introduction to Social Psychology* that gave serious attention to the far from simple connection between trying and doing or not-doing. Dewey at the time of the experience described below was fifty-nine years old, easily the best-known and most influential US philosopher, a man with reason to be confident of his cognitive powers.

> In bringing to bear whatever knowledge I already possessed – or thought I did – and whatever powers of discipline in mental application I had acquired in the pursuit of these studies, I had the most humiliating experience of my life, intellectually speaking. For to find that one is unable to execute directions, including inhibitory ones, in doing such a seemingly simple act as to sit down, when one is using all the mental capacity which one prides himself upon possessing, is not an experience congenial to one's vanity. But it may be conducive to analytic study of causal conditions, obstructive and positive. (1932, p. xvii)

Dewey is describing what happened in the course of a lesson in psychophysical re-education given by F.M. Alexander. It doesn't matter for the moment why, but what Alexander asked Dewey to do was to inhibit his usual manner of sitting down and to substitute new directions, which if successful would bring him into the chair with his head, neck and back in a balanced relationship (roughly to sit down without tensing his neck or sticking out his buttocks). What could be simpler than sitting down in a chair? Or more difficult than sitting down with the head, neck and back in a particular relationship? The failure Dewey experienced is an everyday occurrence in the life of athletes, artists, actors and artisans: everyone whose work involves skill knows that just because you tell yourself to do something in a particular way doesn't mean you can. If all it takes to produce a perfect golf swing, for instance, is to tell yourself how to swing the club, links would be crowded with sub-par golfers. A cognitive command might have been sufficient to get Dewey into the chair, but his brainpower proved helpless to enable him to get into the chair in the way he wished. The critical insight for social psychology, worked out by Dewey in *Human Nature and Conduct* (1922), involves extending the notion from athletes, artists, actors and artisans, where it is obvious, to social behaviour, where it is not. However, once stated, it should become obvious. For whereas Liza Doolittle could quickly learn what a duchess might say and do at an Embassy reception, she could not pass as a duchess until she had the skill to say the words and do the movements in a convincingly duchess-like way. Ways of behaviour cannot be reliably produced until they are mastered, much as a skill is mastered.

Why can't anyone who is capable of memorizing the lines and pronouncing the words give a convincing stage performance? Why can the performance of an understudy differ so from the performance of the star? They say the same words and do the same movements. Don't they? A close look at the stage actor's task will reveal what is missing from most behavioural accounts. The art of acting involves being able convincingly to produce bodily, vocal and emotional ways of behaving. The player's task underlines the twofold nature of behaviour: each behaviour has two components – *what* is done and the *way* in which it is done. Everything done must be done in some way. That is, people don't just sit down, they must sit down in some fashion. An actor does not simply say, 'O, what a rogue and peasant slave am I!' He says it in the way his Hamlet must say it at that moment, on that night, before that audience.

'People don't just sit down' except when the action is incompletely or abstractedly described. Modern psychology has abstracted, has removed essential features of, both the term 'behaviour' and term 'habit'. Behaviour has come to mean *what* an organism does and habit to mean *what* an organism does repeatedly. The uses are abstractions which both ignore the twofold nature of behaviour and change radically the common language meaning of the terms. None of the five definitions of 'behaviour' in the *Oxford English Dictionary* (1887) refers to what is done. The first definition is characteristic: '1. Manner of conducting oneself in the external relations of life; demeanour, deportment, bearing, manners.' Common use of the term 'habit' (as reported in the *OED*) also emphasizes the way things are done:

> Holding, having, 'haviour'; hence the way in which one holds or has oneself, i.e. the mode or condition in which one is, exists, or exhibits oneself, (a) externally; hence demeanour, outward appearance, fashion of body, mode of clothing oneself, dress, habitation; (b) in mind, character, of life; hence, mental constitution, character, disposition, way of acting, comporting oneself, or dealing with things, habitual or customary way (of acting, etc.), personal customs, accustomedness.

Psychologists eviscerated the terms with the highest of motives. The abstractions no doubt came about in an effort to simplify what goes into a stimulus and a response – particularly in animal work. Motive makes the abstractions no less pernicious. For social behaviour the essential component was excised. Behavioural *whats* have been studied as if the way something is done is of no interest. As if the words of the script and the movements prescribed by stage directions encompassed all of behaviour. As if the way the words are said and movements done are superfluous.

But you don't have to be a psychologist to engage in behavioural abstraction. You can, if you wish, ignore the *way* and 'just' sit down, 'just' swing the golf club, 'just' say the words. Looked at from a social point of view, the *what* component of behaviour can be called a 'discretionary task' (Mixon, 1980). These tasks are commonly at people's discretion because they can do them. That is, anyone can sit down, swing a golf club, pronounce words and do the thousands of other things members of a particular society learn and are expected to do. There are exceptions, of course. Some people cannot – because of disability, lack of opportunity, or whatever – do *all* of the things expected. But, generally speaking, societies depend on people being able to do a very large number of behavioural *whats*. And because everyone can do them, such discretionary tasks do not need explanation. They are of no psychological interest. A possible exception is interest in exploring differences in the discretionary tasks expected by various societies. But aside from cross-cultural analysis, behaviour becomes psychologically interesting only when the *way* component is present. People are not expected to be able to do *whats* in the same way. The *way* we sit down, swing a gold club, say words is habit/skill-dependent and varies greatly from person to person.

Cognitive explanations can appear plausible because of the seemingly direct connection between a cognition (that is, a command, intention, or whatever) and the execution *when common discretionary tasks are used as examples*. However, cognitive explanations lose even surface plausibility when we look at behaviour in its full sense. The seemingly direct connection between command or intention and execution simply is not there.

Dewey devoted the entire first section of *Human Nature and Conduct* to ways of behaving (which he called habits) and their workings. The discussion, which is not complete until the book ends, is worthy of any psychologist's attention, even the attention of those who have difficulty with Dewey's way of writing. Dewey contrasted his use of the term 'habit' (which is not unlike the *OED* definition quoted earlier) with the tendency to limit its meaning to repetition:

> Repetition is in no sense the essence of habit. Tendency to repeat acts is an incident of many habits but not of all. A man with the habit of giving way to anger may show his habit by a murderous attack upon some one who has offended. His act is nonetheless due to habit because it occurs only once in his life. The essence of habit is an acquired pre-disposition to *ways* or modes of response, not to particular acts except as, under special conditions, these express a way of behaving. (1922, p. 42)

One of Dewey's chief contributions to the understanding of habit is his insistence on its skill-like nature. Unlike Ryle, who had reason to emphasize the *difference* between intelligent capacities and mechanical habits, Dewey wished to point out the element of intelligent capacity or skill in habits. Mere 'blind habit' did not much interest him except as something that might possibly be transformed into a skill (or intelligent capacity).

Habits, as ways or modes of response – unlike abstracted *whats*, which can break down easily into stimuli and responses – are not convenient and easy to use as units of analysis. Habits do not usually come in neat, time-bound units. They share a common difficulty with motor skills:

> The difficulty is that while the idea and the reflex are excellent concepts for describing behaviours that naturally break into discrete units, they are not nearly as satisfactory for describing behaviours that are essentially continuous. (Irion, 1969, p. 2)

Difficult or not, habit as a unit of analysis offers decided advantages over the units commonly used by social psychologists. Social psychology, throughout most of its history, has been a cognitive discipline. The components of its key term 'attitude', for example, are taken directly from the tripartite division of mind: cognitive, emotional and conative. Cognitivism is not avoided by changing the meaning, as some writers do, of conative from 'will' to 'behaviour', nor when a person's attitude is measured by a discretionary task – typically by checking an attitude scale. Not just attitude research, but very nearly all of experimental social psychology employs discretionary tasks as dependent variables. Although lack of psychological interest is sufficient reason for not using discretionary tasks as dependent variables, it is not the only reason. Anyone can do them: participants, for example, can check an attitude scale anywhere they please. Thus, rather than being determined by the independent variable or variables, the outcome is in the control of the participant. Experimenters know this, so they attempt to trick the participants into giving a 'valid' response by various forms of deceit, but succeed only in producing results impossible to interpret and in creating serious problems for their truthful colleagues (Mixon, 1977). Deception as a 'control' is an ethical and methodological disaster. Luckily for the future of serious research, habit's skill-like nature makes the construction of 'habit scales' on the model of attitude scales unlikely. It would be as absurd as measuring a motor skill by asking people to agree or disagree with statements about their degree of skill.

Gordon Allport could hardly have been more wrong. In a historical essay on social psychology, Allport devotes two paragraphs to Dewey's conception of habit and concludes that Dewey claimed too many attributes for habit and that the notion was too vague. The concept *attitude*, Allport claimed, 'filled the need Dewey felt' (1968, p. 59). But attitude and habit – at least as social psychologists have defined attitude – are radically different concepts. Attitude is cognitive; habits involve the entire psychophysical being.

We can, of course, conceive of cognitive habits. And they appear to pose special difficulties because of the seemingly direct connection between command or intention and acts, when it comes to cognitive acts. Dewey denies a privileged connection:

> ... we are likely to suppose that ... control of the *body* is physical and hence is external to mind and will. Transfer the command inside character and mind, and it is fancied that an idea and the desire to realize it will take immediate effect. After we get to the point of recognizing that habits must intervene between wish and execution in the case of bodily acts, we still cherish the illusion that they can be dispensed with in the case of mental and moral acts. Thus the net result is to make us sharpen the distinction between non-moral and moral activities, and to lead us to confine the latter strictly within a private, immaterial realm. But in fact, formation of ideas as well as their execution depends upon habit. (1922, p. 30)

It may be that the notion of discretionary tasks will help here. When we abstract behaviour, when we 'just' sit down, swing a golf club, pronounce words, there does seem to be a direct connection between command and execution. There is a parallel in cognitive matters, for cognitive behaviour can be abstracted too. When the command is, '2 × 2 = ?' or 'Who issued the Behaviourist manifesto in 1913?' the connection between command and execution seems direct. But if the command is 'Write an essay in the style of William Hazlitt' or 'Write an essay on the early days of Behaviourism', the direct connection is no longer even seemingly there. Even an exhaustive familiarity with the writings of Hazlitt will not guarantee that I can write in his style. And encyclopaedic knowledge about Behaviourism is no guarantee that I can write or even think about it in a coherent or lucid way, or in any particular fashion. Ways, styles of thinking, are just as skill-dependent as ways of moving, speaking, etc. If we wish to think in the way a Zen master thinks, for example, we must master the skill. We can't simply decide to do it.

An alternative to cognitivism would be anything that puts cognitive studies in their place. Place is important. As Ryle took care to demonstrate, the Ghost isn't there. Mind should be studied, but should be studied where it lives: 'the chessboard, the platform, the scholar's desk, the judge's bench, the lorry-driver's seat, the studio and the football field are among its places' (Ryle, 1949, p. 51). Ways of thinking are interesting in themselves and are part of behaviour. So much depends upon how they are studied and what's made of them. The claim that behaviour can be *explained* only by appeal to internal cognitive processes cannot be taken seriously. Explanation that leaves out, for example, ways of moving, speaking, feeling and all the external contingencies is curiously impoverished. People simply are not (even by analogy) machines impervious to environment and controlled by cognitive processes. You can think in a particular way only if you can, you can perceive in a certain way only if you can, you can perform an action in a particular way only if you can, you can speak in a certain way only if you can, you can express emotion in a certain way only if you can . . . and no amount of cognitive processing will make a bit of difference to those *cans*. The only way you can do these things in a certain way is to gain the skill. And that, ordinarily, takes time and practice.

Another way of understanding the importance of ways of behaving or habits is in terms of ends and means. A command or intention to do something is to command or intend an end. Habits are the means. Dewey couldn't sit in a certain way because he lacked the skilled means. The same with the golfer and actor. Liza couldn't go straight to the Embassy reception because she lacked the means to succeed. To think that cognitive processes alone can do anything is, in Dewey's terms, to engage in magical thinking – to think that the wish alone can produce the end: 'The principle of magic is found whenever it is hoped to get results without intelligent control of means . . . ' (1922, p. 27).

An alternative to cognitivism would first of all give up the notion that any part can explain the whole – at least with an organism as complex as a human that lives in an environment as intricate and as encroaching as ours. Cognitive 'explanation' masks the important questions: How can we do what we intend to do? How and why do we fail? How can we develop habits that serve as effective means? How does one type of habit interact with or influence another type? By asking such questions, unimagined influences and relationships become subject to study. For example, actors can tell us that the way a character perceives influences expression. And the way a character expresses influences the way and what of perception.

Dewey said that the early lessons with F.M. Alexander produced 'the most humiliating experience of my life, intellectually speaking'. Yet Dewey went on having lessons for the rest of his life – over thirty years. What kept him going? On a vulgar level he persevered because the lessons helped keep him healthy and young (Dykhuizen, 1973). And no skill is ever entirely mastered. At another level Dewey stated that ideas he held in an abstract and theoretical way were given concrete significance and substance by study and friendship with Alexander. The effect of the lessons on his philosophy was so powerful that E.D. McCormack could write a persuasive dissertation (1958) which makes a strong case for the proposition that the key to Dewey's post-1916 writing lies in understanding the work and influence of Alexander.

What did Alexander teach? Well, for one thing, he taught the importance of 'use' – a concept which maps somewhat on to what Dewey called 'habit', and I call 'ways of behaviour'. He wrote of 'faulty sensory appreciation', which means that use (habit) influences, even seriously distorts, perception. That is, for example, my senses may tell me that my neck muscles are free and relaxed when they are in fact shortened and tense. Alexander emphasized the futility of 'end-gaining', which means going directly for an end without mastering the means to gain it. Describing the Alexander experience has baffled the best writers – and Alexander taught some pretty good ones (e.g. Bernard Shaw and Aldous Huxley). It involves a *relationship* between head, neck and back. When the relationship works, Raymond Dart's (1947) simple term 'poise' describes the state. The experience provided for the pupil by the teacher involves being and moving in a lighter, freer and more integrated way than imagined possible. And the lessons are directed towards giving you the capacity to be and move that way yourself. (For a fuller discussion see any of F. Matthias Alexander's four books [1918, 1924, 1932, 1941], or a more recent account of Frank Pierce Jones [1976].)

> The Alexander technique is a method of re-education that is psychophysical in the sense that it brings about a change in the person as a whole, by introducing a change in his total pattern of reaction. It is not an attempt to reeducate the mind by way of the body or the body by way of the mind. It is a method for changing and redirecting on a conscious level the background of postural tone which underlies and makes possible all orderly motion. A change in this fundamental pattern is a total change, and it affects the character of any activity whether that activity is mental or physical. (Jones, 1953)

I think that Jones's description is a good one and that, furthermore, it provides an apt model for other habit change. A change in any kind of habit will influence the character of any activity. However, in the absence of the kind of study undertaken by Alexander, we cannot assume that a change in habit will be a change for the better – except, Dewey might argue, in the case of changing a mechanical habit into a flexible one, or what Ryle would call an 'intelligent capacity'. In most cases, how the activity is influenced is an empirical question. How, for example, might a change in the way we speak influence the way we hear?

The ground, as you see, has shifted from one type of explanation (can cognitive processes *explain* behaviour?) to questions of assessing the effects of changes of habit on 'a change in the person as a whole'. And it is, I think, much better ground for social psychology to be on, for it would allow us to look seriously at, for example, Alexander's method of re-educating or reintegrating habits, and to ask questions like: What restrains or limits our capacity to act? (Dewey's 'obstructive' condition). What can enhance our capacities? (Dewey's 'positive' condition). In other words, when we cannot, how can we? Or to what extent can we take responsibility for our habits and thus our actions? (Mixon, 1980). The shift is from an attempt to use an internal process to explain the doings of a whole to an attempt to understand the workings of the whole; from questions of linear causality to an interest in negative restraints, and limits on action. That is, one asks 'not why one particular thing happened but instead why everything else did not happen' (Ogilvy, 1979, p. 26).

Unfamiliar territory for most psychologists, but not lonely. Many of us are aware that our colleagues in the natural sciences long ago stopped talking the sort of causal language we indulge in. Looking for limits on actions is more interesting, and more useful – especially for those who wish, like Hamlet, to do something they cannot do.

References

Alexander, F.M. (1918), *Man's Supreme Inheritance*, New York and London: Dutton.
Alexander, F.M. (1924), *Constructive Conscious Control of the Individual*, London: Methuen.
Alexander, F.M. (1932) *The Use of the Self*, New York: Dutton.
Alexander, F.M. (1941) *The Universal Constant in Living*, New York: Dutton.
Allport, G. (1968), 'The historical background to modern social psychology', in G. Lindsey and E. Aronson (eds), *The Handbook of Social Psychology*, vol. 1, Reading, MA: Addison-Wesley.
Dart, R.A. (1947), 'The attainment of poise', *South African Medical Journal*, **21**, 74–91.
Dewey, J. (1922), *Human Nature and Conduct: An introduction to social psychology*, New York: Holt.
Dewey, J. (1932), Introduction, in Alexander, *The Use of the Self*.
Dykhuizen, G. (1973), *The Life and Mind of John Dewey* Carbondale and Edwardsville, IL: South Illinois University Press.
Irion, A.L. (1969), 'Historical introduction', in E.A. Bilodeau and I.M. Bilodeau (eds), *Principles of Skill Acquisition*, New York: Academic Press.
Jones, F.P. (1953), 'Psychophysical re-education and the postural reflexes', lecture given at the Science Weekend, Bard College, NY, May.
Jones, F.P. (1976), *Body Awareness in Action: A study of the Alexander technique*, New York: Schocken.
McCormack, E.D. (1958), *Frederick Matthias Alexander and John Dewey: A neglected influence*, unpublished doctoral dissertation, University of Toronto.
Mixon, D. (1977), 'Why pretend to deceive?', *Personality and Social Psychology Bulletin*, **3**, 647–53.
Mixon, D. (1980), 'The place of habit in the control of action', *Journal for the Theory of Social Behaviour*, **10**, 169–86.
Ogilvy, J. (1979), *Many Dimensional Man: Decentralizing self, society, and the sacred*, New York: Harper & Row.
Ryle, G. (1949), *The Concept of Mind*, London: Hutchinson.

4
Frederic Bartlett and the rise of prehistoric psychology*

Alan Costall

Editors' introduction

Most textbooks on cognitive psychology would include the British psychologist Frederic Bartlett among the early 'pioneers'. His concept of schema is still seen as an important basis upon which to explain the active, structuring role of the individual in remembering. Furthermore, he is often given credit for stressing the importance of social factors in cognition. It is only recently, however, that researchers have begun to appreciate the radical position Bartlett adopted in his earliest work: human cognition, he argued, is irreducibly social. A very significant series of publications has recently appeared that pursue this theme, by challenging the notion of 'memory' as an internal and individual process and to place it instead within its social context (see Butler, 1989; Casey, 1987; Connerton, 1989; Middleton and Edwards, 1990):

> . . . it is in the world that memories are begotten, and it is in the world that they find their natural destiny. To acknowledge this is to de-center and de-individuate remembering as we usually think of it – namely the possession of individual selves – and it is to consider that things, not just representations of things, may be thoroughly steeped in memory. (Casey, 1987, p. 311)

As the following chapter explains, Bartlett did not pursue his important insights. His interests in the social foundations of cognition became increasingly marginalized in his attempts to promote psychology as both an academic and an applied discipline.

---

* Based on a contribution to the symposium 'Bartlett and the Psychology of Human Cognition', Annual Conference of the British Psychological Society, University of St Andrews, 2 April 1989. I am very grateful to Professor Ian M.L. Hunter for his helpful comments and recollections.

References

Butler, T. (ed.) (1989), *Memory*, Oxford: Blackwell.
Casey, E.S. (1987), *Remembering: A phenomenological study*, Bloomington and Indianapolis: Indiana University Press.
Connerton, P. (1989), *How Societies Remember*, Cambridge University Press.
Middleton, D. and Edwards, D. (eds) (1990), *Collective Remembering*, London: Sage.

* * *

It is only if we interpret individual to mean pre-social that we can take psychology to be prehistoric . . .
(BARTLETT, 1923, p. 12)

Bartlett's psychological career

The establishment of psychology as a university discipline in Britain was by no means easy. McDougall recalled his cool reception at Oxford in 1904, as Wilde Reader in Mental Philosophy:

> The post had its drawbacks. It was, I think, T.H. Huxley who said that, if he had to devise a punishment for a very wicked scientist, he would condemn him to be a professor of science at Oxford. If I had been recognized as a teacher of science, my punishment would have been light; for by that date science was well established at Oxford. But I was neither fish, flesh, nor fowl. . . . The scientists suspected me of being a metaphysician; and the philosophers regarded me as representing an impossible and non-existent branch of science. (McDougall, 1930, p. 207)

Conditions at Cambridge were better, though hardly perfect. Yet by the time Bartlett graduated in the Moral Sciences Tripos in 1914, Ward, Rivers and Myers had helped begin to clear the way. Most notably, the Cambridge Laboratory of Experimental Psychology had been formally opened in May 1913, although Myers, its new director, received no salary, and even contributed a considerable amount towards its foundation (Bartlett, 1965).

When Bartlett graduated, he felt torn between anthropology and psychology, but Rivers, his director of studies at St John's, argued that he could painlessly resolve this dilemma by opting for psychology. He was assured that this was the ideal choice since psychology, especially a knowledge of psychophysical methods, would be an essential preparation for anthropological studies (Bartlett, 1937b, p. 105; see also Bartlett, 1936). Bartlett seems to have been convinced by this reasoning (cf. Bartlett, 1937a, pp. 416–17), and in 1914 he took over from Cyril Burt as Assistant in the Psychological Laboratory. When the First World War began he was effectively left in charge, since Rivers and Myers left to join the army as doctors, whilst Bartlett, who was unfit for active service, remained behind.[1] At the end of the war, Rivers made a definite move into anthropology, and Myers, having been made Reader on his return, soon left to set up the new National Institute of Industrial Psychology in 1922. Myers had been disappointed by the grudging reception he felt Cambridge had given to psychology; indeed, there was no guarantee that his position as Reader would outlast him, so he delayed his departure until he had ensured that Bartlett would succeed him (Bartlett, 1965; Broadbent, 1970b). Thus by 1922, at the age of thirty-six, Bartlett was the most senior representative of psychology at Cambridge: Myers had left; Rivers had died; and Ward, who was still around, had lost interest (Bartlett, 1936). Glittering prizes eventually followed for Bartlett, and these included the new Chair of Experimental Psychology established in 1931; an FRS in 1932; a CBE in 1941; and even a knighthood in 1948.

As Donald Broadbent has stressed (1970a, p. 1), Bartlett's impact upon British psychology was not only crucial but also historically unique. Given the scale of modern psychology as an academic discipline and a profession, it would no longer be possible for any one person to exert a comparable influence. Bartlett entered the subject at an early stage, yet at a time when there was indeed a subject to 'enter', and when the initial hassles had been to some extent resolved. He was fortunate, certainly, to have Myers to help advance his career, passing on to Bartlett not only his readership at Cambridge but also the editorship of the *British Journal of Psychology* in 1924. In addition, as many commentators have remarked, he was highly effective on committees and shrewd in placing people, so that after the Second World War his students held what Broadbent describes as 'the lion's share of the Professorships of Psychology in Britain' (Broadbent, 1970b, p. 3). This was not simply a matter of lack of competition. To quote one aggrieved party:

> When I started in psychology, there was an absolute monopoly, like a feudal supremacy, of the 'Oxbridge' tradition. Almost by divine right, chairs in Great Britain or the Commonwealth would be allocated to graduates from Cambridge. (Oxford came into this much later, having been prevented from

42 Against Cognitivism

setting up a proper 'school' for a long time.) There were one or two exceptions, like Rex Knight in Aberdeen; such 'colonials' were occasionally tolerated. But, for the rest, there was an iron curtain around academia that no outsider from London or Redbrick could penetrate. . . . The feudalism is still there, but it is dying. (Eysenck, 1980, pp. 159, 173)[2]

Bartlett retired in 1952, but remained very active; he published his book on thinking in 1958, and continued to serve as a consultant and on committees (Broadbent, 1970b, p. 7). He died in 1969, shortly before his eighty-third birthday. But of course, his influence persists. The people appointed under his regime have themselves helped to determine subsequent priorities and appointments in the discipline. In addition, his ex-pupils were largely, if not exclusively, responsible for establishing that somewhat Masonic organization the Experimental Psychology Society, which once, at least, played an important power-broking role within British academic psychology (cf. Alice Heim, cited in Buzzard, 1971, p. 3).

In stressing these facts about the 'politics' of the British scene, my purpose is not to downplay Bartlett's real scientific contribution. My point is this: given that Bartlett was bound to have some kind of an impact, why did that impact take the form it in fact did? Why did only some of Bartlett's proposals concerning the status of human cognition, and not others, take hold?

Bartlett as a 'pioneer' of cognitive psychology

The idea of a 'cognitive revolution' – an abrupt overthrow of a totally unified 'behaviourism' – is surely overplayed. As the standard histories have unwittingly shown, there are just *too many* 'early pioneers' of modern cognitive psychology. Yet there can be no question that psychology has taken a distinctly cognitive turn, nor that Bartlett played some significant role in preparing the way. Thus Colin Crampton, presents Bartlett as steering Cambridge psychology through the 'mysticism' of Freud, the 'sterility' of Watson, Hull and Ebbinghaus, the seductions of Gestaltism, towards an 'atheoretical, eclectic and concrete psychology'. In doing so, Crampton continues, he 'managed to anticipate many of the central ideas of today's cognitive psychology' (Crampton, 1978, p. 372). This view of Bartlett as a 'straight' cognitive psychologist is widely presented in the textbooks, and certainly finds impressive numerical support from the current citation statistics for his text *Remembering* (1932) (see White, 1983, p. 426). Yet, as I shall now explain, there are a number of different ways in which Bartlett might be regarded as a pioneer of modern cognitive psychology.

A psychology of the higher mental functions

The most obvious and general sense in which Bartlett was a pioneer of cognitive psychology is the simple fact that from the outset his psychological work concerned 'the higher mental functions'. Yet the presentation of Bartlett as a kind of martyr – 'a solitary psychologist working in Britain . . . keeping the cognitive faith' (Gardner, 1987, p. 114) – is perhaps somewhat far-fetched. After all, benighted does not usually mean the receipt of a knighthood!

As early as 1929, in his contribution on 'Psychology' for the *Encyclopaedia Britannica*, Bartlett cheerfully portrayed current psychology as follows:

> *Everywhere* in psychology the main drift appears to be away from atomistic and mechanical types of explanation towards a recognition of the unique, though complex, activities and patterns of activity which govern and direct all highly developed human conduct and feeling, and gradually build up the constructions of human knowledge. (Bartlett, 1929b, p. 256, emphasis added)

Bartlett saw himself as part of a wide group of researchers within psychology (such as the Gestaltists and European functionalists) concerned with human cognition. In addition, of course, he was familiar with the anthropological work being carried out on this topic.

Knowing as a constructive process

Stagner follows Neisser (1967) in identifying a more specific and substantial contribution that Bartlett has made to modern cognitive psychology:

> Bartlett earned his status as the founding father of cognitive psychology [for] . . . his view of memory as a transformational process (in which the item as recalled may have only a modest resemblance to the original stimulus material). (Stagner, 1988, pp. 438–9)

Neisser (1967), in his very influential text *Cognitive Psychology*, had sought to capture this sense of the knower as a constructive agent by appeal to Hebb's analogy of the palaeontologist imaginatively re-creating an entire animal from a few bare bones (Hebb, 1949, p. 47).[3] This image of the knower as processing or reconstructing basic data which are meaningless, or at best ambiguous or incomplete, is one which has long dominated cognitive psychology. This is taken to be the main theme of Bartlett's book on remembering by most later commentators – including Bartlett himself (Bartlett, 1973, p. 140).

A naturalistic approach

Bartlett's third contribution to modern developments in cognitive psychology concerns his continued insistence that the experimenter should not lose sight of the world beyond the laboratory. Indeed, the value of what Stagner (1988, p. 437) calls a 'naturalistic approach' is increasingly recognized within cognitive psychology, and has certainly been taken up enthusiastically by Neisser in his reaction against cognitive boxology (e.g. Neisser, 1976). Again, I do not mean to question Bartlett's role in all this, but rather to suggest that his position was a good deal more complicated than is typically portrayed. For in his 1932 book we find Bartlett, having just lampooned Ebbinghaus for the artificiality of his experiments, himself presenting not only strange, inconsequential 'stories' like the 'War of the Ghosts' (hardly everyday reading material for the people he was studying) but also schematic pictures presented at minimal exposures, and most shocking of all – inkblots! Now of course Bartlett was no fool and, I think, largely realized what he was doing, which was to employ a kind of 'lesion' study in which the 'extirpation' or reduction of meaning in the display forced the people in his experiments to 'mobilize' all their resources in their continual effort after meaning. Yet, although he stressed that it was a method which can be employed only 'with the very greatest caution' (Bartlett, 1932, p. 6), I suspect that Bartlett sometimes confused himself (and no doubt others) about its use.[4]

There is, however, a second and rather distinct sense in which Bartlett is supposed to have pioneered a 'naturalistic approach', and this concerns the strong *practical* orientation of his later work, especially during the Second World War. But it is not at all obvious to me that this kind of practical orientation in itself ensures 'ecological validity' in the current sense of this term. Many real-life situations can be pretty artificial and odd. Indeed, the important role of applied psychology is surely primarily that of a troubleshooter helping us to cope with the peculiar problems posed by modern life. For example, the research of the 1960s and 1970s on memory for digit sequences, which now strikes many students as highly abstract and esoteric, started out, at least, as highly relevant to practical situations, such as the design of all-digit telephone codes. Confusion arises only – and it so often does – when such problem situations are treated as representative and of fundamental, theoretical importance.

The social and cultural context of human cognition

Most recently, Bartlett has been taken as a significant contributor to the project for a cultural psychology of cognition. Thus Derek Edwards and David Middleton (1987) have argued that Bartlett's book *Remembering* can be viewed not as a 'major forerunner' of the information-processing approach but, alternatively, as a 'foundation' for a broader view which treats cognition functionally and within its cultural context:

> Bartlett was truly concerned with . . . the inherently social basis of mentality itself. It made no sense to Bartlett to isolate the components of mentality as consisting in the Platonic division of cognition, affect and conation. Mentality was driven by the criteria of functional adaptiveness to social conditions and contexts of everyday existence. The full force of Bartlett's critique of the theory of mental faculties has been lost in a tradition which, while citing him as an antecedent, takes as its subject-matter individual mentality, defines for investigation a cognitive component, and proceeds to divide this methodologically invented entity into its component stages, levels and processes. *It is not Bartlett's legacy that cognitive social psychology . . . and the study of individual memory . . . have become so widely separated.* (Edwards and Middleton, 1987, pp. 89–90; emphasis added; cf. Douglas, 1987)

My purpose, in the remainder of this chapter, is to examine this claim in some detail.

Remembering

The full title of Bartlett's classic 1932 text is *Remembering: A study of experimental and social psychology*. There is indeed, as many commentators have noted, a good deal of discussion in this book of the social and cultural context of cognition. But Bartlett makes it clear that his 1932 book was transitional, for by the time he was writing it he had already moved beyond what he calls his 'conventionalization phase' (Bartlett, 1958, p. 144). As he explained, the First World War had interrupted the sequence of his thought, and he then came across Head's notion of the schema which led him to place a new emphasis upon 'constructive imagination and thinking' (p. 148). As I shall try to explain, the schema concept, despite its promise, readily lent itself to an internalized and 'privatized' treatment of mentality. Although Bartlett continued to publish occasionally on anthropology and social psychology (e.g. Bartlett, 1937a, 1939, 1943), closer research contacts with engineers and physicists, especially during the Second World War, were to lead to a dominant interest in perceptual-motor skills, and the new appeal of cybernetic and computer analogies. Broadbent (1970b, p. 8) has suggested that this new technology provided just the language in which to formulate Bartlett's insights, a view with which Bartlett, in public at least, concurred (Bartlett, 1955, 1958).[5] The upshot was not that Bartlett relinquished his conviction of the importance of social context, but that his anthropological concerns became increasingly marginalized and separated from his experimental work:

> Social psychology was one of my leading interests when I was more or less beginning my psychological career, and it has remained a leading interest ever since, although influences over which I could have no direct control made it necessary for me to turn to other fields of investigation. (Bartlett, 1957, p. 72; cf. Zangwill, 1970, p. 80)

It would be a mistake, I suggest, to view these other pursuits as merely displacing Bartlett's work in social psychology. The move towards the study of people-minding-machines (see Bartlett, 1957, pp. 53–5) surely set a standard of method and a role for psychology against which social psychology could only appear as rather 'soft' science. The situation of psychology at Cambridge within a faculty of biological sciences – a development which Bartlett himself had encouraged – inevitably reinforced this trend.[6]

Bartlett, in his treatment of the social in *Remembering*, comes across as distinctly uneasy, especially in comparison to his earlier writings. For example, when he explains that the group can influence the individual both directly, through the actual presence of other people, and also *indirectly*, through the influence of the group's beliefs, conventions, customs, traditions, and institutions, he seems far from happy with the implication:

> .... this is, theoretically speaking, rather troublesome, because it seems to mean that *everything* in psychology belongs to social psychology, except idiosyncrasies and such forms of reaction as are immediately and dominantly determined by physical stimuli. (Bartlett, 1932, p. 243; emphasis added)

Furthermore, although Bartlett's continued interest in the anthropological problem of 'conventionalization' is evident, his handling of it is distinctly evasive. Indeed, his experimental methods were hardly best suited to reveal the social dimension. As he himself had earlier put it:

> No doubt many of the most potent influences which help to determine the nature and direction of conventionalisation in daily life are definitely social in origin. And such influences are not clearly brought out by the type of experiment the results of which I propose to discuss in the present paper. In these experiments subjects effected their reproduction of the presented material rather as isolated individuals than definitely as members of a group. (Bartlett, 1920a, pp. 30–1; see also Douglas, 1987, p. 88)

But an important tension also existed at the level of theory. For Bartlett, the concept of schema served to capture a parallel between the process in which 'new material is assimilated to the persistent past of the group' (p. 280) and the way in which an individual person deals with new information. But the problem is that these two processes, the social and the individual, remained in 'parallel' (p. 309). They were not integrated in any serious way. Instead, as Northway has noted, 'the schema and the social group [are treated by Bartlett] as two separate forces influencing remembering' (Northway, 1940a, p. 325; see also p. 321). Northway puts the blame for this particular source of difficulty in Bartlett's treatment of the schema upon his 'familiarity with Rivers's work and his early and continuing interest in anthropology' (ibid., p. 321) and, in fact, she recommends the solution largely adopted later within cognitive psychology – which is, of course, to treat 'social background' as a separate 'factor' which operates ultimately at the level of the individual schema – i.e. at the level of 'what the subject constructs from the material'.

There is indeed within Bartlett's 1932 book a serious conflict between the individual and the social which requires resolution. But, contrary to Northway's claim, I suggest that it was Bartlett's individualized concept of schema that caused the trouble. It displaced and obscured the radical proposals concerning the relation between the social and the individual presented in his earlier book, *Psychology and Primitive Culture* (1923).

Psychology and Primitive Culture

There can be no question that an important issue throughout the history of academic psychology has been that of disciplinary autonomy. Bartlett was alert to the problem of how to define psychology so as to distinguish it safely from philosophy, physiology and sociology. Significantly, his text *Remembering* begins with a discussion of how a distinctively psychological approach to psychological experiment is an improvement upon that adopted by the physicist, the physiologist or the philosopher (Bartlett, 1932, pp. 1–2). However, the hostility of philosophers to psychology does not seem to have been so profound at Cambridge as it was for a very long time at Oxford (see Crampton, 1978, pp. 254–5) and the Cambridge physiologists were positively supportive from the outset (though on their own terms, as Myers discovered). By 1926, as Bartlett explained:

> [The Psychological Laboratory had been organized into a new Faculty structure] and placed where it properly belonged, with Physiology, Biochemistry and Pathology, as one of a group of 'biological sciences', . . . Very nearly all the subsequent changes have grown out of this one. (Bartlett, 1937, p. 108)

The problem of defining a niche for psychology as a *cognitive* psychology did, however, pose itself clearly – from the direction of anthropology, and social science more generally. As we shall see, Bartlett explicitly addresses this problem in *Psychology and Primitive Culture* (Bartlett, 1923). The book was based on a series of lectures given at Bedford College for Women in 1922, which Bartlett had undertaken mainly on the advice of Rivers (for related publications of this period, see Bartlett, 1920a, b, 1925, 1927b, 1928, 1929a). Bartlett's purpose was not to argue for a distinctive kind of primitive mentality, and in fact he strongly rejected this notion (see also Bartlett, 1927b). Instead, he presented examples based on primitive societies to extract general principles about the relation between the individual and the group. And in undertaking this task he inevitably confronted the question of how psychology, as a distinct subject, relates to sociology and anthropology. This question had already been raised in stark form not only by Durkheim and the French School but also, within psychology, by Wundt. And their answer had been clear: an *individual* psychology of the higher mental functions was a contradiction in terms, for human cognition was irreducibly cultural and historical by its very nature.

Bartlett takes on what he calls 'the time-honoured question of the relation between sociology and psychology' at the very outset of his book. He refers to Rivers, who had insisted that the sociologist could – and indeed should – disregard psychological facts, and 'rigorously confine his attention to purely social determination' (Bartlett, 1923, p. 25). Bartlett agrees with this position as far as the sociologist is concerned, and provides plenty of examples of group processes, such as the elaboration of rituals (see pp. 161, 206–8, 212–13), where there is 'no necessary connexion with conscious purpose, and [the result] is, in fact, rarely or never foreseen by any individual (p. 161; see also Bartlett, 1928). But he insists that the argument does not work in reverse. Psychology cannot divorce itself from sociology, for that would tempt us to do exactly what we should avoid – seek explanations which 'always . . . go back to the individual as he may be pictured to exist outside of any social group' (p. 8). For Bartlett saw (as clearly as had Wundt and Durkheim) that such a conception of individual psychology would properly amount to little more than sensory psychophysics or, as Jahoda (1982, p. 40) has recently put it, 'a very impoverished residue'.

This same point has, of course, been echoed, especially within the British scene, by the many philosophical critics of the pretensions of scientific psychology. Their implication was that psychology should be confined to this ahistorical residue. Interestingly, Collingwood – to my mind one of the most effective and engaging of these critics – did envisage the following possible development for psychology as an essentially historical inquiry:

[One] idea of a mental science would be, to use Comte's famous distinction, 'metaphysical', depending on the conception of an occult substance underlying the fact of historical activity. . . . [The] alternative idea would be 'positive', depending on the conception of similarities or uniformities among [the facts of historical activity] themselves. According to this idea, the task of mental science would be to detect [through historical interpretation] types or patterns of activity, repeated over and over again in history itself. . . . [It] can have no guarantee that the laws it establishes will hold good beyond the historical period from which its facts are drawn. . . . If it tried to overcome this limitation by drawing upon a wider field, relying on ancient history, modern anthropology, and so on, for a larger basis of facts, it will still never be more than a generalized description of certain phases in human history. It will never be a non-historical science of mind. (Collingwood, 1945, p. 222)

Although Bartlett's approach to psychology centred upon the person, he put little store on what the individual thinks, feels or desires, but rather on what he called the 'conditions of behaviour'. As he acknowledged, 'it might almost be said that what I am proposing is a form of behaviourism' (1923, p. 269).[7] However – and in this respect he felt that he differed from behaviourism in its dogmatic form – Bartlett insisted that some of these conditions are genuinely social, and should be recognized as such. In his treatment of these conditions of observable human responses there is a clear counterpart to his later concept of schema, but one which seems even closer to that of Ward and Lotze, their view of memory as '[not] a mere precipitate of impressions, a storing up of injected copies of things . . . [but] a kind of scheme, a plan of action, . . . the power of acting again in the way in which one acted before, with a recognition of the fact that the action is qualitatively like a previous action' (Peters, 1962, p. 595; see also Northway, 1940a, b). Thus Bartlett, in his 1923 book, invokes the concept of 'tendencies'; these tendencies are, as he puts it, 'correlative' with the situation and do not imply the existence of any underlying, permanent mental structure (Bartlett, 1923, pp. 273–4). Bartlett's discussion here certainly takes a distinctly 'mutualist' turn. Indeed, it is this early concept of tendency which most clearly relates to the sense of 'schema' developing in modern PDP research:

Schemata are not 'things'. There is no representational object which is a schema. Rather, schemata emerge at the moment they are needed from the interaction of large numbers of much simpler elements all working in concert with one another. Schemata are not explicit entities, but rather are implicit in our knowledge and are created by the very environment that they are trying to interpret . . . [In] the conventional story, schemata are stored in memory. Indeed, they are the major *content of memory*. In our case, *nothing stored corresponds very closely to* a schema. What is stored is a set of connection strengths which, when activated, have implicitly in them the ability to generate states that correspond to instantiated schemata. (Rumelhart, Smolensky, McClelland and Hinton, 1986, pp. 20–1)

Yet the problem of relating the social and the individual *seems* to emerge even in this early treatment, for Bartlett gives the impression of setting up a dualism between what he calls group difference tendencies and individual difference tendencies. These are presented as though they were mere analogues, the former being to the group what the latter are to the person (see pp. 245, 251). But in fact, Bartlett believed that he was demonstrating in this book, a programme for relating the social to the individual, and this was not the one generally assumed within psychology, the 'precarious . . . inference from knowledge of how individuals react separately to what they will do when they come together' (p. 279). Instead, he was promoting an approach to the individual as necessarily nested within a social order. We discover, as it were, the individual – what is individual – *within* the group (pp. 279–80). We start with those conditions which are general to all groups, then consider those processes which are specific to the group, such as particular modes and mechanisms of the transmission and maintenance of culture. Only then, he insists, may we 'legitimately attempt to go further', if indeed the group is sufficiently open to direct observation – i.e. 'try to trace what are the variations of individual attitude in regard to the specialised social responses':

> If we can do this successfully for all our problems we have taken the final step in the development of a complete social psychology. For we have now effected a union between that study of the individual as such which is the concern of general psychological investigation, and that account of the psychical conditions of behaviour in the group which social psychology sets itself to pursue. (Bartlett, 1923, p. 280)

Conclusion

If, as Slobodin has suggested, Rivers was concerned with the 'ethnology of cognition' (Slobodin, 1978, p. 25), then Bartlett's early writings could be said to present a social anthropology of cognition.[8] What made his approach distinctly psychological, however, was his emphasis upon the *person* within a social group. Edwards and Middleton (1987) have rightly drawn attention to this neglected aspect of Bartlett's work. What I have tried to show in the present chapter, however, is that the real statement of Bartlett's anthropological approach is not to be found in his book *Remembering*, but in his earlier work. *Remembering* is a transitional work, which certainly points to his earlier, cultural perspective but also towards an individualistic and mechanical view of cognition, which Bartlett himself, in his increasingly 'official' role as a leader of British psychology, came to promote. In his contribution on 'Memory' for the *Encyclopaedia Britannica*, written at the end of his life, he appears to accept, if not the terminology, then the agenda of the new cybernetic approach. He makes no reference whatsoever to the social or cultural:

> By the early 1960s it was uncertain whether this latest of all approaches, in its bearing on memory, would . . . do little more than introduce a new and perhaps more exact vocabulary for the expert. The critical questions remained as they had been ever since remembering began to be investigated: how to understand and reconcile the conflicting demands for the accurate and literal reinstatement of events and experiences at the time they 'go into storage', and the equally urgent requirement that when they come 'out of storage' it should be in forms sufficiently flexible to meet the challenges of a constantly changing world. Questions of the nature of the location of the persistent effects of original experiences ('traces') had been subjected to an enormous amount of research. (Bartlett, 1973, p. 140)

If we are to treat Bartlett as a 'pioneer', it is as a pioneer of *two* approaches to cognition, at odds with one another. There is the familiar kind of cognitive psychology which either disregards the social and cultural or, at best, 'privatizes' them within our heads (see Lave, 1988, pp. 90–1), and there is a radical alternative that Bartlett also helped to define. The subject of this psychology remains the individual – but as nested within a social order, a participant in a social world.

Notes

1. In his teens, Bartlett had contracted pleurisy; he had studied largely at home, and it was for health reasons that he had not started his Cambridge degree until he was getting on for twenty-five.
2. This problem was compounded (as Eysenck himself notes) for London graduates; Cambridge, with its strong experimental emphasis, was dismissive of the psychometric orientation of the London course.
3. Note that Hebb himself was referring to *tachistoscopic* perception.
4. The tendency to treat 'effort after meaning' as a projection of meaning rather than as a process of discovery – or, better, negotiation – also derives from Bartlett's anthropological background. Bartlett was committed to the view that cultural change, whilst social in origin, originates from *outside* the group, since he largely followed Rivers's assumption that cultural change in primitive cultures is driven primarily through external contacts with other cultures (see Bartlett, 1929a). (Complex societies differ mainly in that change can also occur through contacts between sub-groups.) For this reason, it was

natural to use alien materials which did indeed require the recipients to *make* their own kind of sense of them.
5. In *private*, he could be more outspoken. In a letter congratulating Michotte on the publication of his book on causality in America, Bartlett wrote:

> I hope that its appearance in English in the USA will distract some at least of the brighter young people there, away from some of the rather fruitless and trivial things they seem to do now, towards the vital and basic problems you have shown how to tackle. . . . Sometimes it seems to me that we have got into a jam, with overmuch information theory which tends towards preoccupation with interminable somewhat small detail and conducts most of us away from a study of the more humane interests. (Bartlett, 1963)

6. In a very relevant paper, Kuper (1990) provides a more general account of the isolation of British psychology and anthropology. He, too, notes this relegation of social psychology (p. 410) and makes the further, important point that the psychology of the emotions and psychotherapy were effectively 'banished' from university psychology courses. Kuper also stresses the importance of isolationist developments within mid-century British social anthropology. Bartlett himself, however, was familiar from the outset with the long-standing arguments within anthropology and sociology for a separation from psychology. As I explain, his early writings attempted to counter them by insisting on a *unilateral* dependence of psychology on sociology.
7. See Bartlett (1927a, 1955) for comments on Watson and on stimulus–response psychology.
8. The distinction between ethnology and social anthropology comes from Radcliffe-Brown (a student of both Rivers and Haddon). According to this distinction, ethnology is the historical study of origins (how things came to be as they are) and social anthropology the functional study of how things work and what they mean at the present time (see Beattie, 1969).

References

Bartlett, F.C. (1920a), 'Some experiments on the reproduction of folk-stories', *Folk-Lore*, **31**, 264–93.
Bartlett, F.C. (1920b), 'Psychology in relation to the popular story', *Folk-Lore*, **31**, 264–93.
Bartlett, F.C. (1923), *Psychology and Primitive Culture*, Cambridge: Cambridge University Press.
Bartlett, F.C. (1925), 'The social function of symbols', *Australasian Journal of Psychology and Philosophy*, **3**, 1–11.
Bartlett, F.C. (1927a), 'Critical notice: Behaviourism, by John B. Watson', *Mind*, **36**, 77–83.
Bartlett, F.C. (1927b), 'The psychology of the lower races', *International Congress of Psychology, 8th Groningen 1926, Proceedings and Papers*, Groningen: Noordhof.
Bartlett, F.C. (1928), 'Social constructiveness', *British Journal of Psychology*, **18**, 388–91.
Bartlett, F.C. (1929), 'Psychology of culture contact', in *Encyclopaedia Britannica*, 13th edn, vol. 29, London: Encyclopaedia Britannica Co. Ltd, pp. 769–70.

Bartlett, F.C. (1929b), 'Psychology', in *Encyclopaedia Britannica*, 13th edn vol. 30, London: Encyclopaedia Britannica Co. Ltd, pp. 255–7.
Bartlett, F.C. (1932), *Remembering: A study in experimental and social psychology*, Cambridge: Cambridge University Press.
Bartlett, F.C. (1936), 'Autobiography', in C. Murchison (ed.), *A History of Psychology in Autobiography*, vol. 3, Worcester, MA: Clark University Press, pp. 39–52.
Bartlett, F.C. (1937a), 'Psychological methods and anthropological problems', *Africa*, **10**, 401–20.
Bartlett, F.C. (1937b), 'Cambridge, England: 1887–1937', *American Journal of Psychology*, **50**, 97–110.
Bartlett, F.C. (1939), 'Suggestions for research in social psychology', in F.C. Bartlett, M. Ginsburg, E.J. Lindgren and R.H. Thouless (eds), *The Study of Society: Methods and problems*, London: Kegan Paul, pp. 24–45.
Bartlett, F.C. (1943), 'Anthropology in reconstruction', *Nature*, **152**, 710–14.
Bartlett, F.C. (1955), 'Fifty years of psychology. Paper based on two lectures given at Oxford 1955', *Occupational Psychology*, **29**, 203–16.
Bartlett, F.C. (1957), *Some Recent Developments of Psychology in Great Britain*, Istanbul: Baha Matbaasi.
Bartlett, F.C. (1958), *Thinking: An experimental and social study*, London: George Allen & Unwin.
Bartlett, F.C. (1963), Letter to Albert Michotte, Cambridge, 18 August.
Bartlett, F.C. (1965), 'Remembering Dr. Myers: First Myers lecture', *Bulletin of the British Psychological Society*, **18**, 1–10.
Bartlett, F.C. (1973), 'Memory', *Encyclopaedia Britannica*, vol. 15, Chicago: William Benton, pp. 138–40.
Beattie, J. (1969), 'A.R. Radcliffe-Brown (1881–1955)', in T. Raison (ed.), *The Founding Fathers of Social Science*, Harmondsworth: Penguin, pp. 178–87.
Broadbent, D.E. (1970a), 'Sir Frederic Bartlett: An appreciation', *Bulletin of the British Psychological Society*, **23**, 1–3.
Broadbent, D.E. (1970b), 'Frederic Charles Bartlett, 1886–1969', *Biographical Memoirs of Fellows of the Royal Society*, **16**, 1–13.
Buzzard, R.B. (1971), 'Sir Frederic Bartlett, C.B.E., M.A., LL.D., D.Sc., D.Phil., D. Psych., F.R.S. 1886–1969', *Occupational Psychology*, **45**, 1–11.
Collingwood, R.G. (1946), *The Idea of History*, Oxford: Clarendon Press.
Crampton, C.R. (1978), 'The Cambridge school: The life and work and influence of James Ward, W.H.R. Rivers, C.S. Myers & Sir Frederic Bartlett', unpublished PhD, University of Edinburgh.
Douglas, M. (1987), 'A case of institutional forgetting', in her book *How Institutions Think*, London: Routledge & Kegan Paul, pp. 81–90.
Edwards, D. and Middleton, D. (1987), 'Conversation and remembering: Bartlett revisited', *Applied Cognitive Psychology*, **1**, 77–92.
Eysenck, H.J. (1980), 'Autobiography', in G. Lindzey (ed.), *A History of Psychology in Autobiography*, vol. 7, San Francisco: W.H. Freeman, pp. 153–87.
Gardner, H. (1987), *The Mind's New Science: A history of the cognitive revolution* (paperback edn), New York: Basic Books.
Hebb, D.O. (1949), *The Organization of Behavior*, New York: Wiley.
Jahoda, G. (1982), *Psychology and Anthropology: A psychological perspective*, London: Academic Press.
Kuper, A. (1990), 'Psychology and anthropology: The British experience', *History of the Human Sciences*, **3**, 397–413.

54 Against Cognitivism

Lave, J. (1988), *Cognition in Practice: Mind, mathematics and culture in everyday life*, Cambridge: Cambridge University Press.
McDougall, W. (1930), 'Autobiography', in C. Murchison (ed.), *A History of Psychology in Autobiography*, vol. 1, Worcester, MA: Clark University Press, pp. 191–224.
Neisser, U. (1967), *Cognitive Psychology*, New York: Appleton-Century-Crofts.
Neisser, U. (1976), *Cognition and Reality*, San Francisco: W.H. Freeman.
Northway, M.L. (1940a), 'The concept of the "schema" (Part I)', *British Journal of Psychology*, **30**, 316–25.
Northway, M L. (1940b), 'The concept of the "schema" (Part II)', *British Journal of Psychology*, **31**, 22–36.
Peters, R.S. (1962), *Brett's History of Psychology* (revised edn), London: George Allen & Unwin.
Rumelhart, D.E., Smolensky, P., McClelland, J.L. and Hinton, G.E. (1986), 'Schemata and sequential thought processes in PDP models', in J.L. McClelland, D.E. Rumelhart and the PDP Research Group (eds), *Parallel Distributed Processing: Explorations in the microstructure of cognition*, vol. 2, Cambridge, MA: MIT, pp. 7–57.
Slobodin, R. (1978), *W.H.R. Rivers*, New York: Columbia University Press.
Stagner, R. (1988), *A History of Psychological Theories*, New York: Macmillan.
White, M.J. (1983), 'Prominent publications in cognitive psychology', *Memory & Cognition*, **11**, 423–7.
Zangwill, O.L. (1970), 'Obituary notice: Sir Frederic Bartlett (1886–1969)', *Quarterly Journal of Experimental Psychology*, **22**, 77–81.
Zangwill, O.L. (1972), 'Remembering revisited', *Quarterly Journal of Experimental Psychology*, **24**, 123–38.

5
The rhetorical-responsive nature of mind: A social constructionist account
John Shotter

Editors' introduction

The critic of cognitivism – having pointed out its weaknesses, examined its shaky historical roots, and indicated plausible alternative – is still confronted with the embarrassing question of why it is so popular. Why does it seem a plausible account of the mind to so many psychologists? It is not, we believe, because it is true, but because there are powerful cultural and political forces that support it. In this chapter, John Shotter examines the nature of this support with the aid of recent theoretical developments in social psychology especially social constructionism, and the new rhetoric.

According to social constructionism, the categories we use when talking and thinking about the world are neither simply a reflection of that world nor a mental construction. Certainly they are constrained by the physical world and human capacities; but the finer details are the product of a long co-evolution of a society and its setting, and are absorbed during acculturation, especially learning to talk (Coulter, 1979; Gergen, 1985). The ordinary way we talk about mind – with its categories of perception, consciousness, memory, thinking, etc. – may instil in us a strong conviction that these reflect universal realities; but a quick look at the languages of mind of other cultures or the distant past of our own will reveal differences that should give us cause to doubt (Lock and Heelas, 1980).

An important boost to social constructionism has come from philosophy, with the recognition that language is constitutive of human social life and has many functions besides description (Wittgenstein, 1953). One function is persuasion, which is the subject matter of rhetoric. Until recently rhetoric has had a bad name, probably because it has been viewed as a dishonest substitute for logic and scientific demonstration. It is true that verbal techniques of persuasion can be used for bad ends, but widespread skill in rhetoric (the ability to put one's case effectively and dispassionately) is also necessary for a just democracy (Vickers, 1990). Billig has recently argued (1987) that classical treatises on rhetoric have more to teach us about thinking than modern research in the laboratory. The current emphasis on individual problem-solving in experimental studies of thinking is misleading; thinking should be studied where it primarily occurs – in the social settings where people talk and argue about themselves and the world, and learn to establish their identities through 'social accountability' (Shotter, 1984).

It is now widely recognized that rhetoric plays an important part in the construction and maintenance of all social institutions, including science. Cognitive science is certainly no exception. On the credit side, this new coalition has been as successful as it has because its proponents have often put their case well, and seized the opportunities offered. In so doing they have appealed to the traditional scientific virtues, mechanical precision and testability, as well as a commensurability both with physics and, up to a point, with the traditional categories of the mind. Less publicly, they have benefited by appealing to more questionable social demands. Treating people as machines can serve the interests of bureaucratic, industrial and military organizations, and these have provided the financial support necessary to launch cognitive science.

References

Billig, M. (1987), *Arguing and Thinking: A rhetorical approach to social psychology*, Cambridge: Cambridge University Press.
Coulter, J. (1979), *The Social Construction of Mind*, London: Macmillan.
Gergen, K.J. (1985), 'The social constructionist movement in modern psychlogy', *American Psychologist*, **40**, 266–75.
Lock, A. and Heelas, P. (eds), (1980), *Indigenous Psychologies*, London: Academic Press.
Shotter, J. (1984), *Social Accountability and Selfhood*, Oxford: Blackwell.
Vickers, B. (1990), 'The recovery of rhetoric: Petrarch, Erasmus, Perelman', *History of the Human Sciences*, **3**, 415–42.
Wittgenstein, L. (1953), *Philosophical Investigations*, Oxford: Blackwell.

* * *

Following Billig (1987) and Billig *et al.* (1988), I shall argue that cognitive psychology is not so much a well-formed *system* of thought as a set of dilemmatic 'themes' very much in tune with the (common-sense) political ideology of our times – liberal individualism (Sampson, 1981, 1988). Because of this it constitutes a fertile site for a whole range of still unresolved arguments. As Best (1986, p. 31) says in his introductory textbook, 'the revolutionary period [in cognitive psychology] is not yet over'.

Turning to the focal themes of cognitive psychology, we find a concentration upon the disengaged, instrumental modes of thought and action that characterize our modern age (Taylor, 1989). In cognitive psychology it is expressed in the assumption that all action follows from thought, and that thought is best described as a sequential process of problem-solving taking place inside our heads, consisting in a series of transformations of some abstract codes, representative at some stage of objects or events in the world. It is this feature that is shared by all the versions of cognitive psychology (both strong and weak) known to me – I shall variously refer to it as cognitivism or as the computer model. Although, as Gergen (1989) points out, cognitivism is a great liberation compared with the rat-psychology of behaviourism, it still represents a radical limitation of the range of topics in psychology into which it is deemed legitimate to inquire.

Social accountability and identity

In this chapter, I would like to try to change that state of affairs: to open up the debate to take into account a whole new range of topics to do with the *social* nature of human beings. I want to argue that instead of operating in a disengaged, impersonal, mechanistic and systematic manner, our cognitive abilities[1] reflect the same essentially personal, ethical and rhetorical considerations in their functioning as those influencing the transactions between people out in the world. Thus my approach here can be seen as a chapter in the current attempt to formulate a less cognitive[2] (i.e. more socially responsive and rhetorical) social constructionist psychology, in which what was formerly attributed only to individuals (and located within them) is seen as arising out of the negotiated relationships between them (Billig, 1987; Coulter, 1979, 1983, 1989; Gergen, 1982, 1985, 1989; Harré, 1983; Shotter, 1984).

Central to my argument will be the claim that such an approach is required if we are to give a proper account of a central feature of such relationships: that they occur between people with distinctly unique *identities* – a fact we acknowledge in a number of different ways in our everyday affairs. I shall discuss this in terms of the rights and responsibilities we assign to first-person agents in social life, to do with distinguishing (in at least some spheres of their own conduct) between those of their activities for which they themselves can be responsible and those which they just happen, outside of their own agency, to control. In Western societies, we assign this right to adults when they become capable (unlike their children) of speaking for themselves – i.e. when they become *responsible* and capable of justifying or warranting at least some of their actions if challenged by others to do so, according to how they are 'placed' or 'situated' in relation to those others. In being both responsible for their own position and responsive to the positions of the others around them, adults can both *answer for* themselves in the world and *address* their answers to others (Bakhtin, 1984; Shotter, 1989a). It is both the answerability and addressivity implied in the first-person perspective, and the understanding of these abilities in the functioning of social life, that cognitive psychology leaves unanalyzed. An 'information-processing system' without an identity, without an understanding of who it is and how it is 'placed' in a social situation, cannot be held responsible for its actions; and without that possibility, it could never play the part of a genuine person in everyday social life at large.

Thus, I want to argue that: (1) The computer model fails to characterize the way in which people's everyday actions are always 'situated' or 'placed' within a *social* and *moral*, as well as a historically developed, *political* order, actual or imagined; (2) that the maintenance in good repair of that order is due to the *social accountability* of those 'within' it; (3) that such accountability depends upon a first-person ability to distinguish eventualities for which one is oneself responsible, and those which lie outside one's own agency to control; and (4) that one's motivation to be responsible in this way is sustained by the fact that one's *identity* is at stake in one's actions, for one is *oneself* morally committed in them (both to others and to oneself) to be who one 'claims'[3] oneself to be. Computers, lacking any sense of being individually and *personally* 'placed' in relation to those around them – to their 'parents', their 'friends', their other 'kith and kin', their 'mothers-in-law', their 'bosses' and 'subordinates' and, indeed, to all the others both in and outside their community to whom they are morally bound in one way or another – would lack the practical-moral (Bernstein's [1983], term) social knowledge required to act in a socially responsible and responsive manner. In being socially 'unplaced', computers are unable to relate their actions either to a self-known, situated 'I', or to situated others. In short, they are unable to be accountable in their conduct to others.

Elsewhere (Shotter, 1984) I have explored implications of these issues in terms of the 'social accountability thesis': the claim that our understanding and experience of our 'reality' are constituted for us very largely by the ways in which we *must* talk in our attempts to account for the things and events within it – where a part of that reality is ourselves. And I say 'must' because our ways of accounting have a *morally coercive* quality to them, in the sense that a failure properly to account for ourselves can lead to us not being accounted a fully socially responsible person, and thus to us being denied further access to certain important arenas of social life. Here the issue is important for us because, clearly, we cannot always just speak and act as we please; often we must act 'into' a moral (or better, moralistic) context containing, amongst other groups, certain powerful and authoritative others – for us in psychology, we must persuade our professional colleagues. And should we say or do anything *they* judge to be inappropriate in some way, we run the risk of them sanctioning us (we will find it difficult to get a job) – unless, perhaps, we can provide them with an account which justifies the behaviour which they first found suspect. An important implication of this, though, is that if the ways in which we must account for ourselves are limited in any way – if they are selective, and emphasize some factors at the expense of others – then our grasp upon the factors influencing our sense of ourselves will be biased in the same way. Thus what is at issue here is not a simple matter of whether what we say 'corresponds' with the world in some way or not, but of whether, in making use of currently accepted ways of making sense (cognitivism), we help to maintain them, or whether, in attempting to talk in different ways, we 'give currency' to other patterns of social relationship and forms of mentality than those it upholds.

Within the context of the social accountability thesis, then, we can see that the 'currency' of the computer metaphor in psychology is not so much wrong as limited or inadequate. Indeed, as Sampson puts it, cognitive psychology

> is true insofar as it accurately represents the reality of a given sociohistorical era or group. [But] it is false insofar as that truth may itself be a systematic distortion which serves the interests of some groups over others. (Sampson, 1981, p. 731)

Its function is 'to reproduce the existing nature of the social order' (*ibid.*, p. 730) by ensuring that all further developments take place within its terms – the notions of detached, disengaged, disembodied, atomistic, individualistic knowing we have listed above. Its apparent adequacy, however, is based (I want to claim) upon a mistaken image of ourselves which arises out of the limited forms of discourse we allow ourselves in professionally approved, academic psychology, and the way in which that approval – as Billig *et al.* (1988) point out – is drawn from certain 'dilemmatic themes' intrinsic to the current 'lived ideology' embedded in the common sense of our culture. To have currency, our accounts of human conduct must make sense in terms of the themes provided by a liberal humanistic ideology. And until recently, this has introduced a systematic distortion into our discussions: it has made 'rationally-invisible'[4] to us just the ethical, rhetorical and other sociohistorical processes within which we, between ourselves, create and maintain our present social order. For the very nature of our social psychological interaction with each other has created within us our sense of ourselves as wholly psychologically alone. It is this linguistically created illusory sense of ourselves as self-contained individuals (in contrast to the 'socially sustained individuality' prevalent in some other cultures – see, e.g., Shweder and Bourne, 1982) which, I feel, lends 'common-sense' support to the computer as an adequate model or metaphor of mind.

None the less, changes are clearly afoot, and in what follows I want to explore the new emphasis upon the rhetorical, responsive, socially situated, and especially the non-systematic, two-sided nature (see below) of processes of common-sense thought. But I also want to explore why the information-processing approach we currently take to the study of the mental capacities of individuals seems to us so 'natural',[5] so to speak, and hence so impervious to critical argument. In other words, if the social accountability thesis is true and our ways of life and forms of talk are mutually constitutive, with what forms of life and ways of making sense in our society does cognitivism correspond? Thus first, in attempting to illuminate the aspects of the 'lived ideology' which motivates the continued attraction of the computer metaphor in psychology, I shall explore the non-rhetorical, non-ethically responsive vocabulary at the heart of the 'cognitive revolution'. I shall then turn to a discussion of a couple of classical but everyday situations in Western society in which the intelligent conduct of responsible individuals is reduced to impersonal routines: both F.W. Taylor's (1947) application of Adam Smith's views about the division of labour to the constitution and control of a workforce, and Weber's (1964) notion of the bureaucracy as a rational ordering of social relations. The way will then be clear for an examination of the rhetorical nature of thought, and its conduct within an argumentative context of justification and criticism. This will enable us to see why it is that computers must fail to capture the nature of those everyday circumstances in which we act, not with *conviction* (according to principles) but by being *persuaded* (by 'good reasons') – where, to quote Perelman and Olbrechts-Tyteca (1969, p. 28), we can 'apply the term *persuasive* to argumentation that only claims validity for a particular audience, and the term *convincing* to argumentation that presumes to gain the adherence of every rational being'. To turn first, then, to rationality without an audience.

The 'cognitive revolution'

Over the last twenty years or so, academic psychology has undergone what many think of as a profound and exciting revolution, a 'cognitive revolution'. The traditional behaviourist paradigm has been almost wholly abandoned; the mental is no longer scorned as unscientific. There is a revival of psychological (and philosophical) interest in the human mind – an interest in the supposed mental *processes* and *states* believed to be occurring in the heads of individuals, which are said to mediate between the reality 'out there' and our subjective experience of it. Old and abandoned philosophical interests can once again be pursued, it is claimed, but now in novel and scientific ways – this new work has, for example, so Dennett (1981, p. 119) says, 'broken the back of an argument which has bedeviled philosophers and psychologists for over two hundred years' (what he calls *Hume's Problem* – the problem of personal identity, of the need for an 'interpreter' for representations). What has turned the tables, and apparently reconciled mentalism and materialism, is not only the development of so-called information-processing technology and computers, but the coupling of its development with the claim, initially attributed to Craik (1943), that 'thought models or parallels reality' – to use for the moment the idiom of the cognitive revolution. As a result, many now claim that this is how one should pursue 'a scientific understanding of how the mind works'.

For instance, explicity following Craik, Johnson-Laird (1983, p. 2) outlines his commitment to cognitive science by suggesting that 'the psychological core of understanding . . . consists in your having a "working model" of the phenomenon [in question] in your mind.' Boden (1982, p. 224) makes essentially the same claim:

> [Artificial intelligence research (AI)] studies not the world itself, but the way in which representations of the world can be constructed, evaluated, compared, and transformed.

As Sampson (1981, p. 731) points out, such theorists implicitly make two reductions, a *subjectivist* and an *individualistic* reduction: for they hold that (1) the knower's psychological states, their ideas, or their representations are more important than any of the social or material conditions of their existence; and (2) the evaluation, etc., of their ideas, representations, etc., is wholly an individual matter. It is as if (as theorists) they had access both to 'the world' and to representations of it, and had judged (without further ado) that indeed the latter were proper representations of the former. And many other commentators on what has come to be called the 'representational theory of mind' (Fodor, 1985) have also adopted essentially this same stance. Indeed, they go further and claim that 'the only psychology that could possibly succeed in explaining the complexities of human activity must posit internal representations', to quote Dennett (1979, p. 119). 'It's the only game in town,' Fodor is reputed to have said.

But what is the game? As *I* see it, one of the most significant features of human actions in everyday life is not only their situated, contexted or occasioned nature, but also their normative accountability. That is, in some sense they are not only *made* but *judged* in their making, by both those who perform them and those around them, as to both their social and moral appropriateness to the circumstances of their performance. They are made to 'fit' their circumstances in some way. But in what way? Is it (1) to do with a kind of fittedness which takes into account their *meaning*, their social significance, a socially accountable fittedness? Or is it (2) a mere matter of correspondence in their impersonal shapes or forms?

As Dennett and Fodor – as well as Boden and Johnson-Laird, for that matter – see it, the game seems fundamentally to be of the second type. For as far as the mechanics of computers are concerned, whatever their labyrinthine complexity, the causal relations between their internal changes of state function in terms of one basic operation: that of detecting identities (or their lack) between *patterns* of binary digits. In other words, all matters of meaning must (and, so some claim, can) be reduced to matters of shape. Indeed, without explicitly committing himself to this argument, Fodor (1985, p. 93) outlines its nature thus:

> You connect the causal properties of a symbol with its semantic properties via its syntax. . . . To a first approximation, we can think of its syntactic structure as an abstract feature of its (geometric or acoustic) *shape*. Because, to all intents and purposes, syntax reduces to shape, and because the shape of a symbol is a potential determinant of its causal role, it is fairly easy to see how there could be environments in which the causal role of a symbol correlates with its syntax.

Indeed, it is precisely this reduction of meaning to shape which allows Dennett to claim a solution to what he calls Hume's Problem (Dennett, 1979, p. 122), which he poses as follows: 'something is a representation only *for* or *to* someone; any representation or system of representations thus requires at least one *user* or *interpreter* of the representation who is external[6] to it.' He suggests that we do not need an inner 'I' or 'self' to understand how internal maps or models of the external world should be translated into action, because such inner models can be made to 'think for themselves' – to be, as he says, 'self-understanding'. The need for an inner self or homunculus to make sense of inner representations can be 'discharged', Dennett suggests, by analyzing this 'inner person', – using (to quote him) 'the remarkably fruitful research strategy' of the artificial intelligence (AI) programmer – into a hierarchy of functionaries. Thus the programmer's

A social constructionist account   63

first and highest level of design breaks the computer down . . . into a committee or army of intelligent homunculi with purposes, information and strategies. Each homunculus in turn is analyzed into smaller homunculi, but, more important, into less clever homunculi. When the level is reached where the homunculi are no more than adders and subtractors, by the time they need only the intelligence to pick the larger of two numbers when directed to, they have been reduced to functionaries 'who can be replaced by a machine' . . . [and] if the program works then we can be certain that all homunculi have been discharged from the theory.

Such a self-understanding hierarchy of functionaries, he claims,[7] is what all intelligent activities *are*.

But two comments are relevant: First, as Dennett himself says, what he is describing is a 'design process'. Thus, in his formulation of his account, he executes a sleight of hand which apparently diverts even his own attention, never mind ours, from its main point; for it is the design *process* executed by the AI programmers which requires intelligence. While its *product* may embody the result of intelligent decisions, it still does not possess its *own* intelligence, so to speak – i.e. it is unable to deploy whatever intelligence it has under its own control, thus to be responsible for its own actions. If challenged as to the possibly morally reprehensible nature of 'its' actions it could only, like Eichmann, say it was 'doing its job'; it would not be able to justify *why* its actions were worth doing. It was the programmers who decided the task and what the appropriate 'committees' and 'armies' of basic homunculi should be; and what abilities they should have, and how further they should be interlinked, in order to fulfil that task. Indeed – and this is a second, related point – in this connection we can ask: In such a hierarchy of functionaries as Dennett describes, what is in fact meant by someone being self-understanding? While Dennett's proposals might be appropriate in the context of designing machines to replace people, does his analysis in fact capture what is at stake in accounting for people's intelligent and responsible fitting of their everyday actions to their circumstances? I shall deal with these two issues – the replacement of people by a hierarchy of functionaries and the nature of its self-understanding – in turn in the next two sections.

The division of labour and 'scientific management'

One sphere in which we might explore the replacement of human beings, first by functionaries and then by machines, is in the now considered (in management sciences) anachronistic field of 'scientific management' or 'Taylorism'. In *The Wealth of Nations*, Adam Smith (1776/1921, vol. 2, pp. 301–2) describes one of the more negative results to be expected from the division of labour:

64 Against Cognitivism

The man whose life is spent in performing a few simple operations . . . has no occasion to exert his understanding. . . . He naturally loses, therefore, the habit of such exertion, and generally becomes as stupid and ignorant as it is possible for a human being to become.

Its positive advantage, however, is the 'great increase in the quantity of work, which in consequence of the division of labour, the same number of people are capable of performing' (ibid., vol. 1, p. 9). Thus, for Adam Smith, its institution was a matter of economics. For F.W. Taylor (1947), the originator of 'Taylorism', however, there were other, more political reasons: (1) the centralization of control, and (2) the rendering of the work process independent of craft, tradition and the worker's own skills. And he succeeded in fact in outlining a procedure by which industrialists could appropriate, as he put it, the 'naturally occurring' knowledge in their 'environment', and gain possession of it as a commodity for their own use. Furthermore, he showed how it could be used to separate 'brain work' from 'muscle work' and thus to place the work process under management control, with the work of lower management being brought under the control of higher management, and so on.

Taylor, in analyzing why it was so difficult to manage and control a workforce, realized that it was because it possessed something management lacked: the knowledge and skill to produce the goods. This left the workers with a degree of bargaining power, for:

> The ingenuity and experience of each generation – of each decade, even – have without doubt handed over better methods to the next. This mass of rule-of-thumb knowledge or traditional knowledge may be said to be the principal asset or possession of every tradesman . . . which is not in the possession of the management. (Taylor, 1947, p. 32)

But this state of affairs can be remedied by applying 'the principles of scientific management' in which, as he says,

> The managers assume . . . the burden [!] of gathering all the traditional knowledge which in the past has been possessed by the workman and then of classifying, tabulating and reducing this knowledge to rules, laws and formulae . . . (ibid., p. 36)

Because:

> all the planning which under the old system was done by the workmen, as a result of his personal experience, must of necessity under the new system be done by the management in accordance with the laws of science . . . (ibid., p. 36)

Thus, through the application of scientific methods (but not for scientific

A social constructionist account   65

ends), all this 'naturally' occurring knowledge can be quarried, excavated and itself fashioned into a marketable product. But the 'extraction' process can be applied to the process of management itself[8] also, as Taylor realized, in the form of what he called 'functional management', in which the tasks of management were divided down and distributed, so that each manager had only a single task. And this completes the circle. Management itself becomes subject to a process of manufacture, and can be 'packaged' and marketed as a commodity. We then reach a stage, as Taylor himself put it, where: 'In the past the man has been first; in the future the system must be first' (*ibid.*, p. 7). And to the extent that Taylor's prophecy has come true, instead of the majority of people now living under the domination of the few, all of us live dominated by 'the system' – dominated, in fact, by our techniques of domination.

This, then, is 'Taylorism': the procedure in which a communal stock of knowledge can be mined, excavated and refined into a marketable commodity – where the process of refining can itself, by making use of 'scientifically managed' production processes, be conducted as a manufacturing industry, as a form of what in the attempt to devise 'expert systems' would now be known as 'knowledge engineering'. But as is quite clear, the fully automated manufacturing process which results is the outcome of a great deal of prior social (and intellectual) activity: not only amongst the managers, who must assume the burden of studying and rationalizing the workers' activities, but also amongst all the negotiators, the unionists, the workers, etc., who must arrange all the social circumstances involved in making such transitions possible. All these activities, of course, go unmentioned in Taylor's account.

It is impossible not to notice the similarities between Taylorism's concern with the regimenting and systematizing of rule-of-thumb knowledge in factory life, and an aspect of Dennett's (1979) approach which he calls *type intentionalism*: 'every mental event is some functional, physical event or other, and the types are captured not by any reductionist language but by a regimentation of the very terms we *ordinarily* use – we explain *what beliefs are* by systematizing the notion of a believing-system . . . ' (p. xix). It is only fair to add here Dennett's comment that he cannot rest content with 'type intentionalism' as it stands, 'for it seems' he says, 'to assume something I believe to be false: *viz*, that our *ordinary* way of picking out putative mental features and entities succeeds in picking out real features and entities' (p. xix). Hence he is a type-intentionalist only about a few ordinary mental-entity terms which 'may perspicaciously isolate features of people that deserve mention in a mature psychology . . . [and also those] theoretical entities in a mature psychology that [will] eventually *supplant* [terms

66 Against Cognitivism

such as] beliefs, desires, pains, mental images, experiences . . . ' (p. xx) – when presumably our lives have been regimented and systematized according to the 'mature psychology' of which he speaks.

A Weberian bureaucracy

Let me turn now to another sphere in which the rationalization of human behaviour is at issue: in bureaucracies. Dennett discusses what is required for 'armies' of functionaries to be organized in a way that is 'self-understanding'. Let us explore what his proposals would sound like if they were re-presented in a different context: as social policy for the design of a human institution. Then, I think, what Dennett proposes as a model of our supposed 'internal' processes can itself be seen as modelled upon the notion of a rationally ordered, bureaucratic form of social organization. As he himself says: 'The AI programmer begins with an intentionally characterized problem, and thus frankly views the computer anthropomorphically' (Dennett, 1979, p. 80).

Classically, the 'anthropomorphic' theory of bureaucracies has been outlined by Max Weber (1964, pp. 324–41). He characterized a bureaucracy as consisting in: (1) a hierarchically organized body of specialized, technically qualified functionaries or 'officials', each occupying an 'office' within an impersonal order, to which his or her actions are orientated; (2) in which each is subordinated to those above them while being in charge of those below them; (3) where they obey those in authority not as individuals but as representatives of the impersonal order; (4) where they work by applying general rules to particular cases, and (5) conduct all their business with each other by the continual shuffling of *formal* (i.e. written) documents made out and acted upon according to explicit sets of rules; and (6) where:

> In the rational type [of bureaucracy] it is a matter of principle that the members of the administrative staff should be completely separated from ownership of the means of production or administration. . . . [And] there is a corresponding separation of the place in which official functions are carried out, the 'office' in the sense of premises, from living quarters. (Weber, 1964, pp. 331–2.

To round out his account, it must be added that (1) Weber emphasizes the specialized, technical nature of the knowledge needed by all the functionaries, and their special training, if they are to occupy their 'office' appropriately – at the time he was writing, Taylor's principles of 'scientific management' had not yet been developed, let alone applied to the planning of bureaucratic systems. Only at the 'top' of the hierarchy was demonstrable technical knowledge unnecessary:

A social constructionist account   67

In the modern state, the only 'offices' for which no technical qualifications are required are those of ministers and presidents. . . . Thus at the top of a bureaucratic organization, there is necessarily an element which is at least not purely bureaucratic. (*ibid.*, p. 335)

and (2) the kind of co-ordination that exists between 'officials' is, as he calls it, *imperative co-ordination*, which is defined as 'the probability that certain specific commands (or all commands) from a given source will be obeyed by a given group of persons' (*ibid.*, p. 324).

We now make the reverse analogy, comparing this human institution with a computer. While a bureaucracy may give the appearance of 'thinking for itself', in the sense of not requiring any further direction from external authorities in its operation once designed and established, could it in any sense be said to be thinking 'its own thoughts'? It is such that each functionary in it is directed to execute his or her function by the functionary above, who in turn is directed by the functionary above . . . and so on; while the director at the top is *directed by* . . . by whom? Well, in the Weberian bureaucracy the overall director is a functionary of the state, and it is the state which, from a position outside the system, has laid down the impersonal order to which the director's actions are orientated, while the state itself was often in the thrall of a 'charismatic leader'. Could we, if we lived like this – as embodying within ourselves a hierarchically organized bureaucracy of functionaries orientated towards an impersonal, state order – be said to be 'thinking for ourselves'? I believe not. Far from 'thinking for ourselves', in no sense could any of our actions even be called our *own*. Separated from 'the means of production or administration', we could live and think only as directed by something 'outside' ourselves, by our 'bosses', and they in their turn by their 'bosses', and so on.[9] Such a way of life would not only be dismal, but crazy, crackbrained. For in acting intelligently we must appreciate not only how our actions are related to their circumstances but also how their performance might change our 'position' in relation to the positions of their addressees – their anticipated social consequences. Indeed, it makes no sense at all to talk of either a bureaucracy or a computer as being (politically or ethically) committed to controlling its own social position in its actions in this way.

The rhetorical nature of human thought and action

Above, then, I have been exploring why the information-processing approach we currently take to the study of the mental capacities of individuals seems to us so 'natural', and hence so impervious to critical argument. It seems to conform with certain forms of life and ways of talking currently central within our modern society. No matter how persuasive all the comments above might seem (to some but not to others, according to the kind of people they are), however, none of them can or should be treated as saying anything conclusive about the inadequacy of the computer metaphor.[10] Indeed, no one – not even Dreyfus (1972; Dreyfus and Dreyfus, 1986) – has yet succeeded in conclusively proving the computer's inadequacy. I shall not try to prove it, either, for there are now, I think, good reasons[11] not only for giving up the attempt to find convincing arguments against the adequacy of the computer metaphor, but also for celebrating the fact that none can exist. Why? Because, as the current *rhetoric of inquiry* movement (Nelson and Megill, 1986) is beginning to make clear, convincing 'proofs' do not consist just in the application of a procedure, but also in persuasive testimony (sometimes implicit) that the procedure was correctly applied (Davis and Hersh, 1983; Kline, 1980; Myhill, 1956). Without such testimony the supposed proof is incapable of commanding universal assent, and unworthy of the name proof. In other words (Lewis Carroll's words), logic does not 'seize us by the throat' and just force us helplessly to accept a conclusion; there is always an element of persuasion and consent about it (and other 'socio-historico-psychological' factors too).

Recently, it has been Billig (1987), in his rhetorical approach to social psychology, who more than anybody has shown why we must take the argumentative and responsive nature of thinking seriously. In discussing the cognitivist perspective in social psychology (Billig, 1987, pp. 128–30) he points out (as I have above) that the arguments used by psychologists in favour of 'categorization' and other 'information-processing' procedures are similar to those bureaucrats might use in defence of their office procedures. The arguments refer to the order and efficiency such procedures bring, how they work to make the everyday world manageable by reducing unique, disorderly and contextualized events and actions to decontextualized regularities – indeed, he quotes various cognitive theorists as saying that categorization 'lends organization to our social world' (Hamilton, 1979, p. 56); that it serves 'to stabilize, make predictable and make manageable the individual's view of the world' (Snyder, 1981, p. 183), and so on.

Although Billig also does not think that such arguments are wrong, he does think that they offer a very narrow, unflattering and especially 'a one-sided image, in which thinking has become reduced to the unthinking operations of a filing-clerk' (Billig, 1987, p. 129). For even bureaucrats, never mind ordinary people in everyday life, 'rather than being unimaginative rule-followers, ... are often rule-benders and even rule-creators as well. As they fight their interdepartmental battles, bureaucrats need to show all the skills of witchcraft' (*ibid.*). It is to

A social constructionist account 69

degrade even the intelligence of bureaucrats to think that they need no appreciation of their circumstances in applying their skills aright; that their behaviour can be seen as determined merely by a set of rules.

Upon what does Billig base these claims? Central to his whole approach is a return to the classical concern in the tradition of rhetoric with *topics*, with the 'places of argumentation', the resources from which arguments originate and in terms of which they are fashioned – where what is of outstanding importance is, as Perelman and Olbrechts-Tyteca (1969) point out, that each place of argument has its opposing place:

> It is amazing that even when very general *loci* are concerned, each *locus* can be confronted by one that is contrary to it: thus to the classical *locus* of the superiority of the lasting, one may oppose the romantic *locus* of the superiority of that which is precarious and fleeting. It is accordingly possible to characterize societies not only by the particular values they prize most but by the intensity to which they adhere to one or the other of a pair of antithetical *loci*. (p. 85)

This represents an approach to the nature of knowledge entirely different from that in cognitivism. In cognitivism, knowledge is spoken of, as we have seen, as constituting a system. Here, knowledge is seen as consisting basically in an unorganized collection of (resource) topics, available for arguers (rhetors) to use as best they can. As Billig *et al.* (1988) put it in discussing the nature of a 'lived ideology': 'An ideology is not seen as a complete unified system of beliefs which tells the individual how to react, feel and think. Instead, ideology, and indeed common sense, is seen to comprise contrary themes' (p. 2). Indeed, they say, 'it is not haphazard that common sense contains its contrary themes, or . . . that it possesses its dilemmatic character. The very existence of these opposing images, words, evaluations, maxims and so on is crucial, in that they permit the possibility not just of social dilemmas but of social thinking itself' (p. 7) – they do not just constrain thought, but both motivate and enable it. They are 'the *seeds*, not the *flowers* of arguments', they say, quoting Bacon (1858, p. 492).

Accountability and the first-person perspective

Someone who long ago studied the problem of accountability – the problem of how different people, in different places at different times, justify their conduct to one another – was C. Wright Mills (1940) in a paper he very aptly entitled 'Situated actions and vocabularies of motive'. As he saw it, all human conduct took place in a socially constructed, evaluative context, in which the others in one's social group have a right to judge whether one's conduct 'is fitting' or not, whether it really is directed towards the shared aims (or 'motives') of the group. Hence, if one's actions are thought puzzling or unintelligible, or perhaps illegitimate in any way, then the others have a right to intervene and question it. One justifies one's conduct, Mills suggests, by talking to others about its 'motives' – or, better, by the use of 'motive-talk'. But why should people be satisfied in such circumstances by the use of a form of talk? How does language work to make such a use possible? Words must serve some other function than merely standing for (representing) states of affairs in the world.

Mills emphasized in his paper the need for, and tried to provide, 'an analysis of the integrating, controlling, and specifying functions a certain type of speech fulfils in socially situated actions' (Mills, 1940, p. 904) – an attitude to language which, as we can see, is very congenial to Billig's rhetorical concerns with criticism and justification. Indeed, Mills's approach leads to a quite new appreciation of the basic function of language. For him, its primary function is *not* the representation of things in the world, nor the giving of 'outer' expression to already well-formed 'inner' thoughts; it exerts a material influence upon people's behaviour (including the speaker's). It works to create, sustain and transform various patterns of social relations and, by implication, various forms of mentality or subjectivity. For to use a language *is* to relate oneself to others in some way, and in so doing to determine the psychological character both of oneself and of others. Thus if, in our experience, it seems undeniable that at least some words in our reality do in fact stand for (represent) things, then in this view they do so only *from within* a form of social life already constituted by the ways of talking in which such words are used.

As he put it right at the beginning of his paper (Mills, 1940, p. 903):

> The postulate underlying modern study of language is the simple one that we must approach linguistic behaviour, not by referring it to private states in individuals, but by observing its social function in coordinating diverse action. Rather than expressing something which is prior and in the person, language is taken by the other person as an indicator of future actions.

Hence, motives (or better, 'motive accounts') are, he says,

> imputed or avowed as answers to questions [mostly from others, but perhaps also from oneself] interrupting acts or programs. Motives are words. Generically, to what do they refer? They do not denote any elements 'in' individuals. They stand for anticipated situational consequences of questioned conduct. (Mills, 1940, p. 904)

Speech of a certain type can serve this function because, suggests Mills, learning its use is a part of what it is for us to be socialized into a particular society. In becoming socially competent and allowed to act autonomously (not like a child in the care of an adult) we learn its integrating, controlling and specifying functions,[12] its *normative* force. In its use we learn how to link (our own and other people's responsible) actions to their 'anticipated, normative, situational consequences'. Indeed, as Winch (1958) makes clear, there is a certain 'promissory' quality in much of our speech, in that talking in a certain way at one point in time 'commits' us to 'going on' in a certain way in the future. And we qualify for our adult status by demonstrating that we know how to honour such commitments in our talk and actions. Then we know how to act *routinely* in an unquestionable (by others), intelligible and legitimate manner, thus to qualify for a genuine first-person status. Such a status gives us the right to act in ways which others must take seriously, and either respond to positively or give us good reasons as to why they refuse.

But what actually is involved in acting in a way which makes sense *routinely*, without us continually having to stop to calculate whether our actions are a proper, normatively accountable response to our circumstances? When it comes to accounting for the outcome of any process – whether a cognitive process or otherwise – it is not just a matter of providing a list of *all* the events which as a matter of fact preceded the outcome (Sabini and Silver, 1981). If it were, then amongst the events to be listed in accounting for me writing this chapter would be the fact that while I wrote it I held my breath in many periods for much too long a time. But clearly, such events as these are irrelevant. A way of separating relevant from irrelevant activities is required. There are two distinct approaches to this problem: what might be called (1) the shared *meanings*, and (2) the shared *means* approach.

1. To distinguish relevant from irrelevant activities, one suggestion is that perhaps *criteria* are required, something which one might use as a third-person, external observer to distinguish relevant from irrelevant features – this is the approach implicit in cognitivism. But what are the right criteria? Without a set of *already shared* meanings, we are unable to judge *what* is going on. This approach runs into all the difficulties it was meant to solve. Only if we *already* know in some other way (in some first-person sense) how to recognize the things and activities in question can we judge whether proposed formulations of particular criteria for use by third persons are in any way appropriate.

2. This suggests another approach. Returning to C.W. Mills's views about the accountable nature of conduct on everyday social life, it is

necessary to point out that not *all* everyday conduct is questionable. The conduct of everyday social life is based, it was claimed, upon a right we all assign to each other, as first-person, socially autonomous adults, to have what we say about ourselves taken seriously as meaning what *we* intend it to mean (Cavell, 1969) – as conveying *our* meaning. But this is not because we have a set of agreements about meanings, beliefs or values in common, but because we share a set of societal *resources* (i.e. 'tools', means, ways of talking) which we *must* (morally) use in formulating our thoughts, actions and utterances (Billig *et al.*, 1988). For as Mills (1940) makes plain, when we give accounts we are not merely stating 'reasons', describing or explaining our behaviour (i.e. representing as a type), but creating new ways to guide, mediate, specify further, action which has become 'blocked' in some way. What is important to us about words is that, like hammers and chisels, they are not just stable *forms* but adaptable and changeable *means* for us to use in making *our* meanings.

Indeed, this argument that the first-person status occupies a central position in everyday social life can be carried a step further, to argue that it plays a central part in the conduct of science also. If it were impossible for us as first-person actors to distinguish between that for which we as individual personalities are responsible and that which merely happens to, in, or around us, irrespective of our agency, then not only would everyday life become impossible but so would science. For it would mean that we were unable to sense, when acting in accord with our theories, whether our results accorded with or departed from the expectations engendered by those theories. Thus we would be unable to put any of our theories to empirical test. Without any sense of their own functioning, scientists would be unable to do experiments. No more fundamental basis for deciding the truth of empirical matters exists, nor will one ever be found – in the organizational complexity of matter, say, for how could this ever be established as a true basis? It would still rest upon the basis of us as first persons being able to recognize and articulate the consequences of our own actions.

But even more is involved in the responsible conduct of everyday life than us being able to distinguish our own actions from the happenings around us. For as Mills (1940) makes clear, even when we are all alone, if we are to act responsibly we must be able to make our actions intelligible to ourselves in other people's terms. In other words, we are expected to show in our actions not just an awareness (i.e. consciousness) of our immediate circumstances, but *self*-awareness: that is, we are expected to act in a manner appropriate to interests other than our own immediate idiosyncratic ones, where amongst those interests are the

A social constructionist account   73

first-person rights of others around us. To do that, however, one must become a second person, a recipient of *their* actions, someone who responds to them (Shotter, 1989a). Indeed, first-person rights to speak and act, and have what one does or says taken seriously, are continually in contest. They are continually in contest because there is an intrinsic scarcity associated with them: a 'political economy' is at work because, if I am to be someone else's listener, I cannot be the speaker; if I am to be someone else's reader, then inevitably I cannot at the same time be a writer; and I cannot simply assert my right to be a writer on my own – a writer is useless without readers.

Clearly, although essentially concerned to retain their membership of their society – for it is only in terms of their belonging to it that they have their rights – people act whenever they can to increase their own first-person rights and to reduce their obligations. At every moment, then, 'where' one is, how 'placed' or 'positioned' in relation to the others around one – both in terms of what one has a right to do and in terms of the resources made available to one there – is important knowledge in determining one's momentary action. What we have a right to do in one situation at one moment we have no right to do the next; conditions we have no obligation to satisfy here we must satisfy there. Morally, it just is not open to us to do what we want when we want. Our moral world is clearly an ever-changing sea of opportunities and limitations, entitlements and liabilities, enablements and constraints.

The view of the first person here, then, is of someone always in a seemingly 'given' but changing, socially constructed situation, where the 'openings' to action in such a situation change as the course of one's action changes. If I now ask myself in such a situation: 'What is it like to be *me*?', 'Who and what am I?', I can answer only by describing 'my world', 'my situation': (1) the 'things' I perceive in it; (2) the values I attach to them, how I perceive them, and the reactions I have towards them; (3) the opportunities for action it 'affords' (Gibson, 1979) me; and especially (4) its 'horizon' – i.e. what is not actually 'visible' to me but is reasonable for me to expect in the future. This is my *identity* in the situation, who 'I' am. Indeed, my very use of the word 'I' – in such expressions as 'I think I may be able to see a solution' or 'I feel I have placed myself in difficulties here' – allows me to talk about my 'position' in and within such a changing, socially constructed situation, without characterizing myself in any other way. In this sense, the term 'I' is, as Benveniste (1971, p. 219) says, 'empty', and it becomes 'full' only within the situation of its use. It is precisely this ability – to appreciate its own unique self, its own unique placement among the other unique members of its social group, and the relation between its own desires and whether the justifications it can offer for their pursuit can be supported by 'good reasons' – that computers lack. To repeat what was said earlier: they are unable to relate their actions either to a self-known 'I' and/or to a situated other, a 'you'.

Concluding comments

Why have we not appreciated all this before? Why have we been so uninterested in the rhetorical, responsive and ethical nature of activities in everyday social life? Why have we not appreciated the ineradicable nature of the first-person perspective? And perhaps even more important: Why have we not realized, not just the nature of the subjective misery caused, but the nature of the objective destruction of the intricate, ethically regulated social relationships constitutive of a society of 'free individuals' by the imposition of an external, impersonal, (supposedly) rational order?

Because as professional academics we have, I think, been doubly entrapped: both in a set of professional practices to do with the regimented and systematizing of everyday social life, and by an image invoked in us by the necessity to conduct and report all our professional investigations from within a dominant form of talk – one which suggests to us that 'correspondence with reality' in terms of shape is basically how mental processes work. We have not been able – and in a certain sense rightly so – to speak and act just as we please; we have had to act 'into' the context provided by our professional colleagues. Thus, as I said earlier, what is at issue here is not a matter of whether what we say corresponds with the world in some way but of whether we, in making use of currently accepted ways of making sense, help to maintain the currency of its both individualistic and scientistic communicative practices (Parker and Shotter, 1990). And present in these practices is a way of speaking which confronts us with an inadequate image of ourselves – one which hides from us the social nature of our being.

'A picture held us captive,' said Wittgenstein (1953, no. 115), 'and we could not get outside it, for it lay in our language and language seemed to repeat it to us inexorably.' In fact, as I have suggested above, the image(s) 'in' our languages of psychological explanation are those rendered much more explicit in F.W. Taylor's and Max Weber's accounts of (supposedly) rational (or rationalized) forms of human activity. And what both accounts partially reveal[13] is the nature of the prior social processes (of, in fact, 'political negotiation' *and*, on many occasions, 'political force') necessary to produce such forms, while what they conceal is their own social genesis. As Gergen (1989, p. 464) has put it: on our way towards a fully genuine, socially, historically and politically aware psychology, we must be careful of not 'getting off at the wrong revolution'. The key to a completely new approach can be found, I suggest, in Wittgenstein's (1969, no. 215) claim that 'the idea of "agreement with reality" does not have any clear application'. In other words, we do not *always* check our claims to truth by a procedure of formally comparing representation and reality in terms of their 'shape', but in terms of (many) other, more socially negotiable criteria. Thus, in taking a practical, social constructionist stance, and in attempting to account for the normative accountability of human action, I have been trying to take the 'cognitive revolution' a few steps further, to account for cognitive processes as a product of social processes.

Notes

1. At least, what we *call* our 'abilities'. I say this because cognitivism clearly implies a *realist* stance towards mental processes: that as they have an existence independent of our thought or talk about them, they can be studied by use of the classical, model-building approach. Whereas the *social constructionist* stance sees talk of mental abilities or capacities not as representational, but as socially functional.
2. I say less cognitive rather than non-cognitive, as nobody would want to deny many of the claims and tenets of cognitive psychology – clearly, in many instances (but not always) we *do* have inner mental representations. What I do want to claim, however, is that what are thought of as cognitive *processes* are in fact themselves *products* of essentially sociohistorical political processes, and that the professional hegemony of cognitive psychology prevents the study of this fact.
3. The whole issue is clearly much more complicated than is stated. The discrepancies between who one presents oneself as being and who one feels one ought to be, etc., are investigated by Goffman (1959) – among others, of course.
4. Here I am inverting an expression of Garfinkel's (1967) in which he describes our ways of talking as working to render our everyday world 'rationally-visible' to us, i.e. as consisting of things and events about which it is possible to talk reasonably. But by the same token, such ways of talking also render other aspects of our everyday world 'rationally-invisible' to us; they are unavailable as reasonable topics for discussion.
5. Perhaps at this point we should not forget that the reduction of intelligent conduct to impersonal routines has always been one of the tasks (in certain quarters) of the human sciences.
6. But is this Hume's Problem? Palmer (1987) claims that Hume, in pointing out that he could never catch *himself* at any time without a perception, nor ever observe anything but a perception, was not saying just that he was unable to capture his *self* in thought, but also that his ideas, his thinking, etc., are *internal* (not external, as Dennett suggests) to what and who he is. In other words, claims Palmer, ideas, etc., are intentional all the way through, and thus Hume's Problem (if it is indeed the problem of

intentionality) cannot be solved by making the range of its application smaller and smaller – even adders and subtractors need to be able to warrant, if challenged, that they have acted aright. My own view is that Hume's Problem is not just of intentionality, but also of personal identity.
7. Dennett's views are not easy to divine unequivocally. For instance, in one of his more recent writings he realizes that talk of representations is controversial, and described himself as 'one of the most extreme skeptics about mental representations . . . ' (1984, p. 30). Nevertheless, whether a sceptic about representations or not, he in no way seems to be a sceptic in still talking of 'systems', 'patterns' and 'mechanisms' as central in any understanding of reasoning.
8. It is this form of management, and its 'analytic' counterpart, which is now beginning to lose its attraction (Peters and Waterman, 1982).
9. It is presumably just such a circumstance as this that the peoples of Eastern Europe are, to many people's surprise, revolting against. But as Václav Havel (1986, p. 31) points out, if anyone was surprised, that was because they lived within a system which, by its very nature, had been disconnected from the social conditions of its own existence:

> If every day a man takes orders from an incompetent superior, if every day he solemnly performs ritual acts which he privately finds ridiculous, if he unhesitatingly gives answers to questionnaires which are contrary to his real opinions, and is prepared to deny his own self in public, if he sees no difficulty in feigning sympathy or even affection where, in fact, he feels only indifference or aversion, it still does not mean that he has entirely lost the use of one of the basic human senses, namely, the sense of *humiliation*. On the contrary: even if they never speak of it, people have a very acute appreciation of the price they have paid for outward peace and quiet: the permanent *humiliation of their human dignity*.

10. Indeed, my discussions of Taylorism and Weberian bureaucracies conform to an aspect of cognitivist ideology – they are 'ideal-type' accounts, as Billig's account (see below) of bureaucratic thinking illustrates. Ideal-type accounts 'erase', so to speak, the varied and detailed nature of actual, everyday social phenomena. They work as 'intuition pumps' (Dennett's [1984] term), tending to magnify one facet or other of an issue at the expense of others, tending to push a reader towards certain conclusions.
11. The giving of *good reasons* does not constitute a proof of a claim, for there is always the possibility of finding even better reasons for rejecting it.
12. These views are, of course, very similar to Vygotsky's (1962; Shotter, 1989b).
13. See Braverman (1974) for a discussion of some of the issues involved. One should also, perhaps, not forget the old newsreel footage of the pitched battles between police and workers in America over opposition to the introduction of production-line working. Also, see Doray (1988) who, as a French psychiatrist, has studied the stressful effects on workers of the 'rational madness' of Taylorism/Fordism.

References

Bacon, F. (1858), *Of the Dignity and Advancement of Learning (1605)*, London: Longman.

Bakhtin, M.M. (1984) *Problems of Dostoevsky's Poetics* (ed. and transl. (Caryl Emerson), Minneapolis: University of Minnesota Press.
Benveniste, E. (1971), *Problems in General Linguistics*, Florida: University of Miami Press.
Bernstein, R.J. (1983), *Beyond Objectivism and Relativism*, Oxford: Blackwell.
Best, J.B. (1986), *Cognitive Psychology*, New York: West Publishing.
Billig, M. (1987), *Arguing and Thinking: A rhetorical approach to Social Psychology*, Cambridge: Cambridge University Press.
Billig, M., Condor, S., Edwards, D., Gane, M., Middleton, D. and Radley, R. (1988), *Ideological Dilemmas*, London: Sage.
Boden, M. (1977), *Artificial Intelligence and Natural Man*, Sussex: Harvester.
Boden, M. (1982), 'Formalism and fancy', *New Universities Quarterly*, **36**, 217–24.
Braverman, H. (1974), *Labour and Monopoly Capitalism: The degradation of work in the twentieth century*, New York: Monthly Review Press.
Cavell, S. (1969), *Must We Mean What We Say?*, London: Cambridge University Press.
Coulter, J. (1979), *The Social Construction of Mind*, London and Basingstoke: Macmillan.
Coulter, J. (1983), *Rethinking Cognitive Psychology*, London and Basingstoke: Macmillan.
Coulter, J. (1989), *Mind in Action*, London and Basingstoke: Macmillan.
Craik, K.J.W. (1943), *The Nature of Explanation*, Cambridge: Cambridge University Press.
Davis, P.J. and Hersh, R. (1983), *The Mathematical Experience*, Harmondsworth: Penguin.
Dennett, D.C. (1981), *Brainstorms: Philosophical essays on mind and psychology*, Brighton: Harvester.
Dennett, D.C. (1984), *Elbow Room: The varieties of free will worth wanting*, Oxford: Clarendon Press.
Doray, B. (1988), *From Taylorism to Fordism: A rational madness*, London: Free Association Books.
Dreyfus, H.L. (1972), *What Computers Can't Do: A critique of artificial intelligence*, New York: Harper & Row.
Dreyfus, H.L. and Dreyfus, S.E. (1986), *Mind Over Machine: The power of human intuition and expertise in the era of the computer*, New York: The Free Press.
Fodor, J.A. (1976), *The Language of Thought*, New York: Crowell.
Fodor, J.A. (1985), 'Fodor's guide to mental representation: The intelligent auntie's vade-mecum', *Mind*, **94**, 76–100.
Garfinkel, H. (1967), *Studies in Ethnomethodology*, Englewood Cliffs, NJ: Prentice Hall.
Gergen, K.J. (1982), *Toward Transformation in Social Knowledge*, New York: Springer.
Gergen, K.J. (1985), 'The social constructionist movement in modern psychology', *American Psychologist*, **40**, 266–75.
Gergen, K.J. (1989), 'Social psychology and the wrong revolution', *European Journal of Social Psychology*, **19**, 463–84.
Gibson, J.J. (1979), *The Ecological Approach to Visual Perception*, Boston, MA: Houghton Mifflin.
Goffman, E. (1959), *The Presentation of Self in Everyday Life*, New York: Doubleday.

Hamilton, D.L. (1979), 'A cognitive-attributional analysis of stereotyping', in L. Berkowitz (ed.), *Advances in Experimental Social Psychology*, New York: Academic Press.
Harré R. (1983), *Personal Being: A theory for individual psychology*, Oxford: Blackwell.
Havel, V. (1989), *Living in Truth*, London: Faber & Faber.
Johnson-Laird, P.N. (1983), *Mental Models*, Cambridge: Cambridge University Press.
Kline, M. (1980), *Mathematics: The loss of certainty*, Oxford: Oxford University Press.
Mills, C.W. (1940), 'Situated actions and vocabularies of motive', *American Sociological Review*, **5**, 904–13.
Myhill, J. (1956), 'Some philosophical implications of mathematical logic', *Review of Metaphysics*, **6**, 156–98.
Nelson, J.S. and Megill, A. (1986), 'Rhetoric of inquiry: Projects and problems', *Quarterly Journal of Speech*, **72**, 20–37.
Palmer, A. (1987), 'Cognitivism and computer simulation', in A.P. Costall and A.W. Still (eds), *Cognitive Psychology in Question*, Hemel Hempstead: Harvester Wheatsheaf.
Perelman, C. and Olbrechts-Tyteca, L. (1969), *The New Rhetoric: A treatise on argumentation* (transl. J. Wilkinson and P. Weaver), Notre Dame: University of Notre Dame Press.
Peters, T. and Waterman, R. (1982), *In Search of Excellence*, New York: Harper & Row.
Sabini, J. and Silver, M. (1981), 'Introspection and causal accounts', *Journal of Personality and Social Psychology*, **40**, 171–9.
Sampson, E.E. (1981), 'Cognitive psychology as ideology', *American Psychologist*, **36**, 730–43.
Sampson, E.E. (1988), 'The debate on individualism: Indigenous psychologies of the individual and their role in personal and societal functioning', *American Psychologist*, **43**, 1203–11.
Shotter, J. (1984), *Social Accountability and Selfhood*, Oxford: Blackwell.
Shotter, J. (1989a), 'Social accountability and the social construction of "you"', in J. Shotter and K.J. Gergen (eds), *Texts of Identity*, London: Sage.
Shotter, J. (1989b), 'Vygotsky's psychology: Joint activity in a developmental zone', *New Ideas in Psychology*, **7**, 185–204.
Shweder, R.A. and Bourne, E. (1982), 'Does the concept of the person vary cross-culturally?', in A.J. Marsella and G. White (eds), *Cultural Conceptions of Mental Health and Therapy*, Boston: Reidel.
Smith, A. (1776/1947), *The Wealth of Nations*, vols 1 and 2, London: Bell.
Snyder, M. (1981), 'On the self-perpetuating nature of social stereotypes', in *Cognitive Processes in Stereotyping and Intergroup Behaviour*, Hillsdale, NJ: Erlbaum.
Taylor, C. (1989), *Sources of the Self: The making of the modern identity*, Cambridge, MA: Harvard University Press.
Taylor, F.W. (1947), *Scientific Management*, New York: Harper, first pub. 1918.
Vygotsky, L.S. (1962), *Thought and Language*, Cambridge, MA: MIT.
Weber, M. (1964), *The Theory of Social and Economic Organizations* (transl. A.M. Henderson and Talcott Parsons), New York: Free Press of Glencoe.

Winch, P. (1958), *The Idea of a Social Science and its Relations to Philosophy*, London: Routledge & Kegan Paul.
Wittgenstein, L. (1953), *Philosophical Investigations*, Oxford: Blackwell.
Wittgenstein, L. (1969), *On Certainty*, Oxford: Blackwell.

6
The concepts of the universal in the Cartesian and Hegelian frameworks

Ivana Marková

Editors' introduction

In our everyday activities we deal with *particular* objects, such as a dog or a table, but our knowledge goes beyond particulars to knowledge of universals – to dogs or tables in general. The Platonic explanation of this is that a universal is an essence that exists outside ourselves, an ideal form of which particulars are shadowy copies. Our knowledge of these Platonic forms is mediated by concepts or ideas. According to Descartes, these ideas cannot stem from experience alone. This was disputed by Locke and other Empiricists, and sometimes the reality of essences has been denied altogether, but these criticisms of Plato and Descartes were not truly radical, since they were still presented within the Platonic–Cartesian framework.

In this framework, if universals exist they are fixed entities, whether they are in the mind as concepts, outside in the world, or both. Universals are 'eternal and unchangeable essences of the world' (p. 84), and the mind is structured to discover them. Dualism is built into this view, and when the mind becomes the object of cognitivist inquiry it too is treated as an eternal and unchangeable essence. By contrast, in the Hegelian framework universals correspond to concepts that are the product of human evolution. This is not evolution in a fixed setting, since universals develop in mutual interaction with particulars. Human beings and their settings evolve together. There is an important similarity between this philosophy and social constructionism (this volume, Chapter 5).

The biological version of the Cartesian framework was that the members of a species are held together by a common essence.

I would like to acknowledge most valuable comments and suggestions on previous drafts of this chapter provided by Colin Wright, Arthur Still and Alan Costall.

Darwin undermined this classical view by showing that species are distinguished by descent, and are therefore historical entities that maintain their identity through common descent (c.f. Ghiselin, 1987). Put like this, Darwinian evolution appears to share the Hegelian framework, but neo-Darwinism continued to maintain a kind of eternal universal, by treating the environment as a fixture to which organisms adapt. Correspondingly, cultures are treated as adaptations to a static environment. A more dialectical view, closer to Hegel, is that organisms and environments evolve in mutuality – there is a dynamic relationship as organisms act upon and change the environments by which they are in turn changed through the processes governing evolution. Darwin himself seems to have been ambivalent about this. Sometimes he wrote as though the environment were unchanging, and he has been bracketed with neo-Darwinism by some of the recent critics cited by Marková. But many aspects of his theory run counter to the Cartesian framework of modern biology and stress the active, transformative role of organisms in the evolutionary process (see Costall, 1991).

References

Costall, A. (1991), (forthcoming) 'The 'meme' meme', *Cultural Dynamics*.
Ghiselin, M. (1987), 'Classification as an evolutionary problem', in A.P. Costall and A.N. Still (eds), *Cognitive Psychology in Question*, Hemel Hempstead: Harvester Wheatsheaf.

* * *

In its attempt to establish itself as a science, psychology has long sought to discover so-called *psychological universals*, basic principles of behaviour and mental processes. Although such aims may – at least at first sight – appear relatively clearly defined, a number of questions arise if one starts asking: What kinds of principle qualify as universals? What is the nature of universals? Are they biological, cognitive or environmental in character? By what kinds of method can they be established?, and so on. Answers to these and similar questions depend largely on the concepts of the universal used within particular theoretical frameworks.

In this chapter I shall contrast the concepts of universals in the Platonic–Cartesian and Hegelian philosophies. The choice of these two is not fortuitous. The Platonic–Cartesian philosophy is an explicit and dominant point of reference for much of modern cognitivism (cf. for

Concepts of the universal 83

example Chomsky, 1966; Fodor, 1981). References to Hegelian philosophy, on the other hand, are relatively rare in psychology, although some of the most important Hegelian ideas have been implicitly adopted by psychologists without realizing their original sources (Marková, 1982).

Although I do not accept Hegel's philosophy wholesale, there are two basic reasons for my appeal to him. First, historical; it was Hegel who, in modern philosophy, formulated the principle of the interactional effect of the two mutually dependent factors involved in the concept of *development*. Development is also fundamental in his concept of the universal. Secondly, Hegel's philosophy has been highly influential in the rise of various forms of evolutionism, dialectics, phenomenology, symbolic interactionism, and so on. It is my conviction that psychology would benefit by returning to Hegel's original formulation of the principle of development and human agency because Hegel's formulation, more than any other that came after him, lays bare the fundamental differences between the static, non-interactionist, and the dynamic, interactionist, frames of reference. Moreover, a discussion of Hegel's original ideas of development and agency is important if they are to be understood in the historical context in which they evolved and in separation from the biases imposed by later interpretations and additions. In discussing the concepts of the universal in the two philosophical frameworks I shall emphasize that the Hegelian – i.e. the developmental – conception of the universal in psychology has considerable theoretical and methodological advantages over the Cartesian – i.e. the static – conception.

The Platonic–Cartesian concept of the universal

The assumption that if knowledge is at all possible it must be of entities that are immutable and eternal has a long history in Western culture. The problem, however, is that since the world is changing, and new inorganic, organic and social objects emerge, exist for a while and disintegrate after a period of time, how can one identify what is *unchanging* and therefore true, and separate it from *changing* and ephemeral phenomena? In his attempt to solve this problem Plato developed a theory of Forms. Forms are *universals* existing independently of objects of perception and of minds. They are apprehended by the intellect, while their particular manifestations in individual objects are apprehended by the senses. Examples of Forms are Man, Fire, Motion or Rest. In contrast, an individual man, or an instance of fire, motion or rest takes part in the Form in question. While Forms or universals are immutable and eternal, individual objects change in time. Thus, true knowledge must be of universals only.

If one accepts that knowledge is of entities that are eternal and immutable, the question arises as to how knowledge can be acquired by individual human beings who themselves are neither eternal nor immutable. Plato's response to this problem was that although people themselves are mortal, the human soul is immortal. It is incarnated again and again, and between incarnations it knows everything there is to know and has thus nothing new to learn: 'Seeking and learning is nothing but recollection' of knowledge from the soul's previous lives (Plato, 1961). For example, in Plato's *Meno*, Socrates leads the slave Meno to rediscover for himself what, in fact, he already knows about virtue. In general, if suitably questioned and guided or if given a proper stimulus, any human being is able to recollect *a priori* knowledge, which is independent of learning and experience.

Plato's notion of the universal was adopted in its essence by seventeenth-century Cartesian philosophy. According to Descartes, 'innate ideas are those which account for universals and make universal knowledge possible'. In his letter to Mersenne of 16 June 1641, Descartes says that ideas such as God, Triangle or Mind represent true and eternal essences because they are universals (Descartes, 1970, p. 104). On another occasion he calls universals the primary germs of truth that nature implanted in the human mind (Descartes, 1911a, p. 12). Universals are hidden in the human mind, like the fire in a flint. Just as the fire is revealed only when triggered off by striking the flint on a stone, so universals are revealed only when triggered off by appropriate environmental stimuli (Descartes, 1911b, p. 442).

It is important for our purpose that in the Platonic–Cartesian account universals have both ontological and epistemological significance: they are eternal and unchangeable essences of the world, and they are also capacities of the human mind to acquire knowledge. Thus although, in the Platonic–Cartesian framework, for a philosopher universals in their ontological and epistemological guises amount, ultimately, to the same thing, for a psychologist they appear to have a dual nature, being both something *out in the world* and also something *in the mind*.

The concept of the universal in its dual guise has had a tremendous influence on psychology as it has emerged from philosophy. The subject of psychology is the study of human behaviour and the human mind. Therefore, psychology has taken it for granted that in order to become a science it should search for universals that underlie human behaviour and human mind. In other words, *ontologically* the subject of psychology implies the study of universals *out in the world* – out in the world being, in this case, human mind and human behaviour. Unfortunately, if an ontological universal is an attribute of the human mind, it is liable to be conflated with universals in the epistemological sense. Consider the following examples. The main doctrine of Chomsky's *Cartesian Linguistics* (1966) is that the general principles which determine grammatical structure in particular languages are common to all human languages and are therefore linguistic universals. Universals, consequently, are the properties of Universal Grammar found in all languages. A language as a synchronic system of signs is conceived by Chomskyan linguistics as something *out in the world* – something, therefore, that has ontological significance. At the same time the principles of Universal Grammar are explained by the innateness hypothesis (see also Hawkins, 1988). These principles – which, according to Chomsky, underlie the structure of the human mind – are of biological rather than logical necessity (Chomsky, 1977). In the same vein, Lenneberg (1967) views linguistic universals as innate and invariant capacities of the mind, based on uniform neurophysiological structures.

Fodor (1981) argues and gives evidence that the most plausible rationalist and empiricist theories of concept formation are all based on the assumption of the innateness, not just of capacities of the human mind, but of *primitive concepts*. According to Fodor, both rationalist and empiricist theories assume that primitive concepts such as Red, Line or Angle are innate and that their emergence is 'contingent upon the activation of the sensorium': it is either the structure of the mind in the cognitivists' theories or sensory stimulation in the Empiricists' theories that produce primitive concepts such as Red, Line or Angle. These concepts, therefore, are not learned, and if they are not learned they must be innate. In full agreement with Descartes, therefore, the essential assumption of both rationalist and empiricist theories is that the primitive concepts are hidden in the mind and become available to the knower through appropriate environmental triggering. Fodor labours the point that Rationalists from Descartes to Chomsky all agree that

> the environment of the developing organism actually provides a *poor* inductive basis for the concepts that the organism acquires. . . . All the environment does is provide the triggers that release the information. (Fodor, 1981, p. 280)

The implication of such theorizing is that the conceptual base in human beings is to a considerable degree 'invariant across variation in experience'. Since the mind is structured, *a priori* availability of primitive concepts automatically gives rise to more complex concepts. Although all primitive concepts are triggered, there is nevertheless a hierarchy of triggers, and from this hierarchy the order in which the concepts are acquired can be predicted. Fodor concludes his arguments with the claim that 'everybody is a Rationalist in the long run' because everybody accepts that there must be a primitive conceptual base from which logical constructions of complex concepts arise, while primitive concepts are not learned. The only difference between the rationalism of Descartes and that of Locke is how big such a primitive conceptual base is. One can thus see that at least two questions about universals have been intermingled in psychology: the existence of universals as such and the ways such universals are apprehended by the human mind.

Criticism of the Cartesian concept of the universal in cognitive science

While the clearest expression of the Cartesian concept of the universal in modern psychology is provided by the work of Chomsky and Fodor, the search for cognitive, linguistic and behavioural universals has been prolific in various areas of psychology. At the same time, severe criticism of and objections to the Cartesian concept of the universal have been raised. In considering these I shall draw attention to two issues: first, the tremendous liberality with which the word 'universal' is used in psychology; secondly, the consequent diversity of criticism of the concept of the universal, from attempts to complement the search for universals by the study of individual differences to the outright rejection of the concept of the universal and efforts to substitute for it a concept of a totally different kind. Since the Cartesian concept of the universal has primarily influenced cognitive psychology and psycholinguistics, it is natural that the major attacks have emerged within these subjects.

Concerning the first issue, I would like to point to the multiplicity of meanings of the word 'universal', which conveys totally different things to different researchers. Indeed, one can claim that in some cases these different things have little or nothing in common with each other except, perhaps, for the very word 'universal'. Consider some examples. For Chomsky and Fodor, universals are *abstract* principles arising from the structure of the mind; Comrie (1981a, b) searches for them through the exploration of some *concrete* concepts, performances or expressions. Finnegan (1981) argues that it is not clear how 'universal' a universal should be in order to have the claim to be so called. For Dasen (1981) there are weak and strong universals; Bruner (1981) holds that there are process and outcome universals; and Hardy-Brown (1983) that there are innate and environmental universals. Finally, Feldman (1980) rejects the notion of static universals and claims that universals undergo change. In a similar manner, researchers differ with respect to how they explain universals. While in the 1960s and 1970s the innateness hypothesis was favoured as an explanatory principle underlying universals (Chomsky, 1965, 1977), more recently, semantic (Keenan, 1988), discourse-pragmatic (e.g. König, 1988; Thompson, 1988) and even diachronic explanations recognizing language change are being offered (Bybee, 1988; Hall, 1988).

With respect to the second issue, criticism of the concept of the universal can be discerned at several levels. I shall present only examples of broader levels of such criticism.

At one level, researchers have focused their efforts on finding evidence that language acquisition is not just the triggering off of pre-programmed universals but that the caretakers' speech has a considerable influence upon the way the child acquires language (Snow, 1977). However, as Hardy-Brown (1983) correctly points out, the identification of environmental effects on the child's language acquisition does not challenge the universals hypothesis, since language universals may operate at other levels. Although linguistic variability is now receiving much more attention than previously, the assumptions and associated methodological problems of theories of underlying universals and individual differences have not been sufficiently examined. While both approaches to the study of language acquisition, the genetic and the environmental, are necessary because they provide complementary knowledge, their contributions to language acquisition need to be disentangled. Hardy-Brown suggests that one can represent the dual role of heredity and environment with respect to universals and individual differences in four cells: universals due to heredity, universals due to environment, individual differences due to heredity, and individual differences due to environment. Moreover, she contends, there is also an interaction between genetic and environmental factors affecting variation in language acquisition. In sum, Hardy-Brown argues against the reduction of the role of the environment to that of a triggering-off device, and insists on the importance of both genetic and environmental universals in language acquisition.

Another level of criticism is raised against those who, rather than demonstrate that a phenomenon or relationship is a universal, simply start from the assumption that this is the case, and challenge anyone who questions this assumption to offer a plausible and comprehensible alternative. In the field of cross-cultural research, Jahoda (1981) points out that psychologists conducting studies in the industrialized cultures where the bulk of such work is done are apt to take it for granted that their results would replicate anywhere else in the world. (Jahoda, 1981, p. 43)

For Jahoda, the existence of a universal could be accepted only on the basis of very powerful evidence. Similarly, Comrie (1981a) argues that in order to identify language universals it is essential to explore the whole range of languages. Comrie focuses on universals as formulated on the basis of concrete analyses, and in addition to innateness he is prepared to consider other kinds of explanations for language universals such as functional or pragmatic explanations. Chomsky (1966), however, bases his search for universals on the study of a single language, arguing that language universals should be formulated in terms of abstract structures within the transformational–generative grammars identifiable in any human language.

A third level of criticism attacks the concept of universals itself. Gopnik (1983) argues against immutable conceptual and semantic universals: people's knowledge and concepts change constantly in qualitative ways and cannot be reduced to previous knowledge and concepts. Indeed, no single 'language of thought' in Fodor's (1975) terms can be identified as underlying natural languages. Using examples from science and child development, she argues that neither scientists nor children fit Fodor's idea of a 'language of thought'. For instance, it could be held by a defender of universals that the concepts of Euclidean geometry are innate. Indeed, we have already remarked that Fodor (1981) considers concepts such as Line or Angle to be innate primitive concepts. However, as Gopnik points out, non-Euclidean geometries based on totally different geometrical principles are also conceivable, requiring different 'primitive' concepts. Moreover, evidence from developmental psychology demonstrates that the concepts of young children change dramatically as they obtain more experience, and this evidence strongly contests the supposition that they have a single universal representational system. She concludes her criticism:

. . . if we want to claim that there are universal characteristics of representations and of the way language encodes those representations, we will have to leave children and scientists out of our universe. . . . We might draw an analogy between the study of mental representations and the study of species. . . . The most important fact about species is that they can change, and the principles that explain this change are the most important principles in biology. . . . Similarly, the most important fact about knowledge is that *it* changes. (Gopnik, 1983, 175, 177)

At yet another level, Feldman (1980) rejects the notion of unchanging universals and offers an alternative in terms of changing universals.

Addressing the question of universals in cognitive development, Feldman maintains that Piaget, by his preoccupation with universals, ignores the creative achievements of unique individuals and thus deprives himself of the chance of making real progress in the theory of cognitive development, in particular in his theory of transition rules governing movement from one developmental stage to the next.

There are two essential features of Feldman's approach to the problem of universals. First, he argues for a dynamic relationship between unique and universal achievements, showing that cognitive development may occur within different developmental domains: universal, cultural, discipline-based, idiosyncratic, and unique. These domains form a universal–unique continuum. Only some domains of knowledge are mastered universally – that is, by all humankind; others are acquired by members of particular cultures; still others are achieved by a segment of a culture subject to training; while yet others are acquired by specialists who become masters in their particular disciplines; and finally, there are unique achievements representing an original way of organizing knowledge. Unique achievements, if they are truly creative – i.e. when they make a substantial contribution to knowledge, and individuals other than the originator himself or herself find them significant and important – start their journey towards generality, and thus towards universality. As a result of such a journey, a unique domain may transform an existing body of knowledge and become a new universal. On the other hand, non-creative unique achievements, although they may have similar characteristics to those that are creative, do not become part of universal knowledge and eventually wane away.

The second essential feature of Feldman's approach, following Flavell (1971), is his appreciation of the role of environmental conditions in catalyzing qualitative changes between the domains of development, leading to movement on the universal–unique continuum. In human evolution, he argues, every developmental advancement was once just a unique achievement. However, a unique achievement has the potential to become a critical environmental condition for the next generation, entering the evolutionary and historical journey towards universality.

The above examples of criticism of the Cartesian concept of the universal, and the attempts to modify the meaning of the word 'universal', all represent an effort to resolve certain fundamental theoretical and empirical problems in present-day psychology. These problems stem from the fact that the Cartesian concept of the universal is static, while psychological phenomena are constantly changing and developing. As a result, there is no coherent framework with respect to the concept of the universal. Indeed, as the cognitive and linguistic theories develop, anomalies that do not fit into existing schemata and explanations accumulate at both theoretical and empirical levels. Consequently the word 'universal' itself, by taking on so many meanings, is becoming meaningless.

The Hegelian concept of the universal

The Hegelian concept of the universal can be understood properly only in the context of *evolutionism* that became the *Zeitgeist* of the second half of the eighteenth century. In philosophy, one of the first major proponents of evolutionism was Leibniz, whose idea of self-unfolding monads extended far beyond the static framework of the Cartesian philosophy. Although Leibniz was not an evolutionist in the present sense of the word, he emphasized that nature does not consist of segregated groupings of phenomena such as rocks, plants, animals and humans, but instead is full of *transitions* from one kind of phenomenon to another that connect them all. For Leibniz, as for the majority of eighteenth-century philosophers and scientists, evolution was based on the idea of pre-formation – i.e. on the onfolding of miniatures of completely developed organisms existing in the wombs of their mothers right back to the beginning of the world. However, ideas of a true development involving the emergence of totally new organisms started to appear in the work of Buffon, de la Mettrie, Maupertuis, and later in that of Lamarck and others. Hegel thus grew up in an atmosphere in which various types of evolutionism had gradually undermined the certainty of the Platonic–Cartesian world of immutable Forms. Moreover, evidence for evolution was coming from biology, palaeontology, physiology and other newly founded scientific disciplines. In accord with this trend, the concept of development became the essential feature of Hegel's philosophy; stability, in contrast, was conceived only as an aspect of a constantly changing and developing world of ideas.

Hegel's (1873) concept of the universal, which is also part of the general evolutionist way of thinking described above, has two essential characteristics. First, universals are not ideas implanted in the human mind innately or *a priori*, but concepts that the human mind itself *produces* through its activity. Secondly, universals or concepts are not static but constantly develop and change through their interaction with particulars. There are no universals as ontological entities existing *independently* of the human mind out in the world.

Let us first turn to Hegel's belief that universals are not implanted in the human mind *a priori*. Just as for Plato and Descartes, so for Hegel, too, universals are concepts. In contrast to Plato and Descartes, however, in Hegel's philosophy concepts are not produced by the human mind in any fixed and final form. As the mind actively explores phenomena, concepts, which are the mind's own products, become more elaborate or, as Hegel says, more *concrete*. While in its origin a concept is *abstract*, i.e. not yet fully developed, in the process of the mind's activity it becomes more elaborate or *concrete*. Hegel (1873, p. 293) maintained that a true universal takes thousands of years to develop fully. For example, he argued that the principle of humanity was not completely recognized until Christianity became established. The Greeks, so advanced in many respects, did not believe that the Barbarians were humans in the same sense as they were themselves. The abolition of slavery in Europe was, according to Hegel, related to the development of Christianity, and thus to the emergence of the true universal of humanity. One must add, though, that the recognition of the universal of humanity did not mean that all humans were guided by it at once and on all occasions after it had appeared. Hegel himself recognized that progress does not proceed along a straight line but may regress before it enters the consciousness of all human beings.

Hegel's idea that the formation of concepts proceeds from abstract to concrete ideas has been adopted in various forms since. If one takes Vygotsky's (1962) theory of the child's acquisition of concepts, a similar point of view emerges. At first the child's concepts are fuzzy, overlapping with each other. Vygotsky refers to such a stage in concept acquisition as *pseudo-conceptualization*. With the child's increasing experience and maturation, proper concepts are acquired. A similar idea to that of evolution proceeding by concretization was also expressed by Spencer, according to whom biological evolution is 'an integration of matter and a progressive change from a relatively indefinite, incoherent-homogeneity to a relatively definite coherent-heterogeneity; and during which the retained motion undergoes a parallel transformation' (in Collins, 1901, p. 47).

The second characteristic of Hegel's theory is that universals – i.e. concepts – develop in the process of mutual interaction with particulars. Hegel argued that the traditional problem of philosophy was that universals were concepts in which particular features of objects were neglected as non-essential. For example, with respect to the universal 'dog', a particular colour, size or psychological characteristic was not part of the universal. A colour, size or psychological characteristic may distinguish one dog from another, but dogs of different colours, sizes or psychological characteristics are still *dogs*; their 'dogginess', the universal, is unaffected by particulars such as different colours, sizes or psychological characteristics.

Hegel, however, strongly objected to such a concept of the universal, calling it a mere phantom and shadow. He argued that the universal 'is not a mere sum of features common to several things, confronted by a particular which enjoys an existence of its own' (Hegel, 1873, p. 292). The universal, on the contrary, is self-particularizing or self-specifying. It means that a universal is real only in so far as it realizes itself in a *particular*, which may be this or that object, or this or that person. Although objects belonging to the same category have certain features in common, each of these common or universal features reveals itself in a particular way in an individual object. The particular, therefore, is the *antithesis* of the universal: there is no universal without a particular, just as there is no particular without a universal. For example, a certain variety of rose may be yellow. However, the yellowness expresses itself differently in each individual blossom, although in many cases the subtle distinctions amongst individual roses may not be noticeable to the untrained eye. However, one must not forget that when one talks about the universal manifesting itself through the particular, one is really talking about the manifestation of the individual's mental activity rather than about universals *per se*. Knowledge evolves through focusing on detail (particular) and from detail to the whole (universal), the two forming an unbreakable dyad in this process.

Hegel's insistence that there are no universals without particulars, just as there are no particulars without universals, must not be reduced to the triviality that both common and individual characteristics of objects are important in concept formation. The relationship between universals and particulars is something given not *externally*, but *internally*. Phenomena that are related internally are defined in terms of each other, just like figure and ground, and cannot be separated from each other as externally related phenomena can. If internally related phenomena are separated from each other, they cease to be what they were before (Harris, 1983; Marková, 1990; Rommetveit, 1990). The more the mind actively penetrates the characteristics of particulars, the more elaborate the concept of the universal becomes. There is no end stage to this developmental process because one can always acquire more knowledge and consider phenomena from other viewpoints.

Hegel's concept of development, however, must be considered primarily as a thought-process rather than a time-process (Ritchie, 1893). The essence of his philosophy consists in the criticism of thought, through which thought self-develops from its less adequate to its more adequate, truer forms. This process of the criticism of thought is a *logical* rather than a time-process. The logic of this process is based on Hegel's so-called oppositions, which enable one to view the relationships between universals and particulars from yet another side. What does it mean to have a concept or universal of, say, a dog? It means

Concepts of the universal   93

being able to identify a particular kind of animal as a dog and to distinguish it from, or *oppose* it to, other animals that are not dogs. In other words, one identifies an object not only by the properties that object has but also by properties it does not have. One learns at the same time both what a dog is and what it is not.

Culler (1976), in his study of Saussure, explains this idea very clearly. Consider a teacher wishing to teach someone what 'brown' is. It would not be a good teaching strategy, Culler argues, to attempt to teach the pupil to master all the browns in the various brown objects of various kinds, and then to test such knowledge by asking him or her to point to all brown objects. The problem with such a strategy is that one does not have a clear criterion for the selection of brown objects. Instead, one should teach the pupil to distinguish brown objects from those that are red, yellow, and so on. 'Brown' is not an independent concept that can be learned separately from others: it can be grasped only in relation to other concepts. Thus, one learns a concept through opposing it to other concepts. Moreover, 'contradiction is the very moving principle of the world' (Hegel, 1873, p. 223). Thought actually *develops* through the critical analysis of concepts in their oppositions. For Hegel, something is dynamic because oppositions keep it moving and acting. If a thing is unable to withstand contradictions, it disintegrates. In this sense, he maintained, the world itself is a contradiction, and therefore a constant 'becoming'.

Hegel developed his philosophy of the thought-process some fifty years before Darwin formulated his evolutionary theory. A variety of features in the two theories are similar (cf. for example Ritchie, 1893), but there is one important difference to which I wish to draw attention. The basis of Hegel's theorizing is the *mutuality* in the interaction between oppositions. In other words, oppositions such as variability and stability, universal and particular, identity and difference, have equal status in their complementary relationship (Marková, 1987). This means that they contribute equally to the process of thought-development and transform both themselves and each other as a result of their mutual interaction. One might ask how their mutual changes can be measured, how one knows that both components contribute the same amount to the final product, and so on. To answer these questions, one must bear in mind that one is not dealing with physical, biological, psychological or other kinds of objects, or with quantities; one is dealing with *concepts*. Hegel's concern is conceptual, not numerical. Any change in one component, however small, produces a change in the concept as a whole.

One can, of course, examine the subject of mutuality of oppositions in terms of physical, biological or psychological phenomena. Let us consider how this subject was conceptualized in Darwinian evolutionary theory, which has been highly influential not only in biology but in every science that has adopted an evolutionary perspective. In contrast to Hegel's concept of development based on the mutuality of effect of the two complementary components – universal and particular – the Darwinian concept of development is based on a problem-solving approach: the organism is viewed as solving a problem given to it by the environment, and by solving that problem the organism changes. The environment, in contrast, remains relatively unchanged. In other words, while Hegel's concept of development is based on the mutuality of the interaction between the two components, Darwin views development as based on an asymmetrical relationship between them, with one changing and the other remaining relatively unchanged. In consequence, following Darwin, most models of evolution are unable to cope with the concept of true interaction.

Recently, however, the idea of a problem-solving relationship between an organism and its environment has been criticized (Goodwin, 1985; Gould, 1977; Lewontin, 1982). Lewontin argues that evolutionary epistemologies wrongly conceptualize the environment as an autonomous something 'out there' that presents a problem which the organism has to solve in order to survive:

> Adaptation is the process of reconstituting the organism to fit the environment. Adaptation may be based on autonomously generated novelties, as in the strict Darwinism of Lorenz and Popper, or it may be a directed pseudo-Lamarckian response as for Piaget, but it is always the organism that responds to the environment and not vice versa. Yet our understanding of the real history of organisms has shown that the asymmetric picture is untrue. Organisms construct and reconstruct their environment, not just in their own heads as Piaget would allow, but in reality, 'out there'. (Lewontin, 1982, pp. 167–8)

He continues that this does not mean, of course, that an organism, in its construction of its environment, can go beyond its capacities. However, if genetic epistemology is to explain real invention in nature, it must be concerned with more than accommodation of the individual to a fixed reality.

It may seem, however, that a truly mutual relationship between an organism and its environment rarely occurs. In the process of evolution individuals become more and more complex, and the environment seems to lose its importance because the various characteristics of the individual appear to unfold according to a predetermined programme when environmental stimuli trigger them off. Indeed, the environment relating to some traits and capacities has been pretty stable for up to a hundred thousand years, a period which appears to be sufficient for the traits and capacities themselves to become highly stable (Schilcher and Tennant, 1984). As information becomes encoded into genes, not only do developing organisms appear not to be affected by environmental variability, but they possess autoregulatory feedback systems 'that buffer out the effect of environmental variation' (Lewontin, 1982, p. 155). For example, if the wing of the Drosophila embryo is damaged, the development of the entire organism stops while the wound heals so that the adult Drosophila emerges unhandicapped. One can appreciate that such examples of autoregulation appear grossly to devalue the role of the environment.

However, as Lewontin argues, a different picture emerges if one leaves the macro-level of the process and turns one's attention to the micro-level. He presents several examples demonstrating minute variations in the development of the organism due to 'developmental noise' or subtle environmental interferences. As he points out, the relationship between genes, environment and organism is highly intricate and diverse and different in various species, organs, tissues or enzymes, with some species developing virtually identically in a different environment while others are exceedingly flexible. One would suppose that these findings have implications for more complex species, in particular for those that have developed self- and other-awareness with the aid of which they exert effect upon their environment.

In conclusion, in Hegel's philosophical framework universals are concepts. As the knowledge of phenomena in question progresses, the concepts that are relevant to such knowledge develop – i.e. they become more diverse, specific and *concrete*, to use Hegel's own terminology. One might, however, object to the notion of dynamic concepts or concepts in flux. How can one grasp any reality using 'developing concepts'? Although the answer to this question had already been implied by Hegel (1807, pp. 54–5), Rommetveit's (1990) notion of a *temporary fixation* suggests a solution. According to this suggestion, in order to examine dynamic phenomena the philosopher or the researcher may, *mentally*, temporarily freeze them. However, it must be understood that such a temporarily fixed conceptualization of a dynamic phenomenon serves only a heuristic purpose and must on no account be mistaken for a concept that properly represents the dynamic nature of the phenomenon itself. Rommetveit maintains that an example of such a temporal fixation of phenomena is the viewpoint of mainstream cognitive science, which is based on the assumptions of Cartesianism. The problem, though, is that cognitivism does not see its viewpoint as in any way temporary, but treats its method as entirely objective and as having universal validity. In assuming that it has emancipated itself from any human concerns such as values and motives and that it presents a pure and neutral scientific point of view, cognitivism deceives itself: 'what appears as *emancipation* from human concerns from within enclaves of scientific enquiry, though, is from a dialogical and co-genetic point of view a *fixation*' (Rommetveit, 1990, p. 94). Thus, according to the dialogical – i.e. *mutualist* – point of view that is guided by the principles of *co-genetic* logic rather than *formal* logic (Marková, 1990), phenomena co-develop together with their environment, as do concepts (or universals) referring to such processes.

Is there a viable concept of the universal for psychology?

We have outlined two philosophical theories of the universal: the Platonic–Cartesian theory, according to which universals are immutable ideas abstracted from particulars and implanted innately in the human mind; and the Hegelian, according to which universals develop through the mind's activity in mutual relationships with particulars. In both accounts universals are *concepts*; as such, they are parts of two different philosophical theories of knowledge. Bearing on the above discussion, in this last section I would like to raise a question concerning the theoretical status of universals in psychology: are psychological universals *concepts*, as they are in philosophy, or are they something else? The answer to this question may explain at least some of the problems related to the multiplicity of meanings of the word 'universal' and the occurrence of the diverse levels of criticism of the Platonic–Cartesian concept of the universal discussed earlier.

With respect to the question of the theoretical status of universals in psychology, consider first the cognitivists' claim that cognitive and linguistic universals are innate. According to Chomsky (1980) this claim implies that universals are biologically predetermined programmes 'not qualitatively different from what we find in the case of the body'. Just as an embryo has a highly specific innate endowment that causes two eyes or two kidneys to develop, so it has a neurophysiological basis for the acquisition of cognitive functions. Thus, according to this account, universals appear to be biological *bases for the acquisition of concepts*, but they are not concepts as such. If one considers Triandis's definition, according to which a universal is 'a psychological process or relationship which occurs in all cultures' (Triandis, 1978, quoted by Jahoda, 1981), then again a universal seems to refer to a variety of psychological phenomena, but not to knowers' concepts as such. Support for my supposition that for Triandis universals are not concepts is to be found in his claim that if such psychological relationships or processes are not found it does not mean that the universal in question does not exist;

Concepts of the universal 97

various methodological errors within a culture and across cultures might be responsible for a failure to obtain particular results. However, while Chomsky clearly considers universals to be innate bases for the acquisition of concepts, Triandis is agnostic as to whether psychological phenomena identified as universals are innate, environmental in character, or what have you.

In contrast to Chomsky and Triandis, for whom universals appear to be bases for the acquisition of concepts, other researchers assume that universals *are* concepts. Thus, Fodor (1981), following Descartes, discusses universals in terms of innate primitive concepts invariant across experience. However, when Descartes refers to innate ideas one can well understand that it was his way of expressing certain thoughts which, in the seventeenth century, could not be expressed in terms of biological encoding or genetics. Does Fodor, in the twentieth century, really mean that it is our conceptual equipment (i.e. knowledge) that is innate, rather than biological bases for the acquisition of concepts? If one accepts a truly developmental point of view according to which all concepts and knowledge undergo qualitative changes during the knower's life because of his or her active involvement in the world, then there is no place for Fodor's 'language of thought' based on immutable primitive concepts. In a similar way Feldman's universals are also conceptual in nature, since they refer to actual knowledge rather than to biological or psychological bases for knowledge, as in the case of Chomsky and Triandis. In contrast to Fodor, however, for Feldman universals are not immutable but undergo changes during the knower's life or during historical and cultural processes in society.

These two different approaches to universals distinguished above – those of *universals as the bases for concepts* and of *universals as concepts* – require different theoretical treatments. If universals are considered to be the bases for concepts rather than concepts themselves, then the question that needs attention is how this genetic endowment is *actualized* – i.e. how does the basis for a concept become a concept? In other words, what is the role of the individual's environment in this process? If, on the other hand, universals are considered to be concepts, it is their relationship with the knower's active involvement with the world that must be the subject of concern.

There is, finally, an additional issue that requires clarification. In psychology, the term 'universal' in the philosophical (i.e. ontological or conceptual) sense has tended to be confused with *universality* concerning the number of objects to which the universal applies. Although universals have been confused with numerical universality in both Chomsky's and Triandis's approaches, Feldman's (1980) theory demonstrates the point especially clearly. For Feldman, universals are supposedly conceptual or ontological. In his unique–universal continuum, a creative novelty sets out on a historical journey by the end of which it is transformed into a new universal. However, the difference between creative novelty at the beginning of the journey and the universal at the end is defined merely by the number of people who adopt the novelty in their own behaviour or mental activities. Thus, while at the beginning of the journey the creative novelty was unique because it was the possession of a single individual, at the end it became universal because it was in the possession of others, possibly of all others. This confusion in psychology between universality in the numerical sense and universality in the conceptual or ontological sense appears to result from theoretical naivety. In the Platonic–Cartesian framework, since concepts were supposed to be totally immutable and all people were creatures of God, it was true by definition that everybody who is a human being must be in the possession of universals. So, transparently, all universals in the ontological sense were also universal in the numerical sense. In psychology, in contrast, the starting point of the inquiry has often been a search for *something* that is universal in the numerical sense. When numerical universality has been demonstrated – and very often, as Jahoda (1981) points out, when it has only been assumed – the existence of an *ontological* universal has been inferred.

For Hegel, in contrast, the existence of a universal is not dependent on the number of people in possession of it, as was made clear in his example of such a universal (or concept) as humanity. From Hegel's position it is conceivable that a universal might be acquired by one person only, as is originally the case with any scientific discovery. Such universals or concepts, of course, become more elaborate through the knower's involvement with particulars, leading to more true and more concrete theories.

As pointed out earlier, Platonic–Cartesian philosophy has always been concerned to discover immutable germs of knowledge, and the search for universals has been ubiquitous in this effort. The preoccupation with the study of universals is also a characteristic feature of the Cartesian cognitive science of today (see, for example, Greenberg, Ferguson and Moravcsik, 1978; Comrie, 1981b; Hawkins, 1988; Keenan, 1988). In contrast, the search for universals and the notion of 'universal' do not figure in the mutualist (dialogical) approaches in language and psychology. The mutualist approaches, as already implied, start with the assumption that change and stability constitute only a temporary fixation of dynamic phenomena and concepts. They are, of course, concerned with the question as to what remains relatively stable and what is changeable in the process of human thought and language. The study of temporarily fixed phenomena and of synchronic systems is important in dialogical approaches (Marková and Foppa, 1990, especially pp. 12–15, 87–95) but they are conceived only as *internally related* with the dynamically and diachronically conceived phenomena.

As for cognitive psychology, based on the Cartesian assumptions, it is important that it should clarify for itself whether it is concerned with universals as the biological and psychological bases for concepts, or with universals as the concepts themselves – i.e. with knowledge itself. In either case it is essential that universals should be reconceptualized in developmental terms. If the focus of psychology is on the bases for concepts, then, one should seek to explain relative stability in both biology and psychology, where it exists, and why some behavioural and mental characteristics have become more stable than others. If the focus of psychology is on universals as concepts, it should seek to explain the relationships between relative stability and variability *with respect to the individual's and societal development of knowledge*. The question, however, is whether Cartesian psychologists can start using the idea of the universals in a truly interactive manner or whether it would not be easier to dispense with the word 'universal' altogether, since the difficulty of dissociating universals from the static assumptions of the cognitivist may prove insurmountable.

References

Bronowski, J. (1970), 'New concepts in the evolution of complexity: Stratified stability and unbounded plans', *Zygon*, 5, 18–35.
Bruner, J. (1981), 'Review and prospectus', in B. Lloyd and J. Gay (eds), *Universals of Human Thought*, Cambridge and London: Cambridge University Press.
Bybee, J.L. (1988), 'The diachronic dimension in explanation', in J.A. Hawkins (ed.), *Explaining Language Universals*, Oxford: Blackwell.
Chomsky, N. (1965), *Aspects of the Theory of Syntax*, Cambridge, MA: MIT.
Chomsky, N. (1966), *Cartesian Linguistics*, New York and London: Harper & Row.
Chomsky, N. (1977), 'Conditions on rules of grammar', in R.W. Cole (ed.), *Current Issues in Linguistic Theory*, Bloomington and London: Indiana University Press.
Chomsky, N. (1980), 'Rules and representations', *Behavioral and Brain Sciences*, 3, 1–116.
Collins, F.H. (1901), *The Synthetic Philosophy of Herbert Spencer*, London: Williams & Norgate.
Comrie, B. (1981a), *Language Universals and Linguistic Typology*, Oxford: Blackwell.
Comrie, B. (1981b), 'The formation of relative clauses', in B. Lloyd and J. Gay (eds), *Universals of Human Thought*, Cambridge and London: Cambridge University Press.
Culler, J. (1976), *Saussure*, Brighton: Harvester.

Dasen, P. (1981), '"Strong" and "weak" universals: Sensori-motor intelligence and concrete operations', in B. Lloyd and J. Gay (eds), *Universals of Human Thought*, Cambridge and London: Cambridge University Press.

Descartes, R. (1911a), 'Rules for the direction of the mind', in E.S. Haldane and G.R.T. Ross (transl. and eds), *The Philosophical Works of Descartes*, vol. 1, London and New York: Cambridge University Press.

Descartes, R. (1911b), 'Notes directed against a certain programme', in E.S. Haldane and G.R.T. Ross (transl. and eds), *The Philosophical Works of Descartes*, vol. 1, London and New York: Cambridge University Press.

Descartes, R. (1970), Letter to Mersenne, 16 June 1641, in A. Kenny (transl. and ed.), *Descartes: Philosophical Letters*, Oxford: Clarendon Press.

Feldman, D.H. (1980), *Beyond Universals in Cognitive Development*, Norwood, NJ: Ablex.

Finnigan, R. (1981), 'Literacy and literature', in B. Lloyd and J. Gay (eds), *Universals of Human Thought*, Cambridge and London: Cambridge University Press.

Flavell, J. (1971), 'Comments on Beilin's "The development of physical concepts"', in T. Mischel (ed.), *Cognitive Development and Epistemology*, New York: Academic Press.

Fodor, J. (1975), *The Language of Thought*, New York: Crowell.

Fodor, J. (1981), *Representations*, Brighton: Harvester.

Goodwin, B. (1985), 'Constructional biology', in G. Butterworth, J. Rutkowska and M. Scaife (eds), *Evolution and Developmental Psychology*, Brighton: Harvester.

Gopnik, A. (1983), 'Conceptual and semantic change in scientists and children: Why there are no semantic universals', *Linguistics*, **21**, 163–79.

Gould, S.J. (1977), *Ontogeny and Phylogeny*, Cambridge, MA and London: The Belknap Press of Harvard University Press.

Greenberg, J.H., Ferguson, C.A. and Moravcsik, E.A. (1978), *Universals of Human Language*, 4 vols, Stanford: Stanford University Press.

Hall, C.J. (1988), 'Integrating diachronic and processing principles in explaining the suffixing preference', in J.A. Hawkins (ed.), *Explaining Language Universals*, Oxford: Blackwell.

Hardy-Brown, J. (1983), 'Universals and individual differences: Disentangling approaches to the study of language acquisition', *Developmental Psychology*, **19**, 610–24.

Harris, E.E. (1983), *An Interpretation of the Logic of Hegel*, Lanham, MD: University of America Press.

Hawkins, J.A. (1988), 'Explaining language universals', in J.A. Hawkins (ed.), *Explaining Language Universals*, Oxford: Blackwell.

Hegel, G.W.F. (1807), *Phenomenology of Spirit* (transl. A.V. Miller), Oxford: Clarendon Press.

Hegel, G.W.F. (1873), 'The encyclopedia of the philosophical sciences, Part 1, The science of logic', in W. Wallace (transl.), *The Logic of Hegel*, London: Oxford University Press.

Jahoda, G. (1981), 'Pictorial perception and the problem of universals', in B. Lloyd and J. Gay (eds), *Universals of Human Thought*, Cambridge and London: Cambridge University Press.

Keenan, E.L. (1988), 'On semantics and the binding theory', in J.A. Hawkins (ed.), *Explaining Language Universals*, Oxford: Blackwell.

König, E. (1988), 'Concessive connectives and concessive sentences: Cross-

linguistic regularities and pragmatic principles', in J.A. Hawkins (ed.), *Explaining Language Universals*, Oxford: Blackwell.
Lenneberg, E.H. (1967), *Biological Foundations of Language*, New York: Wiley.
Lewontin, R.C. (1982), 'Organism and environment', in H.C. Plotkin (ed.), *Learning, Development, and Culture*, Chichester: Wiley.
Marková, I. (1982), *Paradigms, Thought, and Language*, Chichester: Wiley.
Marková, I. (1987), 'On the interaction of opposites in psychological processes', *Journal for the Theory of Social Behaviour*, 17, 279–99.
Marková, I. (1990), 'A three-step process as a unit of analysis in dialogue', in I. Marková and K. Foppa (eds), *The Dynamics of Dialogue*, Hemel Hempstead: Harvester Wheatsheaf.
Marková, I. and Foppa, R. (eds) (1990), *The Dynamics of Dialogue*, Hemel Hempstead: Harvester Wheatsheaf.
Plato (1961), 'Meno', in E. Hamilton and H. Cairns (eds), *The Collected Dialogues of Plato*, Princeton, NJ: Princeton University Press.
Ritchie, D.G. (1893), *Darwin and Hegel*, London: Swan Sonnenschein.
Rommetveit, R. (1990), 'On axiomatic features of a dialogical approach to language and mind', in I. Marková and K. Foppa (eds), *The Dynamics of Dialogue*, Hemel Hempstead: Harvester Wheatsheaf.
Schilcher, F. von and Tennant, N. (1984), *Philosophy, Evolution, and Human Nature*, London: Routledge & Kegan Paul.
Simon, H.A. (1969), *The Sciences of the Artificial*, Cambridge, MA and London: MIT.
Snow, C.E. (1977), 'The development of conversation between mothers and babies', *Journal of Child Language*, 4, 1–22.
Thompson, S.A. (1988), 'A discourse approach to the cross-linguistic category "adjective"', in J.A. Hawkins (ed.), *Explaining Language Universals*, Oxford: Blackwell.
Triandis, H. (1978), 'Some universals of social behavior', *Personality and Social Psychology Bulletin*, 4, 1–6.
Vygotsky, L.S. (1962), *Thought and Language*, New York: Wiley.

7
Cognitivism:
A phenomenological critique
Neil Bolton

Editors' introduction

In Europe, phenomenology generally means the philosophy or method originated by Husserl (1859–1938), while in the States it often means a method of psychology based upon describing the contents of mind (Jennings, 1986). Neil Bolton's phenomenology stems from Husserl, while Shanon (Chapter 13) refers to a phenomenology that is closer to descriptive psychology. Husserl set out to give an exact description of the structures in consciousness that are necessary to constitute the world as we experience it. He devoted a lifetime, many books and even more unpublished manuscripts to this task, but failed in his initial goal. This was because, as he himself discovered, all experience is a product of historical and cultural setting (the *life-world*), which cannot itself be explained in terms of experience. His 'failure', however, proved to be one of his most important contributions, for the origins of experience came to be sought in the nature of the *life-world*, rather than in the structures of a pure consciousness. This has given rise to powerful arguments against cognitivism (Merleau-Ponty, 1962) which so far have been ignored rather than answered.

Neil Bolton uses his own development of such arguments to examine modern cognitivism. Cognitivism studies mental phenomena as abstractions, which may be useful as a strategy and even necessary for certain purposes. The fundamental mistake is to treat these abstractions as the sole reality, by forgetting the living context from which they are taken. By making this error cognitivism has become, as Bolton puts it, 'a form of life which admits no alternative since any alternative must be something other than psychology' (p 104).

References

Jennings, J.L. (1986), 'Husserl revisited: The forgotten distinction between psychology and phenomenology', *American Psychologist*, **41**, 1231–40.

104 Against Cognitivism

> Merleau-Ponty, M. (1962), *The Phenomenology of Perception*, London: Routledge & Kegan Paul.

*   *   *

And we: spectators, always, everywhere,
turned toward the world of objects, never outward.
It fills us. We arrange it. It breaks down.
We re-arrange it, then break down ourselves.
Who has twisted us around like this, so that
no matter what we do, we are in the posture
of someone going away? Just as, upon
the furthest hill, which shows him his whole valley
one last time, he turns, stops, lingers –
so we live here, forever taking leave.

RILKE, *Duino Elegies*

Introduction

My argument is that cognitivism is an abstraction from experience that studies mental processes as abstractions. It thus shows a false picture of psychological phenomena, because abstraction needs to be placed within the context of experience. This task has been undertaken within phenomenology.

Cognitivism, through spreading beyond psychology, has come to define both the content and method of approach of that subject. Cognitivism appears to be at once well-established and open-minded, a mature psychological perspective that has overcome an uncertain past. Such confidence is, I believe, unearned. Viewed against the wider perspective of ideas about human being, cognitivism looks perversely narrow and unjustified, secure only because it has isolated itself from other ways of understanding psychological life. Thus cognitive psychologists are able to investigate all experience and behaviour precisely *because* cognitivism itself is not open to scrutiny in all its partiality. Cognitivism is boundless, since it has become a chosen identity, a form of life which admits no alternative, since any alternative must be something other than psychology.

The quotation from Rilke is an example of this 'something other'. The *Duino Elegies* elaborate a way of thinking and feeling about the world that is fiercely opposed to what Rilke called 'the interpreted world' of conventional perception. Cognitive psychologists are unlikely, however, to grant such views any status within psychology: their professional socialization defines poetic vision as outside their subject's frame of reference. And it is not only poetry that is taboo. Cognitive science is also manifestly nothing to do with mythology, history, philosophy or politics as ways in which human beings attempt to make sense of their lives. It has deliberately abstracted itself from human existence at the individual and collective levels, where commitment and choice matter.

The usual justification for this abstraction is the plea of 'scientific impartiality'. It is argued that it is only because psychology has abstracted itself from the politics and poetics of everyday language that it can cast an impartial eye upon behaviour. However, this would be true only if abstraction were merely a methodological ploy that leaves the phenomena of experience intact, as it were, for description and analysis. But abstraction turns experience into abstractions.

The false phenomenology of cognitivism

The most popular view of phenomenology within psychology is to see it as being essentially concerned with conscious experience, with the subject's perception of the situation and with his feelings and introspections. Only the most extreme of behaviourists reject the necessity to take subjective experience into account; consequently, phenomenology can be safely assimilated into an empirical psychology in the form of an account of subjective experience along the lines of personal construct theory (Kelly, 1955), or as broadly supportive of the doctrine that reality is socially constructed (as individuals learn to pool their subjective viewpoints), or as a possibly useful adjunct to cognitive psychology's emphasis upon the role of hypothesis-testing in the construction of the world. A consensus appears to have emerged within contemporary psychology broad enough to encompass the conflicting armies of behaviourists and humanists: a recent president of the British Psychological Society gave this consensus his blessing in his presidential address (Hetherington, 1983).

There is an agreement not only about the content of psychology, but about procedure. The construction of reality can be experimentally studied: the development of hypotheses, limitation of memory, and strategies of information-processing can be described and ultimately summarized through a theory which cuts across the old concerns of subjective experience versus actual behaviour. The programme of this empirical-cum-phenomenological psychology thus readily assumes a substantial material form. The intelligent machine becomes the working model for both behaviour and experience, for the development of computer programs enables us to define operationally the imprecise concepts of human psychology. As MacKay (1951) pointed out, it is useless to say in defence, 'Yes, but you will never get a machine to do X', because the exact delineation of what X is involves an operational specification that could, conceivably, be embodied in a computer program. Thus, notions such as 'intentions', 'perception', 'memory', and so forth can be rewritten, and we can understand how concepts regarded as relating to subjective states of mind can find their rightful place within a science of human behaviour (Boden, 1977). Moreover, the assumption can be made that this level of description of behaviour will one day be matched in some sense against a description at the level of neurophysiology; the two will be seen, in the language favoured by the Gestalt psychologists (Köhler, 1940) and by Piaget (1950), to be isomorphic or 'structurally equivalent'.

It is easy to understand how this consensus should be so appealing. The everyday language of mentalistic concepts can be retained because it can be transmuted into a powerful programme of experimental investigation which, in turn, will ultimately be shown to have a basis in the physical world. There is a definite programme to be completed by a recognizable community of scholars. Of course there are differences of emphasis within the paradigm, but these fade into insignificance in the face of the widespread agreement as to the proper subject matter of psychology and the methods appropriate to that subject matter. In view of this, any criticism of the fundamental assumption of this cognitive-phenomenological world-view are likely to be rapidly dismissed: the strategies employed in defence would themselves make an interesting PhD study, but the commonest response by far is, not surprisingly, 'But I have not yet come across any such fundamental criticism.'

There are, however, some good reasons for not taking these defensive reactions at their face value. First, what we know of the history of science must make us sceptical about any theoretical framework as comprehensive and coherent as the one which dominates modern psychology; at least, caution should lead us to question our framework because there is no reason to believe that the psychological paradigm, in its development and possible decline, is likely to be different from other such perspectives on reality. Second, the very successes of a perspective depend just as much upon the limitations of the assumptions of that perspective as upon its freedom from assumptions. This is a postulate of cognitive psychology itself – the determination of perception by the interpretive framework – and we have no good reason, again, to exclude cognitive psychology from its own laws. Finally, what

Cognitivism 107

psychologists mean by the term 'phenomenology' is strikingly at variance with what phenomenologists themselves mean by this word. As I hope to show shortly, what has been assimilated into psychology as 'consciousness' is, in certain fundamental respects, a contradiction of what consciousness in essence is. Now, this means that in so far as cognitive psychology claims to be a programme for describing and explaining the functioning of consciousness it rests upon a fundamental epistemological mistake, and this mistake cannot be corrected simply by the development of more sophisticated techniques.

In this chapter, therefore, I wish to examine not the false phenomenology that has been found more and more acceptable as psychology has moved away from a narrow behaviourism, but the substance of a philosophical phenomenology that is just as much 'out of bounds' for the new psychology as for the old. I shall argue, as I and others (Bolton, 1978a, b, 1979; 1982a, b; Ashworth, 1981; Giorgi, 1970) have argued before, that a true assimilation of phenomenology to psychology forces a revision of our basic concepts and of the empirical programme of investigation.

True and false phenomenology compared

It is the concept of intentionality, developed in the works of Husserl (1965) and Merleau-Ponty (1962), that at first examination appears to support the case for a parallel between phenomenology and cognitive psychology. Intentionality refers to the essential feature of consciousness, that which is directed towards an object: all acts of perceiving, thinking, remembering, and so forth, have this feature, and from this we may conclude against any simple empiricist theory of consciousness – the mind is active in the construction of reality, so that what must be studied by psychology are the plans, concepts or schemata by which reality becomes organized. The basic assumptions are, then: perception is a constructive process; the process is to be studied as a series of acts (operations); the construction of reality is a cognitive process – emotion may provide the dynamics (in the form of drive or interference as irrational source of behaviour), but the two systems of cognition and emotion may be analyzed independently.

These assumptions, viewed from a genuine phenomenological perspective, can, at best, be accepted as half-truths. They reflect, precisely, half the truth of the dictum that consciousness is essentially directed towards an object – namely, the half that belongs to the subject.

All the differences between cognitive psychology and phenomenology arise from the former assigning priority to the activity of the subject, whereas the latter assigns priority neither to the subject nor to the object (it is not a form of realism any more than it is a form of subjectivism) but to the 'directedness towards an object'. Subject and object are given equal value, as it were, in the determination of reality, for what is real is the product of an active subject and that which is accepted as transcending the activity of the subject. There could not be any object of consciousness without the activity of consciousness, but to talk of it as object implies that it is other than that activity. It is an object of consciousness (an image, a thought, etc.) because it fulfils the intentionality of consciousness, because it allows that intentionality to be confirmed in something other than its own activity. Put less abstractly: we can and do make the distinction between the activity of cognition and that which confirms it; our very mistakes, as Husserl (1977) pointed out, are interludes within the general certainty of the world as confirmation of our thoughts.

Now if this is so, it signifies that we perceive the world in a way that is more fundamental than that envisaged by cognitive psychology. Prior to and transcending the object as the outcome of an interpretation, we are capable of experiencing the object as expression of itself. If we could not experience this, intentionality would be unable to fulfil itself as interpretation. Heidegger (1971) gives voice to this conclusion:

> Not only must that in conformity with which a cognition orders itself be already in some way unconcealed. The entire realm in which this conformity to something goes on must already occur as a whole in the unconcealed. . . . With all our correct representations we should get nowhere, we could not even pre-suppose that there is already manifest something to which we can conform ourselves, unless the unconcealedness of beings had already exposed us to, placed us in, that lightened realm in which every being stands for us and from which it withdraws. (p. 52)

It is this capacity to perceive 'the world as given' which is absent in the constructivist theory of perception, the theory which Merleau-Ponty (1962) challenged in his *Phenomenology of Perception* with the assertion that 'perception is not an act but the background against which all our acts take place'. I have argued elsewhere (Bolton, 1982a) that this capacity of consciousness to allow the object to express its meaning constitutes the aesthetic aspect of experience – the aesthetic, then, may be properly conceived as a fundamental part of all knowing; it is the imagination placing us within the world of objects, not through a series of constructions by which a structure is extended and resolved, but by what Polanyi (1967) called a 'dwelling-in' the object. This 'indwelling' is to be understood as personal knowledge in the sense that what is produced is the outcome of my commitment to it as an identity against which any commitment can be measured. This is what we mean when we talk of the 'directedness of consciousness towards an object'. For the cognitive theorist this directedness flows one way – towards the object which, then, cannot help but become an abstraction: it is created by my mental acts and the condition for its formation is a divorce between the acts and the object; knowing is standing back from something, freeing it from the self's idiosyncrasies. What we know is at once created by us and distant from us. But adopt the view that the object is the ground of our acts, not their outcome, and we must admit that the knower is constituted in the act of knowing by the object as much as the object by the act. To talk of the world as constructed is as true (and as false) as talking of the person as constructed by the world, for self and world are jointly revealed to one another. I am defined by the world as I define the world.

Cognitive theory rests upon the mistake of taking one form of knowing – abstraction – as the model for all knowing (Bolton, 1982b). That abstraction is taken as paradigmatic is not surprising in view of the prevalence of the theory of abstraction (in various guises) in psychological theories themselves – in S–R theory, in Piaget's account of reflective abstraction, and in the sequential programs of information theory (Bolton, 1972, 1977, 1978a). But however significant the capacity of abstraction is in allowing us to distance self from objects and thus conceptualize them, it is only one form of thought and requires itself to be placed in the perspective of other forms in order that both its power and its limitations should be apparent. What phenomenologists refer to as pre-reflective intelligence is the necessary basis for conceptual thought which never succeeds in making do without that openness to the world which is at the heart of our creativity. Cognition as a constructive activity occurs within contexts established as the measure of that activity.

The second assumption – that the constructive process may be studied as a series of acts – is designed to delineate the province of psychology. This discipline forms itself by abstracting mental acts from their context – the world given to us by our involvement in it as that which can be known and valued. Modern psychology, for all the objectivism of its methods, condemns itself to be steeped in subjectivity by the very way in which it supposes that the domain of the mental can be isolated (as one might try to isolate a certain type of virus) from its responsibility and care for the truth of things. In this it is thoroughly Cartesian. This dualism is, oddly enough, nowhere more apparent than in physiological psychology, which reduces the body to a series of physical events that parallel the cognitive processes. (The body in phenomenology, on the other hand [see especially Merleau-Ponty, 1962], is the condition for our being in the world and the mediator of our dialogue with it.) But dualism is only one consequence of psychologism – the reduction of the relation between knower and known to its subjective aspect. The symptoms of this disorder are everywhere: in the reduction of thinking to its strategies, of morality to social conditioning, of language to communication, of art to a moderate state of excitation. What is produced as a result of this study acquires the style of a technical language merely by the fact that it is divorced from the normal human concerns. Thus do psychologists become experts on the human condition!

The only radical alternative to this spurious science is to return to the phenomena themselves in order to develop a taxonomy for the psychological which relates it essentially to the concern for the truth and value of being. Psychology needs to ground itself, as Husserl (1948) pointed out, on a 'regional ontology' – a description of the different ways in which the world can be understood – in order that the empirical accounts of the development and functioning of the mind can be truthful. I have attempted to show (Bolton, 1982b) the force of a taxonomy whose essential elements are imagination, various kinds of abstraction, and faith. Imagination is the most fundamental of these, because it places us within the world as the field of our actions; abstraction is the most clearly powerful, because it results in the achievements of science and technology; and faith is the most necessary, because it is our quest for the ultimate coherence of our actions with the world.

These foundational concepts are at once technical and moral – the founding concepts of psychology cannot be otherwise, since human nature is neither a physical nor a social fact, but exists as concern about its own possibility. This concern is unavoidable but is itself given as possibility and is thus not mechanically accomplished. Man cannot live without truth, Socrates said, but our intellectualism has led us to mistake the meaning of this assertion. It is not an assertion of the power of the rational-cognitive domain over the emotional, but a testament to the continuity which exists between them. What we feel most strongly for is the truth of what we do, and in the truth of what we do, reason and feeling are one. The third major error of cognitive theory lies in its intellectualism, which reduces feeling and motivation to drive or to irrational residue. Thus it can accept as reasonable an account of cognition couched exclusively in terms of information-handling strategies and reinterpret emotional 'states' in terms of those strategies. The relation between learning and value is then seen as a purely extrinsic one, the mechanisms of learning being indifferently true for all value-contexts.

But this is not the case. The true meaning of learning follows from the nature of consciousness as that which is directed towards what can stand as its measure. We can talk interchangeably either of intentionality and transcendence in relation to the objective world or of care and respect in relation to the realm of values. For to know something is to respect it as a reference point for oneself, and it is known only if it is the outcome of our care. Caring *is* the active element in intentionality, respect the submission to reality experienced as transcendent. This is the meaning of learning, not some mechanism of reinforcement or equilibrium, for these are terms which receive their meaning only from our capacity to care and to respect. And we must insist that learning is a social phenomenon, but again not in any reductive sense, because social co-operation demands beings who can present to one another objects which can be cared for. Of course, learning can be mechanical and social forces can determine us without our consent, but to erect these as the cornerstones of a theory of learning is to consent to the aberration and not the norm; in this case the discipline itself becomes symptomatic.

Contemporary psychology represents the triumph of three influences that dominate the Western mind: subjectivism, technology and intellectualism. It construes the mind as comprehensible entirely through a study of its subjective aspect; the life of the mind is seen as a series of operations, so that the success of the discipline rests upon our technical capacity to make explicit the structure of these operations; and this structure can be characterized in purely intellectual terms as, say, problem-solving, information-processing, etc. It is difficult to determine how problematic psychology is in the implementation of this programme (it is, of course, impossible to convince such psychologists that they are in error, as they are safely ensconced within the paradigm), since it is one which generates a great deal of activity which can be satisfying in itself. The best form of criticism is to show the possibility of an alternative programme which differs systematically from that of cognitive psychology in challenging the three prejudices.

The programme of phenomenological psychology

It is true to say, I think, that whilst cognitive psychology has profusely materialized in countless empirical investigations, phenomenology has failed to consolidate itself on the empirical level, having had most recognition in psychiatry – there, chiefly as a therapy rather than a form of investigation. This is, indeed, not surprising in view of phenomenology's opposition to the idea of transforming the mind into a series of operational mechanisms, but it does raise the question: Can there be a phenomenological psychology? Granted that there can be a phenomenology determined by the nature of consciousness itself, and that there ought to be some connection between this study and the experience and behaviour of persons in a variety of situations, how can theoretical phenomenology lead into an empirical programme if it denies the methodological mechanisms necessary to carry out empirical investigations – namely, the operational definition of variables which permits one to study them as mechanical process? The answer to this question can be found only in a radical reappraisal of the very meaning of empirical investigation in the human sciences.

Whilst the first question of modern psychology is undoubtedly: How do we come to know the world?, phenomenology asks: How is it that there is a world to be known? It may be said that the first question takes it for granted that the world exists to be known and thus isolates knowledge as problematic, whereas the second question challenges both the experience of the world as taken-for-granted and our knowing it. But there is a further difference. What is problematic from the psychological perspective is the lack of evidence about the knowing of the world: we do not know how the world is known, but we take it for granted not only that the world exists to be known, but also that we can know how it is known – experiments can be carried out and facts accumulated. But what is problematic for phenomenology about the knowing of the world is not to be resolved in this empirical sense: it is not a matter of tuning in our concepts more finely to the facts, for it is this very activity which is questionable. Remember that phenomenology seeks to find the context in which abstraction can make sense and cannot find its own justification within the realm of concepts thrown up by abstraction. For phenomenology, in its return 'to the things themselves', is an absolute empiricism and cannot accept the partial empiricism of abstraction. This means that phenomenological truth must be expressed in relation to the whole structure of experience and nothing less.

But how is attentiveness to the whole structure of experience translated into a methodology? I have argued that there are three principal components to this structure: imagination, which enables us to enjoy the world as 'lived experience' and defines the boundary between self and world; abstraction from our actions in order to gain insight into their structures; and faith, which is 'ultimate concern' (Tillich, 1957), and seeks the concordance of what is most meaningfully lived with what can be ultimately known. The difference between conventional empiricism and phenomenological empiricism is, therefore, that the former defines its methodology exclusively in terms of what can be known through abstraction, whereas the latter extends the idea of what can be known to include the other ways in which humans exist in the world – chiefly, I believe, through imagination and through faith. Whilst normal science, with all its emphasis upon abstraction, is itself dependent upon imagination for its effectiveness and faith for its motivation, it rarely wishes to acknowledge this. In the physical sciences themselves this refusal is not methodologically damaging, but in the human sciences it results in an abbreviated perspective on the nature of experience and behaviour. To abide by Husserl's dictum that 'a true science follows the nature of what has to be investigated', the phenomenologically minded human scientist must admit imagination, abstraction and faith as methodological criteria in his or her investigation.

Now, it is easy to see that a methodology is a set of rules for allowing the investigator to proceed with an investigation, and that imagination and faith do not fall within this description. We use our imaginations and rely upon faith only when the customary rules fail us! Thus to insist that they should be present in an investigation is to subvert the customary meaning of a methodology. But there is no alternative but to insist upon this: in a genuinely phenomenological investigation, they must be present as expressions of concern that unite the investigator with the investigated. Against the isolation of investigator and investigated necessary to the success of abstraction alone, phenomenology sets the two together in their shared concern; against the partial perspective of abstraction, phenomenology sets the whole structure of experience as imagination, abstraction and faith. A shared concern for the coherence of experience and its ultimate meaningfulness is the only possible ideal for phenomenological methodology.

In normal perception, we see the figure but not the ground; in the methodology of cognitive science we see the force of abstraction, but not the ground from which it eternally arises and to which it returns. Phenomenology asks of us that we see both ground and figure; it demands, in a sense, a reversal of conventional seeing. Similarly, whilst conventional human science assigns priority to pure research, and treats applied fields such as educational and clinical psychology as subservient to the principles established there (roughly following the methodology possible in the laboratory), phenomenology reverses this order of priority. Pure research must be understood within the parameters defined in the applied field. Let us now look at this spectrum of applied to pure.

Phenomenology as therapy

One very common way of viewing therapy is to take it as the necessary outcome of pure research into the normal functioning of the mind.

Psychoanalysis and behaviour therapy provide good examples of such an approach: in both we start from a supposedly sound theoretical basis, which accounts for psychological functioning generally and in mechanical terms, to apply the discovered principles to disturbed cases. And whether we speak of conditioning or of defence mechanisms, it is assumed that both normal and abnormal states follow the same psychological laws. Individual cases can thus be treated by reference to a standard set of prescriptions – a particular kind of behaviour therapy on the one hand; reference to a dictionary of symbolic meanings on the other. For phenomenology, too, there is a continuity between behaviour we call normal and that which we judge abnormal. But it is a continuity born of the fact that we all share the problems of being human, and the therapist succeeds because he or she is more aware of those problems, not because of superior working knowledge of the mechanics of the mind. Success will depend not upon knowledge of specific techniques or of specific and standard symbolic meanings, but on a capacity to return the individual to a condition in which the world as lived is in accord with consciousness of it.

For, as Habermas (1972) and Heaton (1972) have pointed out, disturbed conditions arise when some important part of conscious experience is 'split off' from the normal, direct involvement in the things of the world. Because of this, the person can no longer talk about this experience in a way that combines the rationality of consciousness with the immediacy of lived experience. Imagination and abstraction are no longer united, so that there is no possibility of faith in the potential unity of one's own experience with the nature of the world. The part of experience that is split off has, of course, symbolic significance. All true symbols point in two ways at the same time: they point outwards to transcendent objects and inwards to the subject who constitutes those objects as meaningful. In this sense, they mark the boundary between subjectivitiy and objectivity. Our sanity depends upon our success in establishing the balance between the two, and we should remember as academics that there is a madness of objectivity as well as of subjectivity (Kierkegaard, 1941). The important point here, I think, is that the meaning of symbols is not determined in any straightforward way by either biological or social programming but arises within the whole context of human being as biological-cum-cultural phenomenon.

Vygotsky (1978) has pointed out that beyond a certain stage of development the child recognizes that 'anything can stand for anything else', and this insight needs to be passed on to therapists who believe that the meanings of symbols are absolutely fixed. This has clear implications for therapy. It means that the therapist must discover with the client the meaning of the symbol, the place where the borderline has failed to hold, in such a way as to restore the balance between life and thought. This will not be accomplished through consultation with a theoretical dictionary, it will arise only out of respect for the individual bestowal of meaning and out of concern for its integration within the rational activity of consciousness. Habermas refers to this as a process of enlightenment through self-reflection, and defines this as an 'act through which the subject frees itself from a state in which it had become an object for itself' (1972, p. 247).

There are two major dangers when psychologists discuss therapy and mental illness. One is to romanticize such illness, to see the intensity of experience as an ideal when set against the drab routine of everyday life. The other is to see it simply as aberration, as an extreme departure, and this view tacitly romanticizes everyday life, with its lack of extremes and intense feelings. We avoid both dangers if we state that the significance of mental illness is to show the difficulty of being human, the constant need to balance thought against feeling and inner against outer reality, if faith in one's purpose is to be retained. The therapeutic process reveals not the treatment of pathological conditions or a poetic ideal, but the nature of human existence with its essential, creative tensions – tensions which are lost through both mental illness and conventional everyday life. Because therapy shows us this, it shows the condition to which research must ultimately be referred. This condition can be described only as the context in which research can make sense, since research is formalization which is always partial, for it can never dispense with the human need for faith: it succeeds only in so far as it leaves that untouched.

Phenomenology as applied research

This is why, of course, there is an inevitable tension within applied research – not because of any difficulty in translating the pure into the applied, but because the applied researcher wishes to qualify shared concern by an appeal to 'things as they are'. The method of participant observation, in which the researcher is both at one with the investigated and an observer of them, shows the borderline which is crossed when one passes from 'fellow human being' to researcher. There is a reversal of the natural order of social life, for now he or she participates in order to observe, and seeks to isolate a realm of facts which can function independently of the ontological and existential concerns of both investigated and investigator. But there is no agreement on policy in applied research: the qualitative researcher tries to explore the land from which he or she came; the quantitative researcher does not wish to abandon the marvellous gadgetry of objective investigation.

MacMurray (1961) has shown the necessary relation between these two forms of knowledge, which he calls personal and impersonal. He concludes that personal knowledge is shared concern and requires no external justification, but that impersonal knowledge, which seeks to establish the facts and has to keep its distance from ordinary human involvement, always requires justification through reference to shared concern. One might say: the advances in understanding that come about through the application of operational techniques must always relate to human concerns for the value of life, which themselves transcend all such techniques. And is this not a formula for the continuation of applied research in its present form, for we can be as impersonal as we wish as long as there is some reference, at the end of the day, to the higher ideals? I think not. We will not justify a science of human beings if our programme presupposes an opposition between the activity of being a scientist and that of a human being. Kelly (1955) saw this, but erred in believing the answer lay in human beings being treated as scientists, for there is far more to human being than being a scientist. Human science must be founded upon human being. It must take as its focus that which is central to human being, and in doing this it will be an applied science, for that which is central to human being develops human being.

To say that what characterizes human being is shared concern has several implications for an applied phenomenology. Sharing signifies that we define together what is true and of value. Just as the survival of the species involved the sharing of food and defence (Leakey, 1981), so survival as truthful and moral beings depends upon individuals sharing with one another and thus constituting what they hold to be the truths and principles transcendent to them. These truths are not a matter of indifference to us, but the means by which we define our hold on reality; they have existential and ontological status because they are expressions of the way we live in the world. There is no separation of intellect and emotions in these truths. We are, after Freud, familiar with the idea that the various expressions of a personality are part of a coherent structure (even with its conflicts), so that there are correspondences between emotional and intellectual life. Phenomenological truths are of this order except that they have reference not to an 'inner man' but to human beings in their philosophical dimension of 'being-in-the-world'. Finally, there is no validation of shared concern other than shared concern; there can be no reference to independent criteria or to methodological sophistication as the ultimate court of appeal for the worth of an investigation. There is no alternative to reflection.

What matters, then, in applied research is not a particular set of practices on the part of the investigator or a particular set of conditions of the investigated that must be put right, but the furtherance of the activity of self-reflection, in which participants question and then define the truths and values which they take as their reference points. All fact-gathering is subsidiary to this philosophical purpose, and all methodologies fail unless they culminate in the kind of thought which kindles the imagination and restores faith. We are familiar with Hume's dictum that works which contain no quantitative analysis or causal reasoning should be cast upon the fire, but equally we are all too familiar with that kind of research which contains nothing else. Let us then counter Hume with a challenge to the drabness of mechanical research: if we take in our hand any research report, let us ask: 'Does it contain any metaphor or idea which reveals a reality deeper than the conventional one? No. Does it excite you to a moral involvement in the affairs with which it deals? No. Commit it then to the flames, for it is nothing but information that will soon be superseded by more information!'

We can say that applied human science is necessarily a moral science because it permits us to develop ourselves as human beings. Now, many applied scientists who do not subscribe to the views outlined above would concur with this view. But they would see the enlargement of the moral realm made possible by the accumulation of evidence through the application of appropriate methodology by impartial researchers (see, for example, Broadbent, 1961). They see no need for the therapeutic statement in which truth is not a matter of intellect alone but of the whole person seeking a course to steer by. Indeed, the very prejudices of these scientists – their subjectivism, intellectualism and faith in technology – lead them to judge therapeutic statements as outside the boundary of science, belonging perhaps to literature. And of course, so they are, if human science is defined by these prejudices. It is important to note at this point the interdependence of statements of proper methodology and statements of the true content of a discipline. At any stage in the development of a science, the two go hand in hand. The way in which psychology has defined perception or learning or thinking is related to assumptions about the proper way to study such phenomena – as interior cognitive mechanisms. Therefore, if phenomenological psychology is going to offer an alternative programme of investigation, it will be based upon quite different notions of the nature of psychological phenomena.

Phenomenology as critical science

In fact, the major phenomenological concepts themselves present a coherent challenge to psychological concepts. Merleau-Ponty's (1962) understanding of perception, Heidegger's (1971) view of language, the idea of play for Gadamer (1975), Marcel's (1950) 'intersubjectivity', reject totally the psychologism and intellectualism of the equivalent concepts in cognitive psychology. The most serious error that psychologists make about phenomenology is to see it as an illumination of the conventional psychological concepts through introspection, as though there were certain minor faults only with these concepts, and nothing amiss with their essential nature. However, the illumination phenomenology offers does not leave these concepts intact. Phenomenology is a rethinking of psychological concepts, a disturbance of all that we have unfortunately inherited from both Cartesianism and British empiricism. When Merleau-Ponty defines perception as the background to our acts of interpretation, or Heidegger speaks of language as the revelation of being, what is rejected is the dualism of subject and object, or rather the way of formulating this which the two philosophical movements have in common. For the phenomenologist no priority can be accorded to the Cartesian 'I' or the brute reality of empiricism; self and world are jointly articulated. What a dry statement that appears to be! But it formulates the condition of revelation of being through language and perception.

Consider, as a particular example, the concept of play. This has been defined in psychology in various ways – as the means by which inner conflicts are expressed, as fantasy, as a means of adaptation. No one of these definitions captures the whole of play, because play can be all of these and no doubt more. Gadamer finds the essence of play to be the 'to-and-fro', the experience of movement, as when we talk of the play of light, a play on words, and so forth. I have argued elsewhere that the movement of play that is significant from the point of view of the development of the individual is that which occurs around the boundary-line between self and world, that play helps to maintain this line, and that transitional objects and the symbolic function arise out of this activity of boundary maintenance (Bolton, 1982b). The phenomenological notion of play refers, then, not to a psychological mechanism but to the way in which the person exists in the world. And all phenomenological concepts have this feature: they refer to the original experience in which self and world are constituted and from which the polarities of abstract thought themselves emerge. There is no psychologism in these concepts, no intellectualism either, because there is no false separation of thought from feeling, and there is no mechanism, no operational specification, for them, for they establish the possibility of there being a world within which we can operate.

For the cognitive psychologists this last assertion amounts to an admission of failure; if phenomenology is not reducible to or isomorphic with a set of mechanical operations, they will conclude either that it should be excluded from serious consideration or that it need not be considered because it does not really exist. I think that phenomenologists need not be as brusque as this in dismissing empirical methodology, which, after all, can bring to clarity significant phenomena. However, they must be as robust in rejecting the idea that methodological sophistication provides the means of judging the significance (or existence) of phenomena. But this returns us to our original question: Can there be an empirical study of persons based upon a true understanding of the phenomenon of being human? My own answer to this question is to say that there can be no other true psychology than a phenomenologically guided psychology. However, I hold that phenomenology guides, not by providing a methodology for collecting data, but through developing a form of reflection by which the conceptual and existential significance of these data can be realized.

Empirical psychology sees itself as a natural science and it has become, in a variety of ways, the study of the mind's contingency, abstraction showing how the mind can be construed as subordinate to this or that class of events. There is no doubt that human beings are constrained by any number of such events, which can be traced ultimately to biological or social structures, and that useful information can be gathered. For the phenomenologist, on the other hand, abstraction is only one form of thought, and it is preceded by imagination with its metaphors and transcended by concepts which place us as being-in-the-world. If empirical psychology is the study of the mind's contingency, phenomenology is the study of its freedom, phenomenological reflection showing how abstraction articulates with the 'plunging forward' of the metaphorical imagination and discovers its only possible repose within concepts which return thought to life. Recall what Merleau-Ponty (1962) says of the relationship between the mind's contingencies and its necessary freedom:

> Human existence will force us to revise our usual notion of necessity and contingency, because it is the transformation of contingency into necessity by the act of carrying forward. All that we are, we are on the basis of a *de facto* situation which we appropriate to ourselves and which we ceaselessly transform by a sort of escape which is never an unconditioned freedom. (pp. 170–1).

The idea that guides contemporary cognitive psychology, the mind as an intelligent machine, is, of course, a metaphor, on the basis of which the researcher builds his or her abstractions. Necessarily, phenomenology denies the ultimate validity of this metaphor because, as we have seen, abstraction itself requires to be placed within the broader context supplied by other forms of thought. But we know that a metaphor is not invalidated because it is partial or even because people do not have an explicit recognition of it as a metaphor; the cognitive psychologist is akin to the lover who believes his lady to be 'like a rose' – that she is, implicitly, *not* a rose is just what is valued. Thus, the mistake the cognitive psychologist is likely to fall into is not that of acting on the basis of a metaphor but of theorizing his or her metaphor away – by making the rose an abstraction, as it were. In this way the vision of cognitive psychology is perversely narrow, phenomena being defined and investigated only to the extent that they are abstractions. The difference or contrast, so essential to the life of the metaphor, is lost.

To conclude: phenomenological inquiry is not a technique aimed at particular aspects of experience, at individuals, or even the life-world; it is the discipline concerned with the necessary structure that our thinking about experience must take if it is to make conceptual and existential sense. The exercise of phenomenological thinking should guide an empirical psychology by reshaping psychological theory in the only radical way that such theory can be reshaped – by showing how its limits coincide with the task of developing human sensitivity and concern.

References

Ashworth, P.D. (1981), 'Equivocal alliances of phenomenological psychologists', *Journal of Phenomenological Psychology*, **12**, 1–13.
Boden, M.A. (1977), *Artificial Intelligence and Natural Man*, Brighton: Harvester.
Bolton, N. (1972), *The Psychology of Thinking*, London: Methuen.
Bolton, N. (1977), *Concept Formation*, Oxford: Pergamon Press.
Bolton, N. (1978a), 'The phenomenology of thinking', in A. Burton and J. Radford (eds), *Thinking in Perspective*, London: Methuen.
Bolton, N. (1978b), 'Piaget and pre-reflective experience', in B. Curtis and W. Mays (eds), *Phenomenology and Education*, London: Methuen.
Bolton, N. (1979), 'Being objective about the mind', in N. Bolton (ed.), *Philosophical Problems in Psychology*, London: Methuen.
Bolton, N. (1982a), 'The lived world: Imagination and the development of experience', *Journal of Phenomenological Psychology*, **13**, 1–18.
Bolton, N. (1982b), 'Forms of thought', in G. Underwood (ed.), *Aspects of Consciousness*, vol. 3, London: Academic Press.
Bolton, N. (forthcoming), *Forms of Thought: A study in phenomenology and education*.
Broadbent, D.E. (1961), *Behaviour*, London: Methuen.
Gadamer, H.H. (1975), *Truth and Method*, London: Sheen & Ward.
Giorgi, A. (1970), *Psychology as a Human Science: A phenomenologically-based approach*, New York: Harper & Row.
Habermas, J. (1972), *Knowledge and Human Interests*, London: Heinemann.
Heaton, J.M. (1972), 'Symposium on saying and showing in Heidegger and Wittgenstein', *Journal of the British Society for Phenomenology*, **3**, 42–5.

Cognitivism 121

Heidegger, M. (1971), *Poetry, Language, Thought*, New York: Harper & Row.
Hetherington, J. (1983), 'Sacred cows and white elephants', *Bulletin of the British Psychological Society*, **36**, 273–80.
Husserl, E. (1948), *Experience and Judgement*, London: Routledge & Kegan Paul.
Husserl, E. (1965), 'Philosophy as rigorous science', in *Phenomenology and the Crisis of Philosophy*, New York: Harper.
Husserl, E. (1977), *Phenomenological Psychology*, The Hague: M. Nijhoff.
Kelly, G.A. (1955), *The Psychology of Personal Constructs*, New York: Norton.
Kierkegaard, S. (1941), *Concluding Unscientific Postscript*, Princeton, NJ: Princeton University Press.
Köhler, W. (1940), *Dynamics in Psychology*, New York: Liveright.
Leakey, R.E. (1981), *The Making of Mankind*, London: Michael Joseph.
MacKay, D.M. (1951), 'Mindlike behaviour in artefacts', *British Journal of Philosophical Science*, **2**, 105–21.
MacMurray, J. (1961), *Persons in Relation*, London: Faber & Faber.
Marcel, G. (1980), *The Mystery of Being*, London: Harvill Press.
Merleau-Ponty, M. (1962), *The Phenomenology of Perception*, London: Routledge & Kegan Paul.
Piaget, J. (1950), *The Psychology of Intelligence*, London: Routledge & Kegan Paul.
Polanyi, M. (1967), *The Tacit Dimension*, London: Routledge & Kegan Paul.
Tillich, P. (1957), *Dynamics of Faith*, London: Allen & Unwin.
Vygotsky, L. (1978), *Mind in Society: The development of the higher psychological processes*, Cambridge, MA: Harvard University Press.

8
The contextualism that is behaviour analysis: An alternative to cognitive psychology

Edward K. Morris

Editors' introduction

The following chapter by Edward Morris is concerned with the general tradition of behaviour analysis. His chapter has two main aims: to counter the prevalent view of behaviourism presented by cognitive psychologists (as well as some of their critics — see also Morris, 1989); and to explain that behaviour analysis is itself an important focus of contextualist theory.

Behaviourism, usually with B.F. Skinner as representative villain, figures in most accounts of the *point* of the cognitive revolution. Behaviourism is rejected as S–R psychology, and cognitive psychology is then presented as the alternative — an account of what mediates *between the stimulus and response*, or input and output. Although, in his more popular writings, Skinner did sometimes talk as though the environment functioned as an efficient cause, his basic theory, like Gibson's, rejected the S–R formula. The logic of his fundamental concept, the operant, is 'dialectical'. Not only are the operant and its 'controlling variables' mutually defining, but operant behaviour is treated not as an elicited 'response' but as purposive and intentional activity 'shaped' and constrained by its situation. It was with some justice, therefore, that Skinner complained that it was not behaviourists but cognitive psychologists, with their 'computer-model of the mind, who represent people as machines' (Skinner, 1974, p. 110).

Apart from his role in cognitivist melodrama, Skinner is relevant to the theme of this book in a more positive way. He insisted upon the distinction between contingency-shaped and rule-governed activity, and denied that rules were sufficient or even necessary in the explanation of conduct. Rule-governed activity, he argued, presupposes successful practice, and the existence of a 'verbal community' within which rules are derived and sustained (Skinner, 1957). Operant researchers have recently explored the special, regulatory role of language in human action, and have proposed the concept of rule-governed behaviour as an alternative basis for a psychology of human cognition (see Zettel, 1990). Yet it is a related proposal of Skinner's that places his behaviourism among the most radical alternatives to cognitivism – social constructivism. Skinner's term 'verbal behaviour' is more inclusive than speech and writing, and refers to any activity that is dependent for its effects upon the intervention of others (see Tikhomirov, 1959). He argued that it was only through the mediation of a 'verbal community' that many of the individual skills and abilities presupposed by cognitive psychologists – indeed, consciousness itself – come into being (Skinner, 1957, 1977; see Bloor, 1983, ch. 4).

References

Bloor, D. (1983), *Wittgenstein: A social theory of knowledge*, London: Macmillan.
Morris, E.K. (1989), 'Questioning psychology's mechanism: A review of Costall and Still's "Cognitive psychology in question"', *The Behavior Analyst*, **12**, 59–67.
Skinner, B.F. (1974), *About Behaviorism*, New York: Knopf.
Skinner, B.F. (1957), *Verbal Behavior*, New York: Appleton-Century-Croft.
Skinner, B.F. (1977), 'Why I am not a cognitive psychologist', *Behaviorism*, **5**, 1–10.
Tikhomirov, O.K. (1959), Review of B.F. Skinner, 'Verbal Behavior', *Word*, **15**, 362–7.
Zettel, R.D. (1990), '"Rule-governed behavior": A radical behavioral answer to the cognitive challenge', *Psychological Record*, **40**, 41–50.

* * *

Behaviourism is neither dead nor dying, nor has it succumbed to cognitive psychology. Nor have any successful cognitive–behavioural compromises been reached, for such eclecticism is inherently confusing. It is confusing because contemporary behaviourism and cognitive psychology are incommensurable in their world-views – the former is contextualistic, the latter mechanistic. Worse still for psychology, mechanism is the wrong world-view for its subject matter, and always was, even when behaviourism was mechanistic. The behaviourism that was mechanistic, though, is *not* contemporary behaviourism. Contemporary behaviourism is contextualistic in world-view – a better world-view for the subject matter.

These are strong assertions, for they seemingly turn the history of psychology and the place of contemporary behaviourism in psychology on their heads, but in fact they do not. They turn only the received view of behaviourism on its head. In what follows, I describe contemporary behaviourism as a contextualistic alternative to the mechanism inherent in cognitive psychology. Contemporary behaviourism also offers a basis for critiquing cognitive psychology and for analyzing what it is we call 'cognitive'. That, though, would constitute a treatment different from the one I offer here. Still, some preliminary comments in that regard seem in order.

Contextualism and the content of cognitive conduct

Contextualism dictates no new special means for analyzing cognition. Rather, it offers new perspectives that raise new questions, put aside old questions, and provide new answers. At a philosophical level, contextualism treats cognition and the language of cognition in ways similar to those to be found in contemporary analytic philosophy (see Malcolm, 1977; Ryle, 1949; Wittgenstein, 1953, 1958; cf. Day, 1969a, 1980; Deitz and Arrington, 1984).

At a conceptual level, cognition comprises relationships and activity – not a reified thing (Lee, 1988; Skinner, 1977); cognition is action-in-context – not a mechanistic process that resides in a separate realm (Blank, 1986; Palmer, 1991); perception, cognition and memory are 'direct' – neither mediate (Watkins, 1990) nor stored (Jenkins, 1974; Marr, 1983; Morris, 1989; Skinner, 1977). For a representative behaviour-analytic interpretation of memory and the rememberer, see Palmer (1991); for an analogous interpretation of insight and awareness, see Epstein (1984) and also Morris, Higgins and Bickel (1982). For more explicitly contextualistic and ecological (though behaviourally unsympathetic) treatments, see Hoffman and Nead (1983) and Wilcox and Katz (1981).

Finally, at an empirical level, exactly what a contextualist cognitive research programme might entail cannot at this time be said, but 'theory'-building would probably be simpler and more cumulative; increased attention would be given to contingencies and context, and the activity of the person 'cognizing' (e.g. remembering, problem-solving) would become more explicit (see Watkins, 1990).

What the present chapter offers is an alternative to the contemporary cognitive model of the mind – a model based on the computational information-processing of a machine (see Haugeland, 1981). I develop this thesis first by reviewing the historical record. Second, I examine the implications of mechanism and contextualism for three general meta-theoretical issues. Third, I describe the categorical role of context in contemporary behaviourism. And fourth, I discuss the implications of contextualism for cognition as a process, as opposed to psychological content. I conclude with some observations about the revolution of psychology in the context of the extant world-views. Before beginning, though, I offer two possibly clarifying comments.

The behaviour analysis that is contextualism

First, my thesis that contemporary behaviourism is contextualistic may strike some readers as curious, but contextualism is found in, is supported by, and supports what today is called 'behaviour analysis' (see Hayes, 1988; Hayes and Brownstein, 1986; Hayes, Hayes and Reese, 1988; Morris, 1982, 1988a; H. Reese 1982). Thus, to the extent that behaviour analysis is the one true behaviourism (Day, 1980), contemporary behaviourism is contextualistic in world-view. To be more specific about how the discipline is organized – behaviour analysis is composed of basic, applied, and conceptual programmes of research, which are technically and respectively: the experimental analysis of behaviour (Skinner, 1966; see Catania, 1984), applied behaviour analysis (Baer, Wolf and Risley, 1987; see Cooper, Heron and Heward, 1987) and the conceptual analysis of behaviour (e.g. radical behaviourism – Skinner, 1974; see Lee, 1988; for overviews, see Michael, 1985; E.P. Reese, 1986).

Second, mechanism and contextualism are different things to different people, and thus subject to differing interpretations (Morris, 1988b; Rosnow and Georgoudi, 1986a). For present purposes, my distinctions are drawn from Pepper's (1942/1967) book *World Hypotheses*. Pepper's work is the basis for the major critiques of behaviour analysis as mechanistic (e.g. Overton and Reese, 1973; Reese and Overton, 1970), for counter-critiques that behaviour analysis is contextualistic (e.g. Hayes, Hayes and Reese, 1988; Morris, 1988a) and for the current call to contextualism in psychology more generally (e.g. Rosnow and Georgoudi, 1986b). Enough assertions. Let me begin describing the contextualism in behaviour analysis by examining its history.

A brief history of behaviour analysis

The received view

In the standard account of the history of psychology, behaviourism and mechanism are conjoined through the legacy of Democritus's atomism, the material and reflex side of Cartesian dualism, and Locke's espousal of an epistemological *tabula rasa* – on down through the empiricist and associationist movements in philosophy, from Hume and Berkeley, through to the Mills. With the founding of the first systems of psychology, the thesis of Wundt's and Titchener's structuralism met its antithesis in James's and Angell's functionalism, from which Watson's classical behaviourism emerged, in part, as synthesis. This synthesis, accompanied by its philosophical legacies of reductionism, elementarism and associationism, sought scientific credibility first through an admixture of Comte's positivism and Loeb's operationism, and later through logical positivism.

This rendering of the history of psychology is largely the received and 'presentist' view, both with respect to 'behavioristics' (e.g. Boring, 1950) and contemporary behaviourism (e.g. Mahoney, 1989; *contra* Morris, 1990a). Current historiography, however, questions the narrowness and accuracy of this view (see Morris, Todd, Midgley, Schneider and Johnson, 1990), from which are emerging revised accounts of the history of behaviour analysis (see, e.g. Todd and Morris, 1990).

A revised account

Naturalism and materialism

Behaviour analysis is more accurately traced back to the naturalism of Hellenic Greek philosophy, particularly to Aristotle. Following the Dark Ages, the rekindling of naturalism was influenced – and unfortunately distorted – by various theological interpretations (Kantor, 1963). From this, certain views emerged during the Renaissance and the Scientific Revolution – perhaps most notably Cartesian dualism – that established the paths for the psychology that followed: one path concerned with the immaterial soul-cum-mind, the other with the material body. Neither path, though, characterizes behaviour analysis, for it is neither mentalistic nor materially reductionistic (Ringen, 1976). Indeed, behaviour analysis is focally concerned with the field of purpose and intention (Day, 1976a) – also a major concern of contextualism. Intentionality is a quality of biology and behaviour in context; it is not a quality of inert material (e.g. computer chips), no matter how complexly organized. A cognitive psychology based on a computational metaphor involving inert material cannot thereby explain a biological or behavioural system. It is no more than an 'improved' mechanistic S–R psychology (see Lee, 1988).

Empiricism
The role of British empiricism and associationism in the history of behaviour analysis also requires revision. With respect to empiricism, John Locke's epistemological *tabula rasa* never negated organismic structure and function as sources of individual differences within or across people, nor did it negate the private or inaccessible aspects of what we speak of as feeling, thinking or consciousness. Likewise, neither does behaviour analysis. Biology is taken to participate in all psychological activity: it serves as an ever-evolving context that is necessary, though not sufficient, for behaviour (see Kantor, 1947). Behaviour analysis also acknowledges psychological activity within the skin (Moore, 1980; Schnaitter, 1978), accepting it as a proper, albeit difficult, subject matter (Moore, 1984a; Skinner, 1945, 1974). Moreover, biological and behavioural activity (both public and private) comprise the historical context for subsequent behaviour, which brings a sense of ever-evolving rationalism to the behaviour-analytic account in what is otherwise seen as a strictly empiricist endeavour.

Associationism
Behaviour analysis is also not associationistic (Branch, 1977). Associationism represents a reductionistic and, in one sense, molecular view in which fundamental, universal atomic elements of the mind, computer, or behaviour are taken to exist as *a priori* units of analysis. Multiplied out through contiguity in time and succession, these elements are said to produce and explain complex behaviour, but with complex behaviour still ultimately reducible to them. In contrast, behaviour analysis adheres to a molar perspective in which there are no *a priori*, elementary stimulus and response units (Skinner, 1935). Rather, behaviour is characterized in terms of evolving, co-defining stimulus and response classes (or functions) – their interrelationships being the 'structure' of behaviour (see Bernstein, 1982; Thompson and Zeiler, 1986). Construed thus, these structures are not restricted to any formally defined fundamental units – behaviour ranges from salivation to grand instauration. Only at the molar level does behaviour have psychological meaning (see Day, 1980; Verplanck, 1954).

Structuralism and functionalism
With respect to the first schools and systems of psychology, behaviour

analysis is properly aligned with functionalism (cf. Dewey, 1896; James, 1890; Mead, 1934), especially in its emphasis on the utility and adaptiveness of mind and consciousness – now behaviour. This does not mean that behaviour analysis views structural concerns with antipathy, for at issue is not the correctness of structural versus functional analyses, but rather the nature of the questions asked and the use to which the answers are put. That structural analysis generally lies within the purview of cognitive psychology (e.g. information structures) and functional analysis within the purview of behavioural psychology has unfortunately resulted in the correlation of structural and functional concerns with the disputatious dualism of cognition and behaviour. However, structural and functional concerns do not stand in opposition or conflict; they represent a dichotomy that is orthogonal to the cognitive–behavioural dichotomy (Catania, 1973, 1978), itself a false dichotomy within contextualism.

Positivism and operationism
Under the influence of the Vienna Circle (Carnap, 1935) positivism and operationism became an institutional characteristic of psychology during the 1930s (see, e.g., Stevens, 1939). Psychology was suffering physics envy. The message seemed to be clear at the time: if psychology were to be a real science, it would have to develop objective definitions for its subjective terms, and exclude that which was not empirical or logically definable from its subject matter.

The 'black box' psychology that grew out of these views, though, had several deleterious effects (see Moore, 1980, 1981, 1985). First, although ostensibly objective, the movement did not resolve the mind–body problem. The mind was still taken to exist, but outside the realm of 'objectivist' psychology. This overly restricted the domain of the subject matter to be explained (Moore, 1981; Skinner, 1974). Second, operational definitions and positivistic philosophy became so narrow that ordinary-language terms (e.g. memory) became technical terms, and lost the richness of their shared, everyday meaning. This overly restricted the behaviour that could be understood to an arid truth-by-agreement (e.g. the mechanist's correspondence theory of truth; see Deitz and Arrington, 1984; Skinner, 1945). And third, the movement ignored the role of the scientist in science, thereby failing to account for science as the behaviour of scientists and the products thereof (Creel, 1987; Schnaitter, 1980; Skinner, 1956, 1957, pp. 418–31; Smith, 1986). These are matters of epistemology that cannot be glossed over with the veneer of objectivism (Day, 1983).

Much of psychology has continued in the mould of this operationism and positivism, especially cognitive psychology, but not without protest from Gestalt psychologists, psychoanalysts, phenomenologists, humanists and hermeneuticists. Behaviour analysis also objects to such scientism, and has taken a different path. It adheres to a psychological, not a logical, epistemology, with a line of descent from the inductive positivism of Bacon (1621/1889) and Mach (1883/1960; see Day, 1980; Marr, 1985; Skinner, 1945; Smith, 1986, pp. 259–97) and from an analytic philosophy reflected in the later Wittgenstein (Wittgenstein, 1953, 1958; see Day, 1969a; Deitz and Arrington, 1984; Morris, 1985).

In these views, the problem is not how to make subjective terms objective via logical definitions and operational conventions – or by mechanizing them into rules governing behaviour. Rather, the problem is how to discover and describe the historical and current context in which ordinary-language terms are spoken, because context is what gives those terms their meaning (see Day, 1976b; Malcolm, 1977; Skinner, 1945, 1957). Behaviour analysis does not rule out the subjective or the private as a character of its subject matter; it accepts such qualities as part of behaviour in context. Its epistemology, then, has a phenomenological, even hermeneutical, quality to it that belies the mechanistic distinction between the knower and the known (Day, 1969a, 1977, 1988; see Giorgi, 1975; Kvale and Grenness, 1967).

Pragmatism
What this analysis begs, of course, is a truth criterion. That, though, is found in pragmatism. Not only did James help to establish functional psychology but, with Peirce, he was also central in developing pragmatism as a philosophy and as a method for defining truth and value (James, 1907; Peirce, 1878/1923, 1940). In their hands, as well as those of Dewey (1896) and Mead (1934), pragmatism takes knowledge to be relative, with absolute truth a categorical impossibility. Simply put, 'knowing' refers to behavioural relations, and behavioural relations are a function of their historical and current context. As with any knowing, 'knowing the truth' can never step outside itself (i.e. out of the behavioural stream) for some absolute evaluation because that evaluation, too, is a behavioural relation in context. Under this pragmatic philosophy, the criterion for knowledge and truth is a form of 'successful working', which again reflects a psychological, not a logical, epistemology. Within behaviour analysis, this criterion has become 'effective action' in the description, prediction and control of behaviour (see Day, 1980, 1983; Hayes and Brownstein, 1986; Skinner, 1974; Zuriff, 1985).

The preceding comment warrants clarification, for the place of 'control' in behaviour analysis is commonly misunderstood. For Watson, the goals of behaviourism were the prediction and control of behaviour – control literally for the purposes of social engineering. With control so construed (and 'successful working' so crude), no wonder behaviourism was frightening, and frighteningly narrow, but matters are now different. In behaviour analysis, control is as much an epistemological matter as a practical one – if the two can be separated. It serves knowledge and understanding first, and then, perhaps later, application (see Day, 1969b; Hayes and Brownstein, 1986). This epistemological sense of control is evident in answers to such questions as: What are the conditions under which we say we 'understand' something (e.g. about physics, biology, or behaviour)? The answer: often when we can predict it, but better when we can demonstrate the experimental control of it through the factors of which it is a function. That is, we understand behaviour to the extent that we know how it works – knowledge gained through its analysis, a refined sense of 'successful working'.

Conclusion

Although this account of the history of behaviour analysis is insufficiently developed, the lines of descent show a decided contextual lineage, much different from the mechanistic heritage commonly presumed of it. This account though, offers only hints and suggestions, not direct arguments that behaviour analysis is contextualistic. For this, let me compare and contrast mechanism and contextualism, and discuss their implications for several meta-theoretical issues.

Mechanism and contextualism

According to mechanism, behaviour and environment are reduced, respectively, to stimuli and responses (or input and output), existing as discrete, *a priori* elements out of which the whole of behaviour (or cognition), in all its complexities and qualities, is built. As for causation, the elements are said to act on one another as do mechanical forces, the results of which are chain-like connections between, or sequences of, stimuli and responses (or information being processed). Causation flows from stimulus to response (or from switch to switch) in a manner that is immediate and contiguous. As for truth, its criterion is correspondence: given that knowledge in mechanism is knowledge about the nature of a realist ontology, the truth of that knowledge is found largely in the correspondence between what is hypothesized about the machine (e.g. theories about its structure and processing) and about the machine's operating characteristics (e.g. theory confirmation). Finally, according to the mechanistic view, behaviour is characterized as passive and inherently at rest or inert; it is 'being', not 'becoming'.

As for contextualism, I introduce it more fully in the material to follow, but for the moment offer a brief introduction. In contextualism, behaviour is an act-in-context and must be studied as such, for context gives behaviour its meaning (i.e. its functions). The whole is primary; the elements are derived. The meaning of behaviour emerges from the ever-evolving historic context, as present becomes past for more present – hence the root metaphor of contextualism as the 'historic event'. In the historic event, change is categorical, thereby making the ontology of the psychological present both active and evolving, and obliging epistemology to be relative. Because knowledge about the world is never final but always evolving, the truth criterion is the philosophical 'successful working'. Finally, behaviour is never 'being', but always 'becoming'.

With mechanism and contextualism outlined, I turn to their implications for three meta-theoretical issues – elementarism versus holism, response-based or structural change, and the passive versus active organism – and touch on two others.

Elementarism versus holism

Mechanism adheres to elementarism, representing behaviour and the environment as but collections of materially fundamental, atomic response and stimulus elements (or switches). Complex action is then but an associative compounding of the basic elements and their interrelations, in which identical response elements and identical stimulus elements are taken, respectively, to have identical meanings or functions – such is the character of a machine. In both cases, the whole can always be reconstituted in terms of its parts because the parts are immutable.

Behaviour versus responses
Behaviour analysis is different for at least two reasons. First, behaviour, or the act-in-context, is the unit of analysis, not the spatiotemporally defined response or muscle twitch (or switch) (Skinner, 1935; see Lee, 1988; Midgley and Morris, 1988; Thompson and Zeiler, 1986). A response *per se* is a physiological and anatomical entity, such that the analysis of behaviour in those terms alone would be elementaristic and possibly reductionistic, but superficial in either case.

In contrast, behaviour is a dynamic, active interrelation, in which a response is but one component. The unit of analysis also includes response functions, stimuli, and stimulus functions, all in their current and historical context. The behaviour-analytic view, then, is holistic in that neither responses nor stimuli have meaning, function or significance unto themselves, only in their interdependent relationships with one another and their context. Behaviour analysis knows no stimulus or response elements definable out of context.

Functions versus forms
A second way in which behaviour analysis differs from mechanism pertains to the form–function distinction. Given that responses and stimuli have no inherent function or meaning, then physically identical responses and stimuli need not have the same function or meaning – across or within individuals (Baer, 1982). Indeed, they never can, for every person's history, and hence their present 'psychological' circumstances, are unique and ever-changing. In turn, physically dissimilar responses can have similar functions or meanings, just as physically dissimilar stimuli can (see McKearney, 1977, on equifinality). Individual differences in these form–function relationships are ubiquitous, and the process–achievement, means–end relation between them is forever a dynamic one (see Kantor, 1933).

Response-based or structural change

From a mechanistic perspective, behaviour change involves change in responses over time – a continuous, linear succession of cause and effect, wherein changes in responding are reducible to, and predictable from, their prior forms. In contrast, behaviour analysis focuses on behaviour change as the evolution of interrelationships among stimulus and response functions in context – the interactions being mutual and reciprocal, and constitutive of behaviour's structure. In this sense, behaviour change is broad, generalized change in the organization or structure of behavioural relations, not in mere responses alone (see Lee, 1987).

This 'mutualism' among the relations within the behavioural structure means that behaviour change refers not only to changes in response functions, but also to changes in stimulus functions. The 'psychological fallacy' is to conceive of the environment as something to which people must somehow accommodate their responses. The behavioural (psychological) environment develops in mutual, reciprocal interaction with the behavioural (psychological) organism – there is no parsing of behaviour into person and environment as separable causes, or into the mental and the environmental. Not only does behaviour analysis go beyond dualistic accounts of behaviour, wherein the environment is 'represented' and stored in cognition, it also goes beyond physicalistic accounts in which a realist ontoloty is external to behaviour (see also Gibson, 1979). Instead, the stimulus function of the environment is part of, or internal to, the unit of behaviour.

The passive versus active organism

Within the mechanistic account, causation is characterized in terms of the effects of efficient independent causes on dependent material – material that is otherwise at rest. Stimuli and responses are taken to be linearly sequenced causes and effects. In behaviour analysis, however, the unit of behaviour is characterized as the interrelations among stimulus and response functions in context. These interrelations stand in a strong reciprocal interaction or, better – in Dewey and Bentley's (1949, p. 108) terminology – in a 'transactional' relation with one another; they are mutually implicative (see Keehn, 1980; Krapfl, 1977; Pronko and Herman, 1982). In that both stimulus and response functions continuously contribute to and evolve in behaviour, behaviour is active. Let us look at the implications of this for two related problems: (a) the inadequacy of agent–action locutions and (b) the trait–situationism debate.

The locutional problem

In an organism-based locution, people (or cognition) are the agents that give meaning to their responses and environments. In an environment-based locution, the environment is the agent that gives meaning to stimuli and responses. The first locution, though, makes the environment passive, which it is not, while the second locution makes behaviour passive, which it is not. Neither locution captures the essence of contextualism. They align too closely with the organismic and mechanistic world-views, respectively.

To compound this problem further, the grammatical structure endemic to ordinary English (or 'Standard Average European': Whorf, 1940/1956) generally supports these locutions and their respective world-views. That is, our grammatical structure is disposed to agent–action syntax, to agent nouns (e.g. organisms, representations, structures, memory – and the environment) reified from verbs, adverbs and adjectives (actions and their qualities) and to the priority of things and agents over action and change. Our language simply offers few fluid or unawkward grammatical structures for speaking contextualistically, which makes such talk difficult for speakers and writers, and for listeners and readers. English grammar and syntax are simply mismatched with the subject matter of psychology (Hackenberg, 1988; Hineline, 1980; Lee, 1988), whereas the grammar of Eastern cultures is less so (see Williams, 1986).

The trait–situationism problem

Although behaviour is active, the behaviour-analytic position is not that people are self-actional, autonomous agents. Likewise, though, neither should the environment be seen as an autonomous cause, except perhaps pragmatically (see Hayes and Brownstein, 1986). The tension between these views of causality is at the heart of the trait–situationism debate (and many other false dichotomies, such as nature and nurture; see Oyama, 1985).

In behaviour analysis, stimulus functions and response functions develop historically and exist simultaneously with respect to one another (i.e. they are defined in terms of each other in context). As such, stimulus functions have no more 'control' over behaviour than do response functions – the two are interdependently and mutually defining. A situation does not compel a response to occur except through a person's historically derived response functions for that situation. But neither does a person compel responding, except through the situation's historically derived stimulus functions for the response. Thus, situations do not possess independent or inherent power to control behaviour any more than people possess independent or inherent power for such control. Both are products of ever-changing interactional histories, a point about behaviour analysis commonly misunderstood (e.g. Bowers, 1973).

Interactions may display qualities attributable to personal or situational control, depending on how they are viewed or investigated, but those attributions are shorthand conventions derived from an overemphasis on organismic and mechanistic thinking, as opposed to a contextual world-view. What is even more objectionable is the reification and causal status given to the person as an autonomous, active agent, as per organicism, or to the situation as an autonomous physical form, as per mechanism. Behaviour, of course, can be predicted on the basis of information about people *or* situations (or both, as in an interactional approach), but the ability to do so does not thereby bestow causal power on either (see Keehn, 1980). Such attributions have more to do with the behaviour of scientists than with their subject matter.

Conclusion

These three meta-theoretical issues – elementarism versus holism, response-based versus structural change, and the passive versus active organism – are not the only ones pertinent in psychology today (see Morris, 1988a). For instance, mechanism views behaviour change as a process of continuous, quantitative change. In contextualism, however, change occurs in relation to an ever-evolving historical context, and is thus discontinuous in the sense that the behavioural structure is continuously undergoing qualitative reorganization. That is, when a system of functional stimulus–response interrelations changes, the behavioural structure changes as a whole, hence giving grounds again for denying the pernicious aspects of philosophical empiricism.

Also, in mechanism, the scientific task is to account for behaviour in terms of antecedent–consequent, if–then relations – that is, in terms of independent and dependent variables. Viewed contextualistically, however, behaviour is a systematic interrelation of stimulus and response functions in context, where causal accounts of dependent and independent variables give way to accounts of integrated fields of functional interdependencies. 'Cause' loses its essential meaning when causation becomes the entire field of currently interdependent factors necessary for understanding behaviour (cf. Einstein and Infeld, 1961).

With these meta-theoretical implications now described, I turn to some theoretical and empirical issues. First, having asserted that context is categorical in contextualism, I describe how behaviour analysis takes context into account. After that, I discuss the implications of the contextualist approach of behaviour analysis for cognition as process or content.

Context in behaviour analysis

Psychology has shown, of late, an increased (or renewed) interest in 'context'. This is evinced not only in the discipline as a whole, where much of the focus has had an ecological orientation (Gibbs, 1979; Wicker, 1983), but also in its various sub-disciplines – for instance, in perception, development, social psychology, personality, memory and language (e.g. Gibson, 1979; Jenkins, 1974; see Rosnow and Georgoudi, 1986b).

Within these domains, context usually refers to multiple physical and social determinants of behaviour – that is, to broad, complex and numerous antecedent causes, and to their interplay at various levels of interaction (e.g. personal, social and cultural; see Bronfenbrenner, 1977). To give such conditions their due, however, is not necessarily to embrace contextualism as a world-view (cf. Valsiner and Benigni, 1986). These determinants can be, and often are, handled mechanistically. In contrast, within contextualism, and hence within behaviour analysis, context is categorical. Context imbues behaviour with meaning; the meaning of behaviour emerges from its context. More specifically, stimulus and response functions emerge from their context and from nowhere else, where context is organized into its historical and current sources.

The historical context

The historical context yields a continuously evolving 'present' (see Oyama, 1985). It is what establishes which stimulus and response structures and functions *may* occur in behaviour, and changes in them. Although the historical context is actually irreducible, for expositional purposes I parse it into phylogenic and ontogenic history (see Skinner, 1969). Phylogenic history is the source of species-typic boundaries and preparedness in biological and behavioural structure and function. With respect to behaviour, more specifically, phylogenic history imparts the basic behavioural processes (e.g. operant processes), the initial relationships among some stimulus and response functions (e.g. unconditioned respondents) and variability in both.

Given a phylogenic history, ontogenic history then begets the subsequent individual-typic boundaries and preparedness in biological and behavioural form and function, and variability in both. With respect to behaviour, the ontogenic history is fundamental to the behaviour analysis of such topics as adult–child social interactions (e.g. Redd, Morris and Martin, 1975), reinforcement schedule performance (e.g. Weiner, 1983) and the integration of independently acquired response repertoires (Epstein, Kirschnit, Lanza and Rubin, 1985; Epstein, Lanza and Skinner, 1981; see Wanchisen, 1990). The historical context thereby elucidates some sources of intra- and interindividual differences typically attributed to cognition when stimuli and responses alone provide a seemingly insufficient analysis, and surely they do (see Morris, 1990b). The historical context accounts for much of these inter- and intraindividual differences – differences otherwise attributed to cognition (e.g. cognitive styles and schemata). The latter are effects, not causes.

The current context

Given that the historical context establishes what behaviour *may* occur, the behaviour that *will* occur and *can* occur depend, respectively, on the 'actualizing' and 'enabling' functions of the current context. What will occur (or be actualized) depends on the function of the current context; what can occur (or be enabled) depends on its form or structure. As for the latter, the form or structure of the current context comprises the biological organism (i.e. its anatomy and physiology) and the physical environment (i.e. its ecology), thereby enabling what behaviour can (or cannot) occur. In turn, the function of the current context actualizes stimuli and responses with their previously established functions (i.e. their meaning; e.g. their reinforcing and discriminative stimulus functions).

Whether construed as Skinner's (1931) 'third variables', Kantor's (1946) 'setting factors', or 'setting events' (e.g. Bijou and Baer, 1978), context is of concern to both basic and applied research programmes in behaviour analysis. 'Establishing operations' (Michael, 1982), for instance, actualize the function of certain consequences as reinforcers – for example, water on a hot day, a pencil for a grocery list, or an answer to a question (see Morse and Kelleher, 1977). Establishing operations are essentially the field of motivation and emotion. Likewise, the discriminative function of stimuli is also not inherent in any event; that function is actualized through such factors as 'conditional stimulus control', as in stimulus equivalence (see Sidman, 1986a, b). Stimulus control is essentially the field of cognition.

In clinical research, the leading edge of applied behaviour analysis is 'ecobehavioural analysis', which embraces holism, equifinality and functional analysis – and explicitly focuses on context as an important factor (see Morris and Midgley, 1990). Research on 'setting events', for example, shows that isolated welfare mothers' negative encounters with social agencies at one time of day (a setting event) will actualize some of their children's behaviour later in the day with an aversive function, and induce abuse. Without that setting event, the same child behaviour does not function in this way (see Wahler and Dumas, 1989; Wahler and Fox, 1981, 1982). Changes in the mothers' perception, expectations and feelings of self-efficacy are the consequences of the earlier encounters; they are not mediating causes of the later aversive function or the child abuse. That function is actualized directly.

In either case, the reinforcing or discriminative function of a stimulus is not something cognitively perceived and represented, and then acted upon, but something actualized. Just as Gibson's (1979) theory of perception is a theory of 'direct perception', so too Skinner's theory of behaviour is a theory of 'direct behaviour' – where, in both cases, 'direct' is contrasted with 'mediated'. For Gibson and Skinner, the meaning or functions of stimuli are perceived directly (see Costall, 1984; Morris, 1989).

Summary

In considering context as it does, behaviour analysis clarifies many misunderstandings from outside the field (cf. Bijou, 1979; Todd and Morris, 1983) and provides an account from within of phenomena seemingly dismissed or overlooked: for instance, phenomena such as individual differences that have heretofore been the province of cognitive psychology and personality (see Baron and Perone, 1982; Harzem, 1984). Contextualism offers a fresh new perspective on these issues. It also has an interesting implication for whether cognition is a basic psychological process or a substantive content domain of behaviour.

Cognition as process or content

Behavioural processes, like processes in the other natural sciences, do not refer to any particular kind of activity, but to behaviour-*qua*-behaviour – that is, to content-free behavioural transactions described in abstract terms, as abstract relationships. They refer to classes, properties and relations that transcend the particulars of any specific content.

In behaviour analysis, these processes are the basic principles of behaviour (e.g. reinforcement, punishment and stimulus control; see Catania, 1984, pp. 1–219). These principles are fundamental to all behavioural content, just as the principles of physics, chemistry and biology are fundamental to other everyday, content-specific aspects of our world (e.g. falling leaves, stormy weather and mountain greenery). Behavioural processes are described in technical, extraordinary terms because our knowledge about them is largely 'extraordinary' – that is, beyond ordinary observation, analysis and synthesis (Lee, 1988).

In contrast, behavioural content refers to the particular types or kinds of activities we engage in, described in our everyday natural language (see Deitz and Arrington, 1984, on Wittgenstein's 'language games'). It refers to the content-specific aspects of everyday behaviour-in-context, with respect both to the world in which we live and to our behaving with respect to that world – for instance, private events (e.g. having a toothache, covert problem-solving), daily activities (e.g. posting a letter), personal characteristics (e.g. learned helplessness, self-efficacy), social interactions (e.g. aggressive, altruistic), and emotional and motivational structures (e.g. anxious, manic-depressive, internally versus externally motivated). Behavioural content does not emerge from behavioural processes; it is the product of those processes in social context. It is what we describe in the vernacular, in our everyday ordinary language, because our everyday knowledge of behaviour is largely 'ordinary' (Lee, 1988).

Cognition as content

An ordinary-language account of cognition shows that it, too, falls within the domain of the content of conduct – for example, as thinking and remembering (Deitz and Arrington, 1984; Morris, 1985; Skinner, 1945). These activities are common enough amongst us for a socially shared and conventional language for describing them to develop. In other words – and to use the vulgar behaviourese of an environment-based locution – to say the word 'cognition' is to emit a verbal operant under the discriminative control of the occurrence of certain behavioural relations in context. These relations, in turn, often come under finer control so as to be spoken of as sub-classes of cognition – for instance, as perceiving and categorizing (see Catania, 1984, pp. 252–347).

When we speak of behavioural content, we are speaking of the characteristics and qualities of the world around and within us, and of how we and others behave with respect to that world. Therefore, speaking of behavioural content should be restricted to the characteristics and qualities of behaviour, and hence to adjectives – 'cognitive'; adverbs – 'cognitively'; and verbs – 'cognizing'. We should not be speaking in terms of nouns that purportedly identify some underlying process (e.g. a computational process). The content of conduct is not a 'thing', a cognition or perception; nor are there any content-related processes that are not otherwise behavioural processes. Cognition, then, is what needs explaining; it is not a mechanism that does the explaining (see Ryle, 1949; Schnaitter, 1985).

This view is neither new to behaviour analysis (see Skinner, 1945; cf. Morris, 1988a) nor unique to its philosophy (see Day, 1969a, 1980). Nor is it unique in psychology, where similar positions are taken in other contextualistically grounded perspectives (see, e.g. Costall and Still, 1987; Rosnow and Georgoudi, 1986b). Blank (1986) provides a good illustration:

> Cognizing does not begin and end in one's head or at one's skin; it is not superordinate to our relationships, for our thoughts are our relationships. Attributions, motivation, perception, and personality – what it is to be a person – are *relationships*, not things going on in any one locus, whether that be a stable 'package' of scheme or biological processes or a subjective phenomenological reality. (pp. 121–2)

Process and content conflated

Psychology generally makes two fundamental errors in parsing process and content. First, in the course of making the content of conduct its subject matter (e.g. personality or cognition), psychology operationally narrows and superficially restricts its content domains by inappropriately making technical terms out of ordinary language terms. Second, in seeking explanatory processes for activity in these domains, psychology errs in making them content-specific, such that each domain has its own supposed set of processes – processes largely unrelated to those supposedly being elucidated in the other domains. For example, perception is explained in terms of perceptual processes (e.g. representation), sociality in terms of social processes (e.g. bonding), emotion in terms of emotional processes (e.g. transference) and cognition in terms of cognitive processes (e.g. representation, memory, information-processing). The search for these explanatory processes is considered basic research in mainstream psychology; in behaviour analysis, research concerns behavioural content. In psychology, these processes are explanations; in behaviour analysis, they are content to be explained (Morris, Higgins and Bickel, 1982).

That psychology is divided into these content areas is readily apparent in the organization of its introductory textbooks and its required curricula for undergraduate majors and doctoral candidates, and in the titles of its journals. Psychology, then, is largely a science of mini-sciences, an unreflective pluralism (see Staats, 1981). It has few principles basic to behaviour-*qua*-behaviour – that is, basic to behaviour irrespective of content domain. This is not to say that psychology is devoid of basic principles, but that where they do exist they are usually restricted to specific content areas when they are actually more generic. Nor is this to say that every behavioural process applies equally well to every content domain. Stimulus equivalence (see Sidman, 1986a, b), for instance, may play a greater role in some areas than others (e.g. verbal behaviour; see Hayes, 1987). But these principles are still principles of behaviour, not principles of behavioural content.

This is not an argument against a psychology whose subject matter is the content of conduct. J.R. Kantor's (1924, 1926) interbehavioural psychology, for example, is in large part such a psychology. In contrast, behaviour analysis is mostly a psychology of basic behavioural processes. An appreciation of these differences and a melding of the two might bring better order and cohesion to a psychology whose processes and content domains are often conflated (Moore, 1984b; Morris, 1982, 1984).

Conclusion

The implications and import of behaviour analysis as a contextualistic alternative to cognitive science extend in more directions than one chapter can contend with, but let me close with some observations about – and an extension of – Pepper's (1942) general analysis. Pepper presented four world-views – formism, organicism, mechanism and contextualism – as each relatively adequate and autonomous. Viewed historically, though, they may actually represent different stages in the evolution of science towards an increasingly successful working with its material. I elaborate briefly.

The natural sciences are concerned with the world in which we live, and although these sciences vary in domain (e.g. biology or psychology), in their within-domain content (e.g. social or cognitive psychology) and their research methods (e.g. correlational versus experimental) they are agreed in seeking an account of the behaviour of nature – the behaviour, for instance, of heat, genes and organisms. They may also differ with respect to the progress they have made along the three stages of scientific evolution (see Dewey and Bentley, 1949; Einstein and Infeld, 1938/1961; Kantor, 1946). In the first stage, the substance-property or self-actional stage, events are taken to act under their own power – under their own self-contained, of-their-own-substance, vitalistic power. This is a characterization of the organismic world-view. In the second stage, the mechanical stage, events are described as controlled by physical forces acting on immutable objects. This is the mechanistic world-view. In the third stage, the field-theoretic or transactional stage, the notion of immutable objects is replaced with descriptions of events functioning in dynamic fields. This is largely the contextualistic world-view.

In physics and biology, our understanding of heat and genes has progressed through the three stages. In the substance-property stage, heat was taken to be a caloric substance and genes were accorded inherent, vitalistic power to produce specific phenotypic outcomes. In the mechanical stage, heat was described in terms of the physical energy produced by the causal interaction of immutable particles – the cause–effect physics of classical mechanics. Likewise, in the mechanistic construal of development, genetic outcomes were accounted for in terms of the independent, multiple causation by many different factors. In the integrated-field stage, heat is described in terms of thermodynamics, wherein mass and energy are equatable and thermal activity emerges from specific configurations of the thermodynamic field. Quantum mechanics and relativity theory also illustrate this stage (see Einstein and Infeld, 1938/1961). Similarly in biology: interactions among the biochemical factors (genes included) are described directly as they operate at various levels of structure and function. The developmental-systems perspective illustrates this stage of scientific development (see Oyama, 1985).

As for psychology, the substance-property stage gave us the soul and the mind, and now some thinly veiled cognitive surrogates. The mechanistic stage described physical, casual relationships between environmental stimulation and bodily reflexes, or between input and output – that is, it described both S–R psychology and cognitive science. The third, integrated-field stage is contextualism: behaviour is described in terms of functional interrelationships between organisms and objects in interaction within a field of current and historical contexts (see Kantor, 1946). To this point in the history of psychology, organicism and mechanism have largely vied for supremacy as the only world-views. Contextualism, though, is the bold new alternative – an alternative that is continuing to evolve. This is true both within psychology as a whole and within behaviour analysis – just as it should be in the world-view of contextualism. Within behaviour analysis the contextual themes emerging in basic and applied research, and in conceptual analysis, affirm the essential validity of the evolution of those individual branches of the discipline, which in turn strengthen the discipline's overall contextualistic character. This and more make it a viable alternative to mechanism, and hence to cognitive psychology mechanistically construed.

References

Bacon, F. (1889), *Novum Organum*, Oxford: Oxford University Press (original work published 1621).
Baer, D.M. (1982), 'The imposition of structure on behavior and the demolition of behavioral structures', in D. Bernstein (ed.), *Nebraska Symposium on Motivation, 1981*, vol. 29, Lincoln, NB: University of Nebraska Press, pp. 217–54.
Baer, D.M., Wolf, M.M. and Risley, T.R. (1987), 'Some still current dimensions of applied behavior analysis', *Journal of Applied Behavior Analysis*, **20**, 313–27.
Baron, A. and Perone, M. (1982), 'The place of the human subject in the operant laboratory', *The Behavior Analyst*, **5**, 143–58.
Bernstein, D.J. (ed.) (1982), 'Response structure and organization', *Nebraska Symposium on Motivation, 1981*, vol. 29, Lincoln, NB: University of Nebraska Press.
Bijou, S.W. (1979), 'Some clarifications of the meaning of a behavior analysis of child development', *The Psychological Record*, **29**, 3–13.
Bijou, S.W. and Baer, D.M. (1978), *Behavior Analysis of Child Development*, Englewood Cliffs, NJ: Prentice-Hall.
Blank, T.O. (1986), 'Contextual and relational perspectives on adult psychology', in R.L. Rosnow and M. Georgoudi (eds), *Contextualism and Understanding in Behavioral Science: Implications for research and theory*, New York: Praeger, pp. 105–24.
Boring, E.G. (1950), *The History of Experimental Psychology*, Englewood Cliffs, NJ: Prentice-Hall.
Bowers, K.S. (1973), 'Situationism in psychology', *Psychological Review*, **80**, 307–36.
Branch, M.N. (1977), 'On the role of "memory" in the analysis of behavior', *Journal of the Experimental Analysis of Behavior*, **28**, 171–9.
Bronfenbrenner, U. (1977), 'Toward an experimental ecology of human development', *American Psychologist*, **32**, 513–31.
Carnap, R. (1935), *Philosophy and Logical Syntax*, London: Kegan Paul.

Catania, A.C. (1973), 'The psychologies of structure, function, and development', *American Psychologist*, **28**, 434–43.

Catania, A.C. (1978), 'The psychology of learning: Some lessons from the Darwinian revolution', *Annals of the New York Academy of Sciences*, **309**, 18–28.

Catania, A.C. (1984), *Learning*, Englewood Cliffs, NJ: Prentice Hall.

Cooper, J.O., Heron, T.E. and Heward, W.L. (1987), *Applied Behavior Analysis*, Columbus, OH: Merrill.

Costall, A.P. (1984), 'Are theories of perception necessary? A review of Gibson's *The Ecological Approach to Visual Perception*', *Journal of the Experimental Analysis of Behavior*, **41**, 109–15.

Costall, A.P. and Still, A.W. (eds) (1987), *Cognitive Psychology in Question*, New York: St Martin's Press.

Creel, R. (1987), 'Skinner on science', in S. Modgil and C. Modgil (eds), *B.F. Skinner: Consensus and controversy*, New York: Falmer, pp. 103–11.

Day, W.F. (1969a), 'On certain similarities between the *Philosophical Investigations* of Ludwig Wittgenstein and the operationism of B.F. Skinner', *Journal of the Experimental Analysis of Behavior*, **12**, 489–506.

Day, W.F. (1969b), 'Radical behaviorism in reconciliation with phenomenology', *Journal of the Experimental Analysis of Behavior*, **12**, 315–28.

Day, W.F. (1976a), 'Contemporary behaviorism and the concept of intention', in W.J. Arnold (ed.), *Nebraska Symposium on Motivation*, vol. 25, Lincoln, NB: University of Nebraska Press, pp. 65–131.

Day, W.F. (1976b), 'Analyzing verbal behavior under the control of private events', *Behaviorism*, **4**, 195–200.

Day, W.F. (1977), 'On the behavior analysis of self-deception and self-development', in T. Mischel (ed.), *The Self: Psychological and philosophical issues*, Oxford: Blackwell, pp. 224–49.

Day, W.F. (1980), 'The historical antecedents of contemporary behaviorism', in R.W. Rieber and K. Salzinger (eds), *Psychology: Theoretical-historical perspectives*, New York: Academic Press, pp. 203–62.

Day, W.F. (1983), 'On the difference between radical and methodological behaviorism', *Behaviorism*, **11**, 89–102.

Day, W.F. (1988), 'Hermeneutics and behaviorism', *American Psychologist*, **43**, 129.

Deitz, S.M. and Arrington, R.L. (1984), 'Wittgenstein's language games and the call to cognition', *Behaviorism*, **12**, 7–14.

Dewey, J. (1896), 'The reflex arc concept in psychology', *Psychological Review*, **3**, 357–70.

Dewey, J. and Bentley, A.F. (1949), *Knowing and the Known*, Boston, MA: Beacon Press.

Einstein, A. and Infeld, L. (1961), *The Evolution of Physics: The growth of ideas from early concepts to relativity and quanta*, New York: Simon & Schuster (original work published 1938).

Epstein, R. (1984), 'Simulation research in the analysis of behavior', *Behaviorism*, **12**, 41–59.

Epstein, R., Kirschnit, C.E., Lanza, R.P. and Rubin, L.C. (1984), '"Insight" in the pigeon: Antecedents and determinants of an intelligent performance', *Nature*, **308**, 61–2.

Epstein, R., Lanza, R.P. and Skinner, B.F. (1981), '"Self-awareness" in the pigeon', *Science*, **212**, 695–6.

Gibbs, J.C. (1979), 'The meaning of ecologically oriented inquiry in contemporary psychology', *American Psychologist*, **34**, 127–40.
Gibson, J.J. (1979), *The Ecological Approach to Visual Perception*, Boston, MA: Houghton Mifflin.
Giorgi, A. (1975), 'Convergences and divergences between phenomenological psychology and behaviorism: A beginning dialogue', *Behaviorism*, **3**, 200–12.
Hackenberg, T. (1988), 'Operationism, mechanism, and psychological reality: The second-coming of linguistic relativity', *The Psychological Record*, **38**, 187–201.
Harzem, P. (1984), 'The experimental analysis of individual differences and personality', *Journal of the Experimental Analysis of Behavior*, **42**, 385–95.
Haugeland, J. (ed.) (1981), *Mind Design*, Cambridge, MA: MIT.
Hayes, S.C. (1987), 'Upward and downward continuity: It's time to change our strategic assumptions', *Behavior Analysis*, **22**, 3–6.
Hayes, S.C. (1988), 'Contextualism and the next wave of behavioral psychology', *Behavior Analysis*, **23**, 7–22.
Hayes, S.C. and Brownstein, A.J. (1986), 'Mentalism, behavior–behavior relations, and a behavior-analytic view of the purposes of science', *The Behavior Analyst*, **9**, 175–90.
Hayes, S.C., Hayes, L.J. and Reese, H.W. (1988), 'Finding the philosophic core: A review of Stephen C. Pepper's *World Hypotheses*', *Journal of the Experimental Analysis of Behavior*, **50**, 97–111.
Hineline, P.N. (1980), 'The language of behavior analysis: Its community, its function, and its limitations', *Behaviorism*, **8**, 67–86.
Hoffman, R.R. and Nead, J.M. (1983), 'General contextualism, ecological science, and cognitive research', *Journal of Mind and Behavior*, **4**, 507–60.
James, W. (1890), *Principles of Psychology*, New York: Holt.
James, W. (1907), *Pragmatism*, New York: New American Library.
Jenkins, J.J. (1974), 'Remember that old theory of memory? Well, forget it', *American Psychologist*, **29**, 785–95.
Kantor, J.R. (1924), *Principles of Psychology*, vol. 1, Chicago: Principia Press.
Kantor, J.R. (1926), *Principles of Psychology*, vol. 2, Chicago: Principia Press.
Kantor, J.R. (1933), 'In defense of stimulus–response psychology', *Psychological Review*, **40**, 324–36.
Kantor, J.R. (1946), 'The aim and progress of psychology', *American Scientist*, **34**, 251–63.
Kantor, J.R. (1947), *Problems of Physiological Psychology*, Chicago: Principia Press.
Kantor, J.R. (1963), *The Scientific Evolution of Psychology*, vol. 1, Chicago: Principia Press.
Keehn, J.D. (1980), 'Beyond an interactional model of personality: Transactionalism and the theory of reinforcement schedules', *Behaviorism*, **8**, 55–65.
Krapfl, J.E. (1977), 'Dialectics and operant conditioning', in N. Datan and H.W. Reese (eds), *Life-span Developmental Psychology: Dialectical perspectives on experimental research*, Orlando, FL: Academic Press, pp. 295–310.
Kvale, S. and Grenness, C. (1967), 'Skinner and Sartre', *Review of Existential Psychology and Psychiatry*, **7**, 128–49.
Lee, V.L. (1987), 'The structure of conduct', *Behaviorism*, **15**, 141–8.
Lee, V.L. (1988), *Beyond Behaviorism*, Hillsdale, NJ: Erlbaum.
Mach, E. (1960), *The Science of Mechanics* (transl. T.J. McCormack), LaSalle, IL: Open Court (original work published 1883).

McKearney, J.W. (1977), 'Asking questions about behavior', *Perspectives in Biology and Medicine*, **21**, 109–19.
Mahoney, M. (1989), 'Scientific psychology and radical behaviorism: Important distinctions between scientism and objectivism', *American Psychologist*, **44**, 1372–7.
Malcolm, N. (1977), *Memory and Mind*, Ithaca, NY: Cornell University Press.
Marr, M.J. (1983), 'Memory: Models and metaphors', *The Psychological Record*, **33**, 12–19.
Marr, M.J. (1985), ' 'Tis the gift to be simple: A retrospective appreciation of Mach's *The Science of Mechanics*', *Journal of the Experimental Analysis of Behavior*, **41**, 129–38.
Mead, G.H. (1934), *Mind, Self and Society*, Chicago: University of Chicago Press.
Michael, J.L. (1982), 'Distinguishing between discriminative and motivational functions of stimuli', *Journal of the Experimental Analysis of Behavior*, **37**, 149–55.
Michael, J.L. (1985), 'Behavior analysis: A radical perspective', in B. and L. Hammonds (eds), *Psychology and Learning*, Washington DC: American Psychological Association, pp. 99–121.
Midgley, B.D. and Morris, E.K. (1988), 'The integrated field: An alternative to the behavior-analytic conceptualization of behavioral units', *The Psychological Record*, **38**, 483–500.
Moore, J. (1980), 'On behaviorism and private events', *The Psychological Record*, **30**, 439–75.
Moore, J. (1981), 'On mentalism, methodological behaviorism, and radical behaviorism', *Behaviorism*, **9**, 55–77.
Moore, J. (1984a), 'On privacy, causes, and contingencies', *The Behavior Analyst*, **7**, 13–16.
Moore, J. (1984b), 'Conceptual contributions of Kantor's interbehavioural psychology', *The Behavior Analyst*, **7**, 183–7.
Moore, J. (1985), 'Some historical and conceptual relations among logical positivism, operationism, and behaviorism', *The Behavior Analyst*, **8**, 53–63.
Morris, E.K. (1982), 'Some relationships between interbehavioral psychology and radical behaviorism', *Behaviorism*, **10**, 187–216.
Morris, E.K. (1984), 'Interbehavioral psychology and radical behaviorism: Some similarities and differences', *The Behavior Analyst*, **7**, 197–204.
Morris, E.K. (1985), 'Wittgenstein's language games and the call to cognition', *Behaviorism*, **13**, 137–46.
Morris, E.K. (1988a), 'Contextualism: The world view of behavior analysis', *Journal of Experimental Child Psychology*, **46**, 289–323.
Morris, E.K. (1988b), Review of *Contextualism and Understanding in Behavioral Science*, *The Psychological Record*, **38**, 363–7.
Morris, E.K. (1989), 'Questioning psychology's mechanism: A review of Costall and Still's *Cognitive Psychology in Question*', *The Behavior Analyst*, **12**, 59–67.
Morris, E.K. (1990a), 'What Mahoney "knows"', *American Psychologist*, **45**, 1178–9.
Morris, E.K. (1990b), '*The Behavior of Organisms*: A context theory of meaning', in J.T. Todd and E.K. Morris (eds), *Modern Perspectives on Classical and Contemporary Behaviorism*, Westport, CT: Greenwood Press.
Morris, E.K., Higgins, S.T. and Bickel, W.K. (1982), 'Comments on cognitive

science in the experimental analysis of behavior', *The Behavior Analyst*, **5**, 109–25.
Morris, E.K. and Midgley, B.D. (1990), 'Some historical and conceptual foundations of ecobehavioral analysis', in S.R. Schroeder (ed.), *Ecobehavioral Analysis and Developmental Disabilities: The twenty-first century*, New York: Springer Verlag, pp. 1–32.
Morris, E.K., Todd, J.T., Midgley, B.D., Schneider, S.M. and Johnson, L.M. (1990), 'The history of behavior analysis: Some historiography and a bibliography', *The Behavior Analyst*, **13**(2), 131–58.
Morse, W.H. and Kelleher, R.T. (1977), 'Determinants of reinforcement and punishment', in W.K. Honig and J.E.R. Staddon (eds), *Handbook of Operant Behavior*, Englewood Cliffs, NJ: Prentice Hall, pp. 174–200.
Overton, W.F. and Reese, H.W. (1973), 'Models of development: Methodological implications', in J.R. Nesselroade and H.W. Reese (eds), *Life-span Developmental Psychology: Methodological issues*, Orlando, FL: Academic Press, pp. 65–86.
Oyama, S. (1985), *The Ontogeny of Information: Developmental systems and evolution*, New York: Cambridge University Press.
Palmer, D.C. (1991), 'A behavioral interpretation of memory', in P.N. Chase and L.J. Hayes (eds), *Dialogs on Verbal Behavior*, Reno, NV: Context Press, pp. 261–79.
Peirce, C.S. (1923), 'How to make our ideas clear', in C.S. Peirce, *Love, Chance, and Logic: Philosophical essays*, (ed.) M.R. Cohen, New York: Harcourt, Brace (original work published 1878), pp. 32–60.
Peirce, C.S. (1940), *Philosophical Writings of Peirce*, (ed.) J. Buchler, New York: Dover.
Pepper, S.C. (1942), *World Hypotheses: A study in evidence*, Berkeley, CA: University of California Press.
Pronko, N.H. and Herman, D.T. (1982), 'From Dewey's reflex arc concept to transactionism and beyond', *Behaviorism*, **10**, 229–54.
Redd, W.H., Morris, E.K. and Martin, J.A. (1975), 'Effects of positive and negative adult–child interactions on children's social preferences', *Journal of Experimental Child Psychology*, **19**, 153–64.
Reese, E.P. (1986), 'Learning about teaching from teaching about learning: Presenting behavior analysis in an introductory survey course', in W.P. Makosky (ed.), *The Master Lecture Series*, vol. 6, Washington, DC: American Psychological Association, pp. 69–127.
Reese, H.W. (1982), 'Behavior analysis and life-span developmental psychology', *Developmental Review*, **2**, 150–61.
Reese, H.W. and Overton, W.F. (1970), 'Models of development and theories of development', in L.R. Goulet and P.B. Baltes (eds), *Life-span Developmental Psychology: Research and theory*, Orlando, FL: Academic Press, pp. 115–45.
Ringen, J. (1976), 'Explanation, teleology, and operant behaviorism', *Philosophy of Science*, **43**, 223–53.
Rosnow, R.L. and Georgoudi, M. (1986a), 'The spirit of contextualism', in R.L. Rosnow and M. Georgoudi (eds), *Contextualism and Understanding in Behavioral Science*, New York: Praeger, pp. 3–22.
Rosnow, R.L. and Georgoudi, M. (eds) (1986b), *Contextualism and Understanding in Behavioral Science*, New York: Praeger.
Ryle, G. (1949), *The Concept of the Mind*, London: Hutchinson.

Schnaitter, R. (1978), 'Private causes', *Behaviorism*, **6**, 1–12.
Schnaitter, R. (1980), 'Science and verbal behaviour', *Behaviorism*, **8**, 153–60.
Schnaitter, R. (1985), 'The haunted clockwork: Reflections of Gilbert Ryle's *The Concept of Mind*', *Journal of the Experimental Analysis of Behavior*, **43**, 145–53.
Sidman, M. (1986a), 'Functional analysis of emergent verbal classes', in T. Thompson and M.D. Zeiler (eds), *Analysis and Integration of Behavioral Units*, Hillsdale, NJ: Erlbaum, pp. 213–45.
Sidman, M. (1986b), 'The measurement of behavioral development', in N.A. Krasnegor, D.B. Gray and T. Thompson (eds), *Developmental Behavioral Pharmacology*, Hillsdale, NJ: Erlbaum, pp. 43–52.
Skinner, B.F. (1931), 'The concept of the reflex in the description of behavior', *Journal of General Psychology*, **5**, 427–58.
Skinner, B.F. (1935), 'The generic nature of the concepts of stimulus and response', *Journal of General Psychology*, **12**, 40–65.
Skinner, B.F. (1945), 'The operational analysis of psychological terms', *Psychological Review*, **52**, 270–7, 291–4.
Skinner, B.F. (1956), 'A case history of scientific method', *American Psychologist*, **11**, 221–33.
Skinner, B.F. (1957), *Verbal Behavior*, Appleton-Century-Croft.
Skinner, B.F. (1966), 'What is the experimental analysis of behavior?', *Journal of the Experimental Analysis of Behavior*, **9**, 213–18.
Skinner, B.F. (1969), *Contingencies of Reinforcement: A theoretical analysis*, Englewood Cliffs, NJ: Prentice-Hall.
Skinner, B.F. (1974), *About Behaviorism*, New York: Knopf.
Skinner, B.F. (1977), 'Why I am not a cognitive psychologist', *Behaviorism*, **5**, 1–10.
Smith, L.D. (1986), *Behaviorism and Logical Positivism: A reassessment of the alliance*, Stanford, CA: Stanford University Press.
Staats, A.S. (1981), 'Paradigmatic behaviorism, unified theory, unified theory construction methods, and the zeitgeist of separatism', *American Psychologist*, **36**, 239–56.
Stevens, S.S. (1939), 'Psychology and the science of science', *Psychological Bulletin*, **36**, 221–63.
Thompson, T. and Zeiler, M.D. (eds) (1986), *Analysis and Integration and Behavioral Units*, Hillsdale, NJ: Erlbaum.
Todd, J.T. and Morris, E.K. (1983), 'Misconception and miseducation: Presentations of radical behaviorism in psychology textbooks', *The Behavior Analyst*, **6**, 153–60.
Todd, J.T. and Morris, E.K. (eds) (1990), *Modern Perspectives on Classical and Contemporary Behaviorism*, Westport, CT: Greenwood Press.
Valsiner, J. and Benigni, L. (1986), 'Naturalistic research and ecological thinking in the study of child development', *Developmental Review*, **6**, 203–23.
Verplanck, W.S. (1954), 'Burrhus F. Skinner', in W.K. Estes, S. Koch, K. MacCorquodale, P.E. Meehl, C.G. Mueller, W.N. Schoenfeld and W.S. Verplanck (eds), *Modern Learning Theory*, Englewood Cliffs, NJ: Prentice Hall, pp. 267–316.
Wahler, R.G. and Dumas, J.E. (1989), 'Attentional problems in dysfunctional mother–child interactions: An interbehavioral model', *Psychological Bulletin*, **105**, 116–30.

Wahler, R.G. and Fox, J.J. (1981), 'Setting events in applied behavior analysis: Toward a conceptual and methodological expansion', *Journal of Applied Behavior Analysis*, **14**, 327–38.
Wahler, R.G. and Fox, J.J. (1982), 'Response structure and deviant child–parent relationships: Implications for family therapy', in D. Bernstein (ed.), *Nebraska Symposium on Motivation, 1981*, vol. 29, Lincoln, NB: University of Nebraska Press, pp. 1–46.
Wanchisen, B.A. (1990), 'Forgetting the lessons of history', *The Behavior Analyst*, **13**, 31–7.
Watkins, M.J. (1990), 'Mediationism and the obfuscation of memory', *American Psychologist*, **45**, 328–35.
Weiner, H. (1983), 'Some thoughts on discrepant human–animal performances under schedules of reinforcement', *The Psychological Record*, **33**, 521–23.
Whorf, B.L. (1956), *Language, Thought, and Reality*, Cambridge, MA: MIT (original work published 1940).
Wicker, A.W. (1983), *An Introduction to Ecological Psychology*, New York: Cambridge University Press.
Wilcox, S. and Katz, S. (1981), 'The ecological approach to development: An alternative to cognitivism', *Journal of Experimental Child Psychology*, **32**, 247–63.
Williams, J.L. (1986), 'The behavioral and the mystical: Reflection on behaviorism and Eastern thought', *The Behavior Analyst*, **9**, 167–73.
Wittgenstein, L. (1953), *Philosophical Investigations* (transl. G.E.M. Anscombe), New York: Macmillan.
Wittgenstein, L. (1958), *The Blue and Brown Books*, New York: Harper & Row.
Zuriff, G.E. (1985), *Behaviorism: A conceptual reconstruction*, New York: Columbia University Press.

9
'Graceful degradation': Cognitivism and the metaphors of the computer
Alan Costall

Editors' introduction

Cognitive Psychology in Question (Costall and Still, 1987) largely identified modern cognitivism with the representationalist theory of mind: 'the assumption that, for scientific purposes, human cognitive activity must be described in terms of symbols, schemas, images, ideas, and other forms of mental representation' (Gardner, 1987, p. 39). Representationalism has a long history, but has taken on a modern guise through its linkage with computer technology. While we were preparing our earlier book there were important developments in computer science which, many reviewers insisted, undermined the point of much of our criticism. Cognitive psychology, they claimed, was once more on the move, and abandoning its earlier commitment to representationalism, at least of the kind based on propositional structures. The new research on 'parallel distributed processing' based on artificial networks of simplified neural connections seemed to be moving cognitive psychology away from symbol-based theories, and indeed embracing the radical insights of the 'opposition':

> Paradoxically, the parallelists are using the mechanisms most clearly associated with the Establishment view – powerful electronic computers – in order to put forth a view of perception closer to that embraced by Gibson. . . . [S]everal features of the new approach – its fidelity to the mechanics of the brain, its spurning of complex, symbol manipulation or intricate decision procedures about what step to carry out next, its importation of vast amounts of real world knowledge, and its suggestions about how Gestalt phenomena might emerge from the competition and cooperation of various neural networks – have a Gibsonian ring to them. . . . (Gardner, 1987, p. 321)

Representationalism in psychology appears as an alternative to mechanistic psychology when, in fact, it is a highly elaborate *supplementation* of the traditional stimulus–response formula. The following chapter examines the status of PDP as an alternative to this scheme.

References

Costall, A.P. and Still, A.W. (eds), (1987), *Cognitive Psychology in Question*, Hemel Hempstead: Harvester Wheatsheaf.
Gardner, H. (1987), *The Mind's New Science: A history of the cognitive revolution* (paperback edn), New York: Basic Books.

* * *

Cognitive psychology presents itself as a protest movement against American neo-behaviourism – indeed, a 'revolution' (see Coleman, 1988) leading not only to a new emphasis upon the concepts of structure and organization in psychological explanation, but also to a concern with the problems of the 'higher mental functions'. Yet there are also significant continuities between the new cognitive psychology and the behaviourism it was supposed to have replaced. For example, both share the same conception of their ultimate data ('observable behaviour') and also the same general notion of theoretical explanation in terms of processes intervening between 'input' (stimulus) and 'output' (response). Perhaps, then, there was more than just a nice joke in Miller, Galanter and Pribram's claim that they were 'subjective behaviorists'.[1] In fact, even in the attempt to distance themselves from neo-behaviourism cognitive psychologists were able to draw upon the existing intellectual resources not only of related disciplines, such as anthropology and linguistics, but also of psychology itself (e.g. the work of Bartlett, Tolman, the Gestaltists, and Piaget).[2]

In view of the obvious continuities with the past of psychology, the idea of a cognitive *revolution* is perhaps far-fetched. Nevertheless, cognitivism represents an unprecedented unity of purpose within academic psychology. In part, of course, this has involved the concentration of research upon the study of 'cognition' (although, curiously, the study of thinking remains a poorly developed field). The unity is more apparent, however, at the level of theory: the extensive investigation of the 'computer metaphor'. Indeed, Boyd, in an account of the uses of metaphor in science, identified cognitivism as a particularly striking example:

> [A] concern with exploring analogies, or similarities, between men and computational devices *has been the most important single factor influencing*

postbehaviorist cognitive psychology. Even among cognitive psychologists who despair of actual machine simulation of human cognition, computer metaphors have an indispensable role in the formulation and articulation of theoretical positions. These metaphors have provided much of the basic theoretical vocabulary of contemporary psychology. . . . [They] are theory-constitutive: psychologists do not, generally speaking, now know how to offer literal paraphrases which express the same theoretical claims. . . . [Their] cognitive content cannot be made explicit. (Boyd, 1979, pp. 360–1; emphasis added)

Some might see a nice irony in the fact that cognitivism – so intent upon rendering the tacit explicit – has rested so heavily on metaphors. Boyd himself confidently anticipated that research would eventually determine 'in exactly what respects human beings are like computers' (*ibid.*, p. 362). Yet computer metaphors continue to proliferate, and it must be their proliferation, rather than their clarification, that primarily sustains psychologists in their belief in an intimate theoretical relation between psychology and computer science. This relation has now come to seem so essential that both are primarily regarded as aspects of a single discipline, *cognitive science* (Hunt, 1989a).

The 'computer metaphor'

'Information-processing'

Neisser, in his influential text *Cognitive Psychology* (Neisser, 1967), drew a comparison between the problem of determining the stages and styles of information-processing occurring within a complex system, such as a computer, and those supposedly occurring within a human being. Programs, he argued, have much in common with theories of cognition, since both 'are descriptions of the vicissitudes of input information' (Neisser, 1967, p. 8). Interestingly, however, Neisser rejected the attempts by Newell, Shaw and Simon (1958) to go further than this, and attempt to simulate intelligence on a computer. We should, he insisted, stay with the program analogy very much at the level of *metaphor*:

> It is true that a number of researchers, not content with noting that computer programs are *like* cognitive theories, have tried to write programs which *are* cognitive theories. . . . In a sense, the rest of this book can be construed as an extensive argument against models of this kind, and also against other simplistic theories of the cognitive processes (Neisser, 1967, p. 9)

The development of the information-processing approach within psychology depended as much on the analogy with cybernetic and communication systems as with computers (e.g. Broadbent, 1958; see Vroon, 1987). Although these models made appeal to representationalist concepts such as information, the primary concern was to establish the case for a more abstract, 'structural' level of explanation within psychology – a concern largely shared with developments in neo-behaviourism itself (e.g. Deutsch, 1953). Indeed, Neisser made reference not only to computer science but also to biochemistry and economics as examples of disciplines concerned with relational structures themselves rather than their 'incarnation':

> The same point can be illustrated with quite a different analogy, that between psychology and economics. The economist wishes to understand, say, the flow of capital. The object of his study must have some tangible representation, in the form of checks, gold, paper money, and so on, but these objects are not what he really cares about. The physical properties of money, its location in banks, its movement in armored cars, are of little interest to him. . . . Psychology, like economics, is a science concerned with the interdependence among certain events rather than with their physical nature. (Neisser, 1967, pp. 6–7)

Rules and representations

What has most clearly distinguished modern cognitive theories from the neo-behaviourist accounts of mediational processes is their appeal to representational accounts expressed in terms of *propositions* (Newell, Shaw and Simon, 1958). Now representation and rule-following do indeed pose real and important problems to be addressed by any psychology, but trouble begins as soon as these practices are internalized and privatized in psychological theory so that they *seem* to explain everything else – and there has been a rather long history of that kind of thing. As Fodor has noted, in so far as the computer metaphor entails the representationalist theory of mind, 'the computer metaphor predates the computer by about three hundred years' (Fodor, 1981, p. 140). The representationalist scheme did not depend upon computers for its creation, but computers have played a crucial role in its revival and elaboration.

At the very least, computers have seemed to provide a 'license to talk' in non-physicalist terms (Miller, 1986, p. 205). After all, if computer programmers (i.e. *real* scientists) refer to rules and representations, why should not psychologists? Indeed, the early pioneers of computer science not only *talked as if* the computer were intelligent, but even *designed* the machines partly on the basis of rather informal analogies with psychology (Norman, 1986, p. 534). One might say that the computer scientists were employing a *psychological* metaphor – except, of course, that the terms in which we talk and think about both minds and machines had already become thoroughly intertwined well before the advent of the computer. Psychologists, however, in their references to the *computer* metaphor, readily suppose that the properties they attribute to the computer reside in the machine itself.

To be specific, it seems never to have occurred to many psychologists to question whether *computers* actually follow rules and interpret representations. They have supposed that the computer can, at the very least, serve as an 'existence proof' for the feasibility of representationalist theory.[3] *All* that is at stake, they insist, is the literal or metaphorical status of the rules and representations *in the human case*. Pylyshyn, for example, has been resolutely literal-minded (if not flat-footed) on this issue:

> [For] me the notion of computation . . . is not a metaphor but part of a literal description of cognitive activity. This is not to say that there are not also metaphorical uses of computer concepts. But it seems to me that *computation, and all that it entails regarding rule-governed transformations on intentionally interpreted symbolic expressions, applies just as literally to mental activity as it does to the activity of digital computers*. Such a term is in no sense a literal description of the operation of electronic computers that has been metaphorically transported to the primary subject of mind. (Pylyshyn, 1979, p. 435; emphasis added)

Yet if, as Pylyshyn (1989) has more recently insisted, 'cognition is literally a species of computing' (p. 52), such an analogy can justify *representationalism* only if the computer itself *literally* performs rule-governed transformations on intentionally symbolic expressions (i.e. representations) *interpreted by the computer itself*. Now, the remarkable profusion and diversity of cognitive theories – formulated in terms of schemata, prototypes, scripts or production rules – conveys the misleading impression that this fundamental question must at some stage have been resolved.

In fact, Dennett is one of the few people even to have addressed this problem. He proposed that any system of representation could be broken down into smaller and smaller sub-components to the point where these become so trivial that they can be handled by 'stupid homunculi'. In this way, he argued, '[one] *discharges* fancy homunculi from one's scheme by organizing armies of idiots to do the work' (Dennett, 1981, p. 124). In effect, Dennett tried to explain the problem *away*. But, far from eliminating the problem of intentionality and intelligence, he simply relocated it through his appeal to an analysis – and hence an *analyst* – breaking down the original complex task into its appropriate, minute, 'mindless' components (see Shotter, this volume, Chapter 5; Palmer, 1987).

There is, of course, an obvious similarity between Dennett's proposal and Turing's attempt to formalize and automate thought (see Dennett, 1978, p. 123). Yet it seems unlikely that Turing would have agreed with Dennett (and indeed most psychologists) in supposing that such artificial simulations could count as 'functioning examples of representations that can be said in the requisite sense *to understand themselves*' (Dennett, 1981, p. 123; emphasis added). Turing had been very directly involved in the extreme decomposition of highly complex tasks as a director of code-breaking operations during the Second World War. The majority of the naval staff who assisted in this highly secret work simply did not know – and were not supposed to know – what they were really doing. Indeed, according to his biographer, Turing was 'fascinated' by the fact that they 'could be taking part in something clever, in a quite mindless way' (Hodges, 1985, p. 211).

Turing himself was well aware that the representational status of the computer is *derivative*. The symbols within the machine are not representations *for the computer* but *for the users*. This insight, far from being an incidental observation on Turing's part, was of central importance in his new approach to programming and the design of the early ACE computer:

> In the ACE, one might regard pulses as representing numbers, or as representing instructions. But it was really in the mind of the beholder. . . . One could 'pretend that the instruction was really a number', because the machine itself knew nothing about either. Accordingly, [Turing] was free in his mind to think about mixing data and instructions, about operating on instructions, about tables of instructions being inserted by other instructions of 'higher authority' . . . (Hodges, 1985, p. 327)

In his more recent writings, Dennett has kept rather quiet about his stupid homunculi, and acknowledges the derivative status of the representations in the computer (Dennett, 1989). Representation is a *problem*, not a *solution* – and the problem does not ultimately concern how one representation may be translated into another, but *how representation is possible at all* (see Bickhard and Richie, 1983; Shanon, 1988). If computers appear to constitute 'living' proof that meaning can exist *within* a self-enclosed realm of representations devoid of *any* interpreter, it is because we forget *ourselves* – the people *outside* the machine who invest the symbols with our meanings.

Unconscious inference and assumptions

Representationalism, in itself, is just one aspect of modern cognitivism. An important, related assumption is that both representations and the processes that operate upon them are, for the most part, *unconscious*. Indeed, it is perhaps this schema of 'unconscious processing' that most effectively characterizes modern representationalist theory (see Khilström 1987; Meyering, 1989; Reed, 1989). And, once again, computers have played their part:

> The notion put forward by Helmholtz that perception essentially involves 'unconscious inference' from sensory clues was almost totally resisted for nearly a century; but it has recently emerged in the dramatic and testable form of computer programs for 'scene analysis' of pictures and 'robot vision' . . . (Gregory, 1975, p. 616)

The early 'scene analysis' programs seemed to provide compelling evidence for the role of unconscious inferences at many different levels: the isolation of edges, the identification of individual junctions, the overall reconciliation of the interpretations given to the various junctions, and so on. Furthermore, the fact that these programs capitalized on particular constraints holding in the task environment also seemed to substantiate the traditional notion of 'perceptual assumptions'.[4] Perhaps most persuasive, however, was the complexity of processing that seemed to be required by the simplest of tasks. The possibility that this complexity might reflect an inelegant programming solution or even the intrinsic unsuitability of programs for representing certain theoretical insights has seldom been entertained (cf. Runeson, 1977).

Programming languages may well provide a promising new medium in which to formulate psychological theories (see Fodor, 1968, p. 146); they may even prove critical in capturing certain essential insights – as calculus, for example, proved so important in the development of the science of mechanics. Yet the fact that a system can be modelled by means of a program does not imply that the system is itself running a program, any more than the modelling of planetary motion in terms of calculus entails that the planets themselves are busily solving differential equations in order to stay on course.

The new dualism of software and hardware

According to Johnson-Laird, the computer metaphor is to be regarded as 'a new *reaction* to dualism' in which the 'brain and mind are *bound together* as computer and program' (Johnson Laird, 1988, p. 23, emphasis added; see also Hodges, 1985, p. 291). Yet the curious implication of this 'bond' is that it permits us to treat the software of the mind as *separable* from the hardware of the body, and hence to regard psychology as an entirely autonomous science. Indeed, to treat the mind as an abstract set of instructions that controls the body is simply to reformulate the traditional dualism of mind and body. As James Russell has argued:

[The] analogy between the program and the mind does not stand up to even the most cursory examination because accepting it means accepting a model of the mind as an instruction-giving entity *distinct from any realisation* (*not just from a particular one*) and as influencing the brain, if not through the pineal gland, then through the interface between the brain or 'brain-code' and some kind of mental compiler. It is partly to avoid this kind of embarrassment that proponents of [the computation theory of mind] maintain a degree of ambivalence in their overall aims: an ambivalence between modelling the 'mind' and modelling the brain. (Russell, 1984, pp. 94–5; emphasis added)

None the less, the extensive theoretical work on universal Turing machines and the ideal of a general-purpose computer does create the reassuring impression that the software analogy must have a serious rationale. There is, however, another side to the software analogy – the *hardware* analogy – and this aspect of the comparison between computers and people has been curiously neglected. Yet how could anyone seriously have supposed that the human *body*, with its specific skills and limitations, could be likened to a general-purpose machine whose functioning is *solely* constrained by instructions?

Was Turing serious? His presentation of the 'imitation game' as a test of computer intelligence begins with what seems to be an irrelevant digression: a guessing game, via a computer terminal, where an 'examiner' tries to determine whether a hidden person at another terminal is a man or a woman (Turing, 1950). In fact, as Hodges has explained:

The whole point of this [initial] game was that a successful imitation of a woman's responses by a man would *not* prove anything. Gender depended on facts which were *not* reducible to sequences of symbols. In contrast, [Turing] wished to argue that such an imitation principle did apply to 'thinking' or 'intelligence'. If a computer, on the basis of its written replies to questions, could not be distinguished from a human respondent, then 'fair play' would oblige one to say that it must be 'thinking'. (Hodges, 1985, p. 415)

Yet the imitation game simply begs the basic question of whether intelligence can be reduced to a matter of the sequencing of symbols (see Shanon, 1989, p. 252). Have we been trying to read too much into the Turing test? Was it, after all, just a misleading – perhaps mischievous – thought experiment, relying for its provocative effect upon the unusual limitations placed upon the observer?[5] Hodges has suggested that the imitation game should be understood in relation to Turing's view that the ACE computer was '*imitating* arithmetic, in the sense that an input representing "67 + 45" could be made to guarantee an output representing "112"' (Hodges, 1985, p. 327). Yet there are two ways we could take this proposal. The first is that Turing did not mean us to take him too seriously – that the game is a test of nothing more than the *mere* imitation of intelligence. The second is that we should take Turing and his game *very* seriously as a severe case of methodological behaviourism – the denial of any fundamental distinction between the appearance and reality of intelligence. This would seem to be the implication of Turing's claim that the question of whether machines actually think is ultimately 'too meaningless to deserve discussion' (Turing, 1950, p. 444).

What is certainly true is that Turing's favoured examples of intelligent activity (most notably chess) – as well as his own work in deciphering codes – concerned highly formalized symbolic systems where the 'presence' of the body is indeed minimized. *In relation to such cases*, the Turing test might well seem 'fair play'. It is wise, therefore, to remind ourselves of the wide territory now dominated by the new cognitivism:

[The whole of psychology] . . . has been redefined as the study of cognition. Friendship has become social cognition, affect is seen as a form of problem-solving, new-born perception is subsumed under a set of transforming rules, and psychoanalysis is reread as a variant of information processing. Cognition, the feeble infant of the late Fifties and early Sixties, has become an apparently insatiable giant. (Kessen, 1981, p. 168)

Alongside this remarkable expansion, the metaphor of the computer has itself amounted to a grandiose conceit: the idea that human psychology, in its entirety, can be reduced to the manipulation of symbols. But it would now appear that this scheme is faced with a fundamental challenge, not from its periphery but from its very centre.

Computers v. cognitivism?

If cognitive psychologists have not actually claimed the credit for inventing the computer, the prestige of the new technology has, nevertheless, lent a special credibility to their theoretical position. A recent development in computer science – *parallel distributed processing*, or *PDP* – now threatens the long-standing alliance between computers and cognitive psychology. Greeno (1987, p. 28), for example, has talked of 'counterrevolution', while Schneider (1987, pp. 73, 82) reckons we may be in for 'the largest paradigm shift that most psychologists will see during their careers' (which should certainly be instructive for those of us still confused about Kuhn's concept of 'paradigm').

The PDP approach departs from the familiar structure of programs where explicit symbols are processed in a sequential order. Instead,

160 Against Cognitivism

there is simply a network of interconnected 'nodes' where the strength of the connections changes in accord with various learning rules. Not only is PDP a continuation of an early emphasis within computer science upon systems modelled upon neural structures (see Valentine, 1989; also Hilgard, 1987, pp. 261–5), but it seems to involve a revival of some rather old psychological ideas.[6]

Why, then, the excitement? There have certainly been important discoveries. For example, Hopfield (1982) showed that neural networks with symmetrical connections between nodes will settle down into stable configurations and hence be capable of storing information. Furthermore, the technique of 'the back propagation of errors', proposed by Rumelhart and his colleagues, has provided a solution to the problem of how to train the more powerful networks that include an additional layer of 'hidden units' between both input and output layers (Rumelhart, Hinton and Williams, 1986). The emergent properties of these artificial systems, based on very local principles regulating the connections between nodes, is indeed remarkable. But, after all, psychologists (when they have turned their minds to the matter) have surely always supposed that neural coding by the brain must involve changes in synaptic connections. Furthermore, despite the effect of Minsky and Papert's book *Perceptrons* (1969/1988) in diverting military funding away from neural networks (see Papert, 1988), important research continued in the period up to the recent resurgence of interest (see Cowan and Sharp, 1988, for details).

A good deal of confusion still remains about the relation between PDP models and the more familiar, symbol-based accounts. Is it a question of the *level* of explanation, and, if so, do PDP models really count as cognitive explanations (see Smolensky, 1988)? Or is it a matter of *style*, networks models being formulated in terms of 'probability theory rather than symbolic logic' (Rosenblatt, 1958, p. 388; see also Golden, 1990; Schneider, 1987)?

In fact, the new excitement about neural networks has very much focused upon the work of the 'PDP research group', which includes, among others, Rumelhart, McClelland, Hinton and Smolensky (see Rumelhart, McClelland and the PDP Research Group, 1986; McClelland, Rumelhart and the PDP Research Group, 1986), For these researchers have managed to convey the sense of a *direct* challenge to mainstream cognitive psychology.

First of all, PDP constitutes a move away from a representationalist approach based on explicit symbols in favour of cognitive models framed in terms of a rich network of connections. Knowledge is implicit and distributed across the entire pattern of interconnections: it is 'in' the connections rather than in a change of state of any isolated unit in the system (Rumelhart, Hinton and McClelland, 1986, pp. 75–6). Yet there is also the suggestion that the very idea of representation might need serious reconsideration:

> Schemata are not explicit entities, but rather are implicit in our knowledge and are created by the very environment that they are trying to interpret . . . [In] the conventional story, schemata are stored in memory. . . . In our case, nothing stored corresponds very closely to a schema. What is stored is a set of connection strengths which, when activated, have implicitly in them the ability to generate states that correspond to instantiated schemata. (Rumelhart, Smolensky, McClelland and Hinton, 1986, pp. 20–1)

There is also the issue of rules. Modern cognitivism has systematically obscured the distinction between *following* a rule and merely acting *in accord with* some kind of rule. In recent psychology, this distinction has perhaps been most actively stressed and explored within operant psychology, in terms of the contrast between rule-governed and contingency-shaped action. The PDP approach has now itself presented a significant alternative to rule-based explanation in psychology. In contrast to 'the explicit rule formation' tradition, learning is regarded not as the formulation of explicit rules, but rather as 'the acquisition of connection strengths which allow a network of simple units to act as *though* it knew the rules' (McClelland, Rumelhart and Hinton, 1986, p. 32).

Rumelhart and McClelland (1986b) have attempted to model one of the favourite examples of the proponents of rule-based explanation, the child's acquisition of the past-tense forms of English verbs:

> The child need not figure out what the rules are, nor even that there are rules. . . . Associations are simply stored in the network, but because we have a *superpositional* memory, similar patterns blend into one another and reinforce each other. . . . [The] phenomenon of regularization is an example often cited in support of the view that children do respond according to general rules of language. Why otherwise . . . should they generate forms that they have never heard? The answer we offer is that they do so because the past tenses of similar verbs they are learning show such a consistent pattern that the generalization from these similar verbs outweighs the relatively small amount of learning that has occurred on the irregular verb in question. (Rumelhart and McClelland, 1986b, p. 267)[7]

The PDP account is not, however, to be regarded as a mere alternative, or reformulation, of the rule-based explanation. According to McClelland, Rumelhart and Hinton (1986, p. 12), rules are, at best, 'approximate descriptions' of what is really happening at the level of the micro-structure of the connections (see also Hunt, 1989b). Explicit rules, such as those postulated by linguists, are an unlikely basis for innate knowledge; it is 'implausible that a newborn possesses elaborate symbol systems and the systems for interpreting them required to put these explicit, inaccessible rules to use in guiding behavior' (Rumelhart and McClelland, 1986a, p. 142). But, most importantly, an approach in terms of explicit representations cannot account for the flexibility and open-endedness of cognition – the basic facts of development and learning (see Hanson and Burr, 1990).

The most obvious way, however, in which the PDP approach runs counter to the 'traditional' computer metaphors does not concern rules and representations, but the very idea of a division between hardware and software:

> There is, on this view, no such thing as 'hardwiring'. Neither is there any such thing as 'software'. There are only connections. All connections are in some sense hardwired (in as much as they are physical entities) and all are software (in as much as they can be changed). (Rumelhart and McClelland, 1986a, p. 141; see also Thagard, 1986)

In short, the 'PDP research group' do not sound like cognitive psychologists. They tend to avoid psychological terms in their explanations; they talk, for example, of the networks settling or relaxing into solutions, rather than inferring or even computing them. They also emphasize their efforts to found their work upon analogies with the brain. Yet they have readily caught the interest of cognitive psychologists. Do, then, the claims of PDP – the rejection of explicit symbolic representations and rules, and the denial of the analogy of mind as software – amount to a fundamental challenge to cognitivism?

According to the jargon of PDP, distributed systems have the property of 'graceful degradation'. When these systems are damaged, their 'performance gradually deteriorates . . . but there is no single critical point where performance breaks down' (Rumelhart and McClelland, 1986a, p. 134). Cognitivism is diffuse, and shows just such resilience, for there is much more to this scheme than rules and symbolic representations, or software–hardware dualism. Additional – and much more implicit – assumptions have simply been carried over into the new PDP research.

If the project of cognitive psychology has been to put 'a little wisdom . . . *between the stimulus and response*' (Miller, Galanter and Pribram, 1960, p. 2; emphasis added), the new PDP researchers have reformulated this 'wisdom' in terms of connections. So now, as Bruce and Green have revealingly put it, the most prominent objection to the PDP approach concerns its failure to provide a distinctly 'cognitive or psychological level of theory to stand *between the "stimulus" and the "response"*' (Bruce and Green, 1990, p. 389; emphasis added). But note that the underlying S–R scheme of both mechanistic behaviourism *and* modern cognitivism has been retained, and the problem of 'cognition' is defined as before: how passively received 'inputs' are 'processed'. The very idea that animals might act in and upon their environment – that they might *transform* it – finds no place in the new PDP models. The environment is simply taken for granted. Thus, both traditional cognitive theory and the new connectionism subscribe to animal–environment dualism (Treffner, 1987): they both disregard the *mutual relation* between organisms and their environments. a relation that develops and evolves.

Cognitive psychologists have perhaps been too busy congratulating themselves on not being behaviourists to notice that they themselves treat people as machines (Skinner, 1974, p. 110; see Edward Morris, this volume, Chapter 8). The mechanistic scheme, and computer metaphors in particular, lead us to regard the problem of cognition as nothing other than an internalized re-presentation of the environment. And the PDP approach, despite its holistic claims, repeats this 'fallacy of encapsulation' (Bullock, 1987; see also Woolgar, 1987), the attribution of a property of an entire system to a single location, by failing to see that cognition, as a transformative and social process, is *radically* distributed. Cognition is not to be localized *in* people's heads.

Looking beyond computer metaphors

The point of metaphors is, of course, to indicate relationships, yet metaphors based on human artifacts have a curious distancing effect. They treat things *people have made and use* as though they were entirely independent of us. And metaphors based on the computer obscure the reason why these metaphors – and the new computer technology itself – should have flourished at all:

> [From] its very beginnings research into AI has always been financed by the military-industrial complex, and certain discontinuities in its development can only be explained by the investment of research funds in particular projects and their withdrawal if these projects did not measure up to the expectations of their sponsors. (Scheerer, 1988, p. 18)

A great deal of research money was released by the American Defense Department's various funding agencies when the Western lead in electronic technology no longer seemed secure, most notably after the Soviet launching of *Sputnik* in 1957 and the first manned satellite, *Vostok*, in 1961. The prime concern, of course, was to restore the technological lead, but cognitive psychology was an important beneficiary since it promised to provide a better understanding of scientific thought and creativity, and also, perhaps, to assist in the actual design of 'intelligent' devices. Yet this wider aspect of the 'cognitive revolution' is seldom mentioned in the textbooks, nor given much prominence in the historical accounts (but see Hudson, 1967, p. 120; Hilgard, 1987, p. 237).

Funding is an important but neglected explanation of why cognitive psychologists are so concerned about neural networks. On the one hand, PDP, by proving a novel attraction to the military funding agencies, promises to release substantial, additional finance for research that does pose interesting, intellectual challenges to cognitive psychologists. On the other hand, PDP research is in direct competition for the existing funds that would otherwise be available for the symbol-based approaches:

> The Sloan Foundation, the National Science Foundation, the Office of Naval Research, the Defense Advanced Research Project Agency, and the Air Force Office of Scientific Research all have initiated programs to fund [PDP] modeling. This modeling has caught the interest of basic researchers who wish to understand cognition and biological computing, as well as of applied researchers who want to build better weapon systems. (Schneider, 1987, p. 77)[8]

The real problem with modern psychology is not just a question of theoretical principles, but the interests that structure academic research. Researchers, *whatever their theoretical approach*, are largely restricted to the same sources of funding. Industry or the military provide the funds, and we try to get on with our pure research. And the result is always the same: a psychology centred on machines that dangerously obscures our actual relations to technology.

Notes

1. 'How does one characterize a position that seems to be such a mixture of elements usually considered incompatible? Deep in the middle of this dilemma it suddenly occurred to us that we were subjective behaviorists. When we stopped laughing we began to wonder seriously if that was not exactly the position we had argued ourselves into' (Miller, Galanter and Pribram, 1960, p. 211).
2. See Murray (1980) for an important reappraisal of the 'Chomskian revolution'. The utilization of Piaget's ideas was initially rather hesitant.
3. For example, Baars (1986, p. 14): 'The existence of the computer provides a concrete proof that the commonsense notion of representation is indeed viable, even with all its attendant philosophical difficulties.'
4. There are surely alternative ways of theorizing the role of environmental constraints in perception other than simply popping them into the perceiver's head as 'assumptions'. Nevertheless, these computer vision programs helped to illustrate the crucial importance of constraints in perception – even if the constraints actually invoked were exclusive, for example, to artificial 'blocks worlds' (cf. Dreyfus, 1978).

5. As Russell has put it, 'the correct way to regard the "passing" of the Turing test is as a reflection of the incapabilities of testers, not of the computational system, that is, it is not machines that pass it but people who fail it' (Russell, 1984, p. 100).
6. For useful overviews of the PDP approach, see Graubard (1988), Morris (1989) and Rumelhart (1989); for critical comments on the neurological plausibility of current PDP models, their biological plausibility and their explanatory power, see, for example, Crick (1989), Phillips (1988), Reeke and Edelman (1988).
7. Pinker and Prince (1989) dismiss Rumelhart and McClelland with 'revisionist associationism', yet as far as I can see they never address the basic point. Regardless of the accuracy of the model, does its performance meet Pinker and Prince's unrevised cognitivist criteria for a rule-based system?
8. According to a 1988 issue of *MacWeek*, an American Defense Department official was greeted with cheers by PDP researchers when he compared neural networks to nuclear weapons in their importance, and called for $400 million in research funding (cited in Hintzman, 1990, p. 110). See Weizenbaum (1983) for an early warning of this dangerous development.

References

Baars, B.J. (ed.) (1986), *The Cognitive Revolution in Psychology*, New York: Guilford Press.
Bickhard, M.H. and Richie, D.M. (1983), *On the Nature of Representation*, New York: Praeger.
Boyd, R. (1979), 'Metaphor and theory change: What is a "metaphor" a metaphor for?', in A. Ortony (ed.), *Metaphor and Thought*, Cambridge: Cambridge University Press, pp. 356–408.
Broadbent, D.E. (1958), *Perception and Communication*, Oxford: Pergamon Press.
Bruce, V. and Green P. (1990), *Visual Perception*, 2nd edn, London; Erlbaum.
Bullock, D. (1987), 'Socializing the theory of intellectual development', in M. Chapman and R.A. Dixon (eds), *Meaning and the Growth of Understanding: Wittgenstein's significance for developmental psychology*, Berlin: Springer Verlag, pp. 187–218.
Coleman, S.R. (1988), 'Kuhn's Structure of Scientific Revolutions in the psychological journal literature 1969–1983', *Journal of Mind and Behavior*, **9**, 415–46.
Cowan, J.D. and Sharp, D.H. (1988), 'Neural nets and artificial intelligence, in S.R. Graubard (ed.), *The Artificial Intelligence Debate*, Cambridge, MA: MIT, pp. 85–122.
Crick, F. (1989), 'The recent excitement about neural networks', *Nature*, **337**, 129–32.
Deese, J. (1972), *Psychology as Science and Art*, New York: Harcourt Brace Jovanovich.
Dennett, D. (1981), 'Artificial intelligence as philosophy and psychology', in his book *Brainstorms*, Brighton: Harvester, pp. 109–26.
Dennett, D. (1989), *The Intentional Stance*, Cambridge, MA: MIT.
Deutsch, J.A. (1953), 'A new type of behavior theory', *British Journal of Psychology*, **44**, 304–17.

Dreyfus, H. (1978), 'Empirical evidence for a pessimistic prognosis for cognitive science', *Behavioral and Brain Sciences*, **1**, 105.
Dreyfus, H.L. and Dreyfus, S.E. (1988), 'Making a mind versus modeling the brain: Artificial intelligence back at branchpoint', in S.R. Graubard (ed.), *The Artificial Intelligence Debate: False starts, real foundations*, Cambridge, MA: MIT, pp. 15–45.
Fodor, J.A. (1968), *Psychological Explanation*, Cambridge, MA: MIT.
Fodor, J.A. (1981), *Representations*, Cambridge, MA: MIT.
Gardner, H. (1987), *The Mind's New Science: A history of the cognitive revolution* (Paperback edn), New York: Basic Books.
Golden, R.M. (1990), 'Are connectionist models just statistical classifiers?', *Behavioral and Brain Sciences*, **13**, 494–5.
Graubard, S.R. (ed.) (1988), *The Artificial Intelligence Debate: False starts, real foundations*, Cambridge, MA: MIT.
Greeno, J.G. (1987), 'The cognition connection' (Review of D.E. Rumelhart, J.L. McClelland and the PDP research group, *Parallel Distributed Processing*, *New York Times Book Review*, 4 January, p. 28.
Gregory, R.L. (1975), 'Do we need cognitive concepts?' in M.S. Gazzaniga and C. Blakemore (eds), *Handbook of Psychophysiology*, New York: Academic Press, pp. 607–28.
Hanson, S.J. and Burr, D.J. (1990), 'What connectionist models learn: Learning and representation in connectionist models', *Behavioral and Brain Sciences*, **13**, 471–518.
Hilgard, E.R. (1987), *Psychology in America: A historical survey*, San Diego, CA: Harcourt Brace Jovanovich.
Hintzman, D.L. (1990), 'Human learning and memory: connections and dissociations', *Annual Review of Psychology*, **41**, 109–39.
Hodges, A. (1985), *Alan Turing: The enigma of intelligence*, London: Unwin.
Hopfield, J.J. (1982), 'Neural networks and physical systems with emergent collective computational properties', *Proceedings of the National Academy of Sciences*, **79**, 2554–8.
Hudson, L. (1967), *Contrary Imaginations: A psychological study of the English schoolboy*. Harmondsworth: Penguin.
Hunt, E. (1989a), 'Cognitive science: definition, status, and questions', *Annual Review of Psychology*, **40**, 603–29.
Hunt, E. (1989b), 'Connectionist and rule-based representations of expert knowledge', *Behavior Research Methods, Instruments, and Computers*, **21**, 88–95.
Johnson-Laird, P.N. (1988), *The Computer and the Mind*, Cambridge, MA: Harvard University Press.
Kessen, W. (1981), 'Early settlements in New Cognition', *Cognition*, **10**, 167–71.
Khilström, J.F. (1987), 'The cognitive unconscious', *Science*, **237**, 1445–51.
McClelland, J.L., Rumelhart, D.E. and the PDP Research Group (eds) (1986), *Parallel Distributed Processing: Explorations in the microstructure of cognition*, vol. 2. Cambridge, MA: MIT (refs on vacillation: 120, 121 *et seq.*)
McClelland, J.L., Rumelhart, D.E. and Hinton, G.E. (1986), 'The appeal of parallel distributed processing', in D.E. Rumelhart, J.L. McClelland and the PDP Research Group (eds), *Parallel Distributed Processing: Explorations in the microstructure of cognition*, vol. 1, Cambridge, MA: MIT, pp. 3–44.
Meyering, T.C. (1989), *Historical Roots of Cognitive Science: The rise of a*

cognitive theory of perception from antiquity to the nineteenth century, Dordrecht: Kluwer.
Miller, G.A. (1962), *The Psychology of Communication*, London: Allen Lane.
Miller, G.A. (1986), 'Interview', in B.J. Baars, (ed.), *The Cognitive Revolution in Psychology*, New York: Guilford Press, pp. 200–23.
Miller, G.A., Galanter, E. and Pribram, K.H. (1960), *Plans and the Structure of Behavior*, New York: Holt, Rinehart & Winston.
Minsky, M. and Papert, S. (1988), *Perceptrons: An introduction to computational geometry* (expanded edn), Cambridge, MA: MIT.
Morris, R.G.M. (ed.) (1989), *Parallel Distributed Processing: Implications for psychology and neurobiology*, Oxford: Oxford University Press.
Murray, S.O. (1980), 'Gatekeepers and the "Chomskian revolution"', *Journal of the History of the Behavioral Sciences*, **16**, 73–88.
Neisser, U. (1967), *Cognitive Psychology*, New York: Appleton-Century.
Newell, A., Shaw, J.C. and Simon, H. (1958), 'Elements of a theory of human problem solving', *Psychological Review*, **65**, 151–66.
Norman, D.A. (1986), 'Reflections on cognition and parallel distributed processing', in J.L. McClelland and D.E. Rumelhart (eds), *Parallel Distributed Processing: explorations in the microstructure of cognition*, vol. 2, Cambridge, MA: MIT, pp. 531–52.
Palmer, A. (1987), 'Cognitivism and computer simulation', in A.P. Costall and A.W. Still (eds), *Cognitive Psychology in Question*, Hemel Hempstead: Harvester Wheatsheaf, pp. 55–69.
Papert, S. (1988), 'One AI or many?', in S.R. Graubard, *The Artificial Intelligence Debate: False starts, real foundations*, Cambridge, MA: MIT, pp. 1–14.
Phillips, W.A. (1988) 'Brainy minds: A critical notice of "Parallel Distributed Processing (Vol. 1: Foundations; Vol. 2: Psychological and biological models)", by D.E. Rumelhart, J.L. McClelland and the PDP Research Group, Cambridge: MIT, 1986', *Quarterly Journal of Experimental Psychology*, **40A**, 389–405.
Pinker, S. and Prince, A. (1989) 'Rules and connections in human language', in R.G.M. Morris (ed.), *Parallel Distributed Processing: Implications for psychology and neurobiology*, Oxford: Oxford University Press, pp. 182–99.
Putnam, H. (1987), 'Computational psychology and interpretation theory', in R. Born (ed.), *Artificial Intelligence: The case against*, London: Croom Helm, 1987, pp. 1–17.
Pylyshyn, Z.W. (1979), 'Metaphorical imprecision and the "top–down" research strategy', in A. Ortony (ed.), *Metaphor and Thought*, Cambridge: Cambridge University Press, pp. 420–36.
Pylyshyn, Z.W. (1989), 'Computing in cognitive science', in M.I. Posner, (ed.), *Foundations of Cognitive Science*, Cambridge, MA: MIT, pp. 49–92.
Reed, E.S. (1989), 'Theory, concept, and experiment in the history of psychology: the older tradition behind a "young science"' *History of the Human Sciences*, **2**, 333–56.
Reeke, G.N. and Edelman, G.M. (1988), 'Real brains and artificial intelligence', in S.R. Graubard (ed.), *The Artificial Intelligence Debate: False starts, real foundations*, Cambridge, MA: MIT, pp. 143–74.
Rosenblatt, F. (1958), 'A probabilistic model of information storage and organization in the brain', *Psychological Review*, **65**, 386–407.
Rumelhart, D.E. (1989), 'The architecture of mind: A connectionist approach',

in M.I. Posner, (ed.), *Foundations of Cognitive Science*, Cambridge, MA: MIT, pp. 133–59.
Rumelhart, D.E., Hinton, G.E. and McClelland, J.L. (1986), 'A general framework for parallel distributed processing', in D.E. Rumelhart, J.L. McClelland and the PDP Research Group (eds), *Parallel Distributed Processing: Explorations in the microstructure of cognition*, vol. 1, Cambridge, MA: MIT, pp. 45–76.
Rumelhart, D.E., Hinton, G.E. and Williams, R.J. (1986), 'Learning internal representations by error propagation', in D.E. Rumelhart, J.L. McClelland and the PDP Research Group (eds), *Parallel Distributed Processing: Explorations in the microstructure of cognition*, vol. 1, Cambridge, MA: MIT.
Rumelhart, D.E. and McClelland, J.L. (1986a) 'PDP models and general issues in cognitive science', in D.E. Rumelhart, J.L. McClelland and the PDP Research Group (eds), *Parallel Distributed Processing: Explorations in the microstructure of cognition*, vol. 1, Cambridge, MA: MIT, pp. 110–46.
Rumelhart, D.E. and McClelland, J.L. (1986b), 'On learning the past tenses of English verbs', in J.L. McClelland, D.E. Rumelhart and the PDP Research Group (eds), *Parallel Distributed Processing: Explorations in the microstructure of cognition*, vol. 2, Cambridge, MA: MIT, pp. 216–71.
Rumelhart, D.E. McClelland, J.L. and the PDP Research Group, (eds), (1986), *Parallel Distributed Processing: Explorations in the microstructure of cognition*, vol. 1, Cambridge, MA: MIT.
Rumelhart, D.E., Smolensky, P., McClelland, J.L. and Hinton, G.E. (1986), 'Schemata and sequential thought processes in PDP models', in J.L. McClelland, D.E. Rumelhart and the PDP Research Group (eds), *Parallel Distributed Processing: Explorations in the microstructure of cognition*, vol. 2, Cambridge, MA: MIT, pp. 7–57.
Runeson, S. (1977), 'On the possibility of "smart" perceptual mechanisms', *Scandinavian Journal of Psychology*, **18**, 172–9.
Russell, J. (1984), *Explaining Mental Life: Some philosophical issues in psychology*, London: Macmillan.
Scheerer, E. (1988), 'Towards a history of cognitive science', *International Social Science Journal*, **40**, 6–19.
Schneider, W. (1987), 'Connectionism: Is it a paradigm shift for psychology?', *Behavior Research Methods, Instrumentation and Computers*, **19**, 73–83.
Searle, J. (1989), *Mind, Brains and Science*: The 1984 Reith lectures, Harmondsworth: Penguin.
Shanon, B. (1988), 'Semantic representation of meaning: A critique', *Psychological Bulletin*, **104**, 70–83.
Shanon, B. (1989), 'A simple comment regarding the Turing test', *Journal for the Theory of Social Behaviour*, **19**, 249–56.
Simon, H.A. and Kaplan, C.A. (1989), 'Foundations of cognitive science', in M.I. Posner (ed.), *Foundations of Cognitive Science*, Cambridge, MA: MIT, pp. 1–47.
Skinner, B.F. (1974), *About Behaviorism*, New York: Knopf.
Smolensky, P. (1988), 'On the proper treatment of connectionism', *Behavioral and Brain Sciences*, **11**, 1–74.
Thagard, P. (1986), 'Parallel computation and the mind–body problem', *Cognitive Science*, **10**, 301–18.
Treffner, P. (1987), 'Ecological connectionism and animal–environment mutuality', *1st IEEE International Conference on Neural Networks*.

Turing, A. (1950), 'Computing machinery and intelligence', *Mind*, **59**, 434–60.
Valentine, E.R. (1989) 'Neural nets: From Hartley and Hebb to Hinton', *Journal of Mathematical Psychology*, **33**, 348–57.
Vroon, P.A. (1987), 'Man–machine analogs and theoretical mainstreams in psychology', in W.J. Baker, M.E. Hyland, H. van Rappard and A.W. Staats (eds), *Current Issues in Theoretical Psychology*, North-Holland: Elsevier, pp. 393–414.
Weizenbaum, J. (1983), 'The computer in your future. Review of *The Fifth Generation*, by Edward A. Feigenbaum and Pamela McCorduck', *New York Review of Books*, **30**, 27 October, 58–62.
Woolgar, S. (1987) 'Reconstructing man and machine: A note on sociological critiques of cognitivism', in W.E. Bijke, T.P. Hughes and T.J. Pinch (eds), *The Social Construction of Technological Systems: New directions in the sociology and history of technology*, Cambridge, MA: MIT.

10
James Gibson's ecological approach to cognition
Edward Reed

Editors' introduction

In classical cognitivist theories of perception, physical energy impinging upon the senses is transduced into neural inputs which are then operated upon by cognitive processes to give rise to meaningful perception. Cognition is therefore involved, but is separate from the process of transduction that goes on at the senses. The process is a linear causal chain of a kind that first appeared in the seventeenth-century accounts of visual perception based on the newly discovered retinal image (e.g. Descartes, 1972).

J.J. Gibson's ecological theory is probably the best-known alternative to such cognitivist theories within scientific psychology, but it is still sometimes presented as though it were merely an alternative account of sensory transduction, preliminary to processing by higher-order cognition (Bruce and Green, 1990). On the contrary, the theory includes cognition as much as cognitivist theories do, but in a very different way. Perception in ecological theory involves the active pick-up of information over time, and this has two consequences, which appear most clearly in the case of vision. First the available information is richer by another dimension, since it is no longer confined to the two-dimensional image of the classical account, but consists of transformations over time. So much richer, in fact, that the information picked up is sufficient to specify its sources in the environment, and also what activities they afford an animal (Gibson, 1979). Thus the information itself gives rise directly to meaningful knowledge about potential action, and the significance of the environment for the animal does not have to be added by cognitive elaboration. Secondly, the information that is picked up over time is always a product of directed exploratory activity on the part of the animal, and is a controlling source of further directed activity; thus the information is assimilated to ongoing activities in the very process of being picked up, and in this respect is meaningful from the beginning (cf. Fodor and Pylyshyn, 1981). Either way, there is no room in Gibson's theory for 'meaningless inputs', and therefore no need to appeal to cognitive construction to account for experience.

So there is no need to appeal to unconscious inference in order to explain direct knowledge of the world through perception. But perception is not the only way to gain knowledge. For knowledge is a social matter, and in the case of human beings much of our knowledge is gained indirectly through learning from other people. Furthermore, many of our activities involve the use of symbols and other socially determined sources of meaning. These include the use of money in the exchange of goods, signs and maps in finding our way about the environment, and time measurement through clocks and calendars. This is a relatively undeveloped part of Gibson's ecological psychology, and Edward Reed extends the theory by exploring the processes of indirect knowledge and the part played by representation systems in human activity.

References

Bruce, V. and Green, P. (1990), *Visual Perception: Physiology, Psychology and Ecology*, Hillsdale, NJ: Erlbaum.
Descartes, R. (1972), *Treatise of Man*, Cambridge, MA: Harvard University Press.
Fodor, J.A. and Pylyshyn, Z.W. (1981), 'How direct is visual perception?: Some reflections on Gibson's "Ecological Approach"', *Cognition*, **9**, 139–96.
Gibson, J.J. (1979), *The Ecological Approach to Visual Perception*, Boston, MA: Houghton Mifflin.

* * *

Introduction

James J. Gibson was a highly controversial figure in modern psychology, who excited great passion among proponents and detractors of his theory alike. About the only matter on which Gibson's adherents and opponents have agreed is that his is an anti-cognitive theory of perception (compare, e.g., Michaels and Carello, 1981, with Ullman, 1980). As it turns out, this sentiment – however widely promulgated – is simply and utterly false. Gibson thought of his as a cognitive psychology, and of perception as a cognitive function. It is a fact that Gibson (rightly) dismissed modern 'cognitivism' (e.g. information-processing models, artificial intelligence, cognitive science), with its archaic yet incoherent

James Gibson's ecological approach 173

theory of mental representations operating on stimulus inputs (Reed, 1989a). But Gibson's dismissal of these facile, modish theories was not his position on cognition as such. Ever since the 1950s, when he self-consciously abandoned the response theory of cognition and behaviourism (Reed, 1986, 1988a), Gibson considered his account of perception to be a theory of how animals come to *know* their environments – a theory of cognition. Gibson's last two books (1966, referred to hereinafter as SCAPS; 1979, referred to hereinafter as EAVP) are replete with explicit discussions of the psychological issues concerning cognition, language, memory and imagination, discussions which have been ignored or worse throughout the entire secondary literature on Gibson's work.

When writing EAVP, Gibson (1975, 5–52)[1] made the following note to himself:

Fields of Cognitive Psychology

I. The perception of the environment and its
affordances for behaviour
Learning and the education of attention
Control of locomotion and manipulation
Orientation to the far environment
II. Perception and knowledge at second hand
Pictures, models, toys, (Images)
Experiments with graphic *displays*
III. Knowledge available in language
Speech, writing, concepts, words
Association, traces, memory, learning
Experiments with *verbal* items.

This review will cover all these areas (though not in that order) except the control of locomotion and orientation to the far environment (so-called cognitive mapping), which deserve separate discussions. I have also brought some of Gibson's ideas about knowledge at second hand and about the role of language in knowing under the single rubric of 'representation systems', a term of my own invention, although the idea for it derives from SCAPS. Criticism of Gibson's ideas is here kept to a minimum. My goal in this chapter is to expound a set of profound and novel ideas that deserve serious discussion, not the kind of ignorant dismissal they have received.

The cognitive revolution

Modern cognitive psychology has its roots in behaviourist learning theory. Already in the 1930s and 1940s, Edward C. Tolman was developing his 'cognitive' interpretations of rat maze-learning experiments. In the 1950s, as the ideas of cybernetics and computation theory became widely known, there were the beginnings of a full-scale revolt against the stultifying assumptions of classical learning theory. Cognitive psychology's equivalent of storming the Bastille was Noam Chomsky's (1959) attack on B.F. Skinner's *Verbal Behavior* (1957). Chomsky showed that Skinner's view of language was missing an important aspect of language, namely its *cognitive* function. A language is more than a system of labels or associations, it is more than a complex lexicon of phrases called up at appropriate times by experience and circumstances. A language is also a system of *predication*, which requires a grammar as well as a phrasebook. Language is an evolved specialization for sharing knowledge about the world.

Chomsky's attack on learning theory, and the contemporaneous developments in computation theory, led to a growing realization that the psychology of stimulus, response and association had severe limitations. Human behaviour could not be cut off from human knowledge, which was more than a mere linking of stimuli and responses. Supposedly, human beings 'processed' stimulus inputs, creating grammar-like, rule-based structures for *interpreting* stimuli, or for *planning* future actions (Miller, Galanter and Pribram, 1960). These structures, linked by grammar-like hierarchies of rules and not by experienced associations, came to be called *mental representations*, and cognition came to be viewed as the formation and use of representations according to rule (Chomsky, 1980; Johnson-Laird, 1983).

The so-called cognitive revolution in psychology has thus far *not* challenged the truly basic assumptions of S–R psychology, so much as it has added a new set of assumptions (Reed, 1986b). Cognitive psychologists who study perception do not deny that it is based on stimuli (as Gibson does), but they do deny that association of stimuli (or even Gestalt organization of inputs) is *sufficient* to explain all of perception (Neisser, 1967; Pinker, 1985). Something else is needed: the rule-based processing of inputs into representations. Cognitivists who study action do not deny that it is based on responses, but they question whether the association of responses through innate linkages and learning is all there is to action. Isn't action also based on the rule-governed implementation of routines based upon stored knowledge, such as locomoting around the environment with the aid of a cognitive map (Gallistel, 1980; Requin, Semjen and Bonnet, 1984)? The cognitivists' idea is that a stimulus–response psychology can be made complete only by adding to it a psychology of mental representations or mental models that turn stimulus inputs into knowledge, and organize responses meaningfully (Fodor, 1985; Johnson-Laird, 1983; Pylyshyn, 1984).

Gibson's cognitive psychology also emerged from a critique of S-R psychology, but a very different critique. And where cognitivists attempted to modify and supplement S-R principles, Gibson tried to overthrow them and replace them with an entirely different approach to psychology. The cognitivist critique of learning theory started with the problem of language and the kind of knowledge gained through language, whereas Gibson's critique of behaviourism started with perception and the kind of knowledge it facilitates. Gibson thought his perception-based critique was deeper than the other, and that is why he called for the replacement of S-R psychology, not its supplementation.

Gibson's critique of behaviourism

The behaviourist or response theory of perception – which Gibson, following his teacher Holt (1915), espoused for years – involves the kind of associative principles which Chomsky and others have criticized so effectively. The basic idea is that one does not perceive an object until one has made a discriminative, specific response to it. This may sound odd, but it is actually just a more sophisticated version of the classic and widespread 'touch teaches vision' theory. The child is said to learn to see that a tennis ball is soft by having experience in touching it and subsequently associating those tactile experiences with the visual experiences of round, white (or orange), and so on. Meaningful perception is thus learned perception, and learned perception requires associating sensory stimuli with previous experiences, an association based on behaviour (see J.J. Gibson, 1982, ch. 4.2 for a critique). Just as words are supposed to gain meanings through experienced association, so are sensory inputs.

There are many problems with such response theories of perception. First of all, as Gibson (1933, 1937) long ago showed, visual experiences of the same stimulus can change without *any* responses being made. Second, perceptual learning can be shown to occur without any reinforcement linking stimuli to responses (E. Gibson, 1953). This raises the question (at least for behaviourists) of, third, what kind of reinforcement does occur in perceptual activity (J.J. Gibson, 1958; Woodworth, 1947)? In behaviour, animals and people supposedly repeat and learn those responses which succeed; in perception, observers tend to learn *what is the case*, regardless of the behavioural outcome. The *exploratory* behaviour involved in perception would seem to be of an entirely different order from the *performatory* responses studied by behaviourists (SCAPS, Ch. 2). Fourth, there is the vexed problem of what should count as a stimulus. Behaviourists tended to be glib about this, referring to objects and other animals as stimuli just as readily as they referred to physical energies as stimuli (J.J. Gibson, 1982, Ch. 4.3). Gibson's 1982, Ch. 1.4) discovery that complex energy patterns counted as *information* for perception, combined with his critique of the stimulus concept, and his novel idea of exploratory action, led to his complete rejection of S–R psychology (Reed, 1986a, 1988a).

For Gibson, perception now became not a response to stimuli, or the awareness of the mental representations caused by stimuli; rather, perception was defined as an observer's awareness of the environment, based on information and the active, exploratory pick-up of information. Information is the basis for contact with the environment because it is specific to its sources in the environment. It is *external* to the animal, and various exploratory actions of perceptual systems are required for perception to occur. Observers look, listen, sniff, taste and feel by orientating and moving their heads, hands and other sensory organs. *Neither* the sensory inputs *nor* the motor responses of these organs count as the information; they are simply what enables an observer to detect external information. One can track a moving object by moving one's eyes with a stationary head, or by moving one's head and keeping one's eyes steady, or by combining these two procedures. In each case there are very different stimuli and responses, but the awareness of the moving object can be the same if the information picked up is the same (see Gibson *et al.*, 1958, for experimental evidence).

On this information-based theory of perception the meaningfulness of perception does not derive from any form of association, only from the information actually detected by an observer. Whereas cognitivists explain perceptual knowledge of the world as a construction out of stimulus inputs, Gibson explains it as the ability of the nervous system to home in on useful information: 'Instead of postulating that the brain constructs information from the input of a sensory nerve, we can suppose that the centers of the nervous system, including the brain, resonate to information' (SCAPS, p. 267). This resonance is a circular process that can achieve a state of equilibrium when the information being sought is detected. Perceptual learning is the process of becoming able to differentiate more and more kinds of information, and to increase the range and economy of the detection process (SCAPS, Ch. 13; E. Gibson, 1969). Perceptual learning involves changes in both behaviour and awareness, resulting in improved knowledge. According to the Gibsons, perceptual learning is the fundamental cognitive process.

The modern proponents of cognitive psychology started with certain traditional principles: that stimuli and responses are the building-blocks of behaviour, that stimuli lead to sensations or sensory experiences, and that these stimulus inputs are the basis of our contact with the environment. These assumptions led them to treat cognition as the processing or interpretation of inputs into stored knowledge (representations) which can be accessed or re-called for use in language, memory and thinking. Gibson's rejection of these same assumptions resulted in a radically different definition of both perception and cognition. The novel and unusual definitions he proposed have led to the common contention that Gibson did not have a theory of the psychological processes underlying perception and cognition (see, e.g., Heil, 1979; Ullman, 1980; and see the replies by Reed, 1980; Reed and Jones, 1981). The problem here is that what cognitive psychologists call psychological processes are processes Gibson treated as irrelevant or incidental to cognition, and cognitive psychologists have not yet even considered the processes of cognition discussed by Gibson:

> Associating, organizing, remembering, recognizing, expecting, and naming – all these are familiar psychological processes, and all of them have been appealed to in the effort to explain the growth of knowledge. But all of these processes were first conceived as operations of the mind upon the deliverances of sense, and they still carry some of this implication. They have now been examined, one by one, and I have suggested that, as commonly understood, they are incidental, not essential to the developing process of information pickup. They need to be reinterpreted. The deeper, underlying kinds of perceptual development seem to involve exploration and attention. (SCAPS, p. 283)

To understand Gibson's argument here requires first distinguishing and defining two kinds of cognition – direct and indirect; and, second, analyzing the psychological processes involved in each of these kinds of knowing.

Direct cognition and the varieties of indirect cognition

As Gibson's ecological theory of perception developed, he began to realize just how radical a change in thinking about perception he was proposing. Heretofore, virtually all theories of perception had assumed that the objects of which we are immediately aware are sensory objects, sensations. These subjective objects give us knowledge about the external world, but only after a complex process of inference, association and interpretation is applied to them. In other words, most perceptual psychologists held (and still hold) that what we directly perceive are mental ideas or representations, and it is only indirectly, through the mediation of these representations, that we perceive the external world. Gibson's theory that the perception of environmental objects, places and events is based on ecologically available information challenged this widespread consensus. Thus Gibson began to call his theory a form of direct realism, in that he held it possible to perceive the surrounding environment directly, on the basis of information, and not indirectly, on the basis of sensations and mental representations (Gibson, 1967/1982, Ch. 4.5; Gibson, 1972).

In arguing that it is possible to perceive the world directly, Gibson never argued that mediated, or indirect awareness was impossible – although he was forced to an entirely new definition of indirect perception. He repeatedly made a strong distinction between perception based on information and perception based on language, pictures or other symbols. In SCAPS (p. 91) he wrote

> In this book, a distinction will be made between perceptual cognition, or knowledge of the environment, and symbolic cognition, or knowledge *about* the environment. The former is a direct response to things based on stimulus information, the latter is an indirect response to things based on stimulus sources produced by another human individual.

In EAVP (p. 147) he is perhaps more blunt:

> Direct perception is what one gets from seeing Niagara Falls, say, as distinguished from seeing a picture of it. The latter kind of perception is *mediated*. So when I assert that perception of the environment is direct, I mean that it is not *mediated* by *retinal* pictures, *neural* pictures, or *mental* pictures. *Direct perception* is the activity of getting information from the ambient array of light.

This process of detecting information is a complex one, unfamiliar to most psychologists or neurophysiologists, who have studied only how sensory inputs are processed or transduced, not how external information is detected by active observers (Reed, 1980, 1989b). Gibson devoted the major portion of his second book, SCAPS, to an analysis of the process of pick-up, so only a few of his leading ideas can be summarized here. Most importantly, information pick-up is a process carried out by a functional system distributed throughout an animal's nervous system. Adjustments of peripheral organs, such as turning the eyes and head, play as significant a role in direct perception as the activity of the higher brain centres. Awareness of the environment is based on the adjustment of the animal's entire perceptual system to the information surrounding it. This adjustment includes a range of processes, all of which may be described as the simultaneous extraction of persisting and changing properties of stimulation, invariants despite disturbances of the array of information (EAVP, p. 249). Observers can perceive themselves, their environments, and the changing relationship between themselves and their surroundings. This requires component processes such as delimiting the range of variables in stimulation, establishing co-variations of information across different perceptual systems, distinguishing information specifying the self from information specifying the environment, and extracting information about the affordances of the objects, places, events and other people in one's habitat. All these processes are described in SCAPS (especially Chapter 13). As Gibson emphasizes, these processes are 'postulated to be very susceptible to development and learning. The opportunities for educating attention, for exploring and adjusting, for extracting and abstracting are unlimited' (EAVP, p. 250).

The fundamental hypothesis of Gibson's ecological approach to perception is that where specific information about environmental objects, places, events and people is available and picked up, observers will perceive these things. This is what Gibson means by direct perception, or 'knowledge *of*' the environment. It is tacit knowledge. It is not formulated in pictures or words, for it is the knowledge that makes the formulation of pictures and words possible. However, even though it is tacit, this knowledge of the environment obtained through direct perception is not personal, subjective or private. Information is *available* in the environment, and it can be picked up by many observers. Even a point of view is not private: 'your perception and mine can be identical even though your sensation and mine can never be identical at the same time. The same invariants over time are available to both of us.' When you move around the rectangular table the changing angles of its corners as projected into the optic array co-vary so as to keep the cross-ratio invariant, and the same is true for the optic array at my eyes, although I am not in your position at any given time: 'I cannot occupy your point of observation now, but I can in the future and I could in the past' (J.J. Gibson, 1982, pp. 411–12). Because we live in a *shared* environment, a social environment inhabited by others of our kind, direct perception is not necessarily private. Privacy of perception and action is possible, by means of occluding edges and their use in preventing information from becoming available to others, but that is another story (see EAVP, p. 136).

Any group of socially living animals thus perceives their habitat in common and can, to some degree, perceive the affordances of their environment for their fellows as well as for themselves. Under certain evolutionary conditions they may also develop the ability to act so as to make their fellows aware of relevant environmental facts. Through gestures and displays, information can be selected and presented to others. Humans specialize in the making of optical displays, through facial, manual and postural gestures, and through modifying surfaces with incisions and/or pigments. Humans also specialize in a unique kind of vocal display, speech. According to Gibson (EAVP, p. 42):

> a display . . . is a surface that has been shaped or processed so as to exhibit information for more than just a surface itself. For example, a surface of clay is only clay, but it may be molded in the shape of a cow or painted with the profile of a cow or incised with the cuneiform characters that stand for a cow, and then it is more than just a surface of clay.

Similarly, a sound stream can be modified to provide linguistic information for a cow, and then it is more than just a vocalization, it is a reference to a cow. These 'images, pictures, and written-on surfaces afford a special kind of knowledge that I call *mediated* or *indirect*, knowledge at second hand' (*ibid.*). This indirect knowledge is intrinsically shared, because it involves the *displaying of information to others*. Even when one is talking to oneself, or scribbling notes, information is being made potentially available to other observers. (The special case of so-called 'internalized' speech and imagery will be discussed separately below.)

All displays are made up of *samples* of information in various forms. The following is a tentative list of the modes of mediated visual perception (Gibson, 1976?, 5–75):

1. A sample of the optic array is magnified or minified by an optical device, or its energy level is amplified by a device.
2. Some of the frozen structure in a sample of an optic array is reproduced photographically, or recreated chirographically (drawing, painting, etc.).
3. Samples of optical information are *converted* or *coded* into verbal descriptions.
4. Samples of optical information are *indexed* by an instrument, as with a meter stick.

In all these cases the information on which direct perception can be based is *selectively* adapted and modified in a display. A microscope or a photograph samples a *sector* of the global array, even if they do not necessarily distort that sample. The value of these selected samples of information lies not in the displays themselves, but in what they refer to or *represent*. These mediators are representations; they do not have affordances as objects do, but rather have 'referential meaning' (5–75). They 'consolidate the gains of perception' – a favourite phrase of Gibson's – 'by converting tacit knowledge into explicit knowledge'

(Gibson, 1976, 5–61). One consequence of this concept of indirect cognition consolidating directly gained knowledge is that all of human perception – or at least all of adult human perception – is *socialized*. The process whereby each of us comes to know his or her environment is inherently social, even though we can and do learn about things for ourselves. What we attend to, many of the processes of attention, and all of our various practical activities are in large part results of socialized upbringings. Moreover, each culture (and many groups within a given culture) has its own norms, taboos and techniques concerning both awareness and activity. I have begun to discuss the issues raised by ecological psychology's social orientation to cognition in two recent papers (Reed, 1991).

The knowledge of the shared environment gained through direct perception can thus itself be selected, highlighted, made explicit and shared. A gesture or picture can make you aware of something I have seen that you have never seen, and a word can label unknown things for you, as well as refer to known ones. Often words and representations tend to delimit and stereotype our knowledge of the world. This is because the environment, and the ecological information available in it, is infinitely rich, whereas lexicons are finite and must therefore select and categorize (SCAPS, p. 281). When perception depends on such labels alone it, too, will tend to be stereotyped. For example, the Nazi stereotype of the 'Jew' had profound and horrifying social consequences on the actions and consciousness of Germans (Gibson, 1939). Luckily, perception can depend on information as well as mediating representations, so it is not inevitably stereotyped (Reed, 1988a, Ch. 6).

Indirect awareness has a variety of modes which all have in common the function of making observers aware by means of selecting and sampling information. That sampling may be accomplished through tools, like a telescope or a telephone; or by displays, such as a photograph or a page of text; or through complex coding of ecological information, as in all forms of language (EAVP, Ch. 13). In all cases the awareness can be called indirect because it is different from that based on the direct perception of the display, tool or vocalization. One directly perceives a picture as a marked surface (even though one rarely attends to that aspect of it) and indirectly perceives that it is, say, a portrait of one's mother. The great variety of processes involved in indirect perception therefore have in common this one process of a 'dual awareness' – a simultaneous awareness of the mediator and what it represents. There are thus many levels of visual cognition:

> At all four levels, (1) seeing the man, (2) seeing his picture, (3) reading his name, and (4) reading about him, the information has to be carried in

structured light. There has to be an array with borders, textures, patterns or forms, and this is why the problem of defining the structure of an [optic] array is so fundamental. (SCAPS, p. 244)

Indirect awareness consolidates the gains of direct perception

The various processes of indirect cognition – the uses of depictions, descriptions, symbols and tools for extending awareness – are quite diverse and have barely begun to be studied. They cannot be analyzed here in any depth. Instead, I shall focus on Gibson's fundamental hypothesis: that *indirect modes of cognition consolidate the capacities of direct perception; mediators allow one to make explicit previously tacit knowledge.* It is this hypothesis about the relations between indirect awareness (especially through language) and direct perception that sets Gibson aside from the modern consensus in cognitive psychology. It is virtually a dogma of modern psychology that all meaningful perception is indirect, and is in some ways analogous to language and the use of symbols and representations (Fodor, 1975; Luria, 1973; Marr, 1982). Simply put, the idea is that perception of the world is based on sense inputs. We have direct access to the sense inputs, but these are not meaningful in themselves; they become meaningful only after a complex form of quasi-grammatical or computational processing. Thus, it is argued, meaningful intercourse with the world requires that an observer already has some stored knowledge (either innate, acquired, or both) that can be used to interpret inputs. On this theory there is *no* direct experience that is truly meaningful. The relation between direct and indirect processes in cognition is analogous to the old idea of the relation between matter or substance and form: the sense inputs are the matter out of which meanings are carved by 'higher' psychological processes (Fodor, 1985).

The ecological approach to direct perception rejects the basic assumptions from which this cognitivist consensus has sprung. *If* ecological information is available, and *if* animals have evolved nervous systems capable of picking it up, then – or so Gibson's hypothesis goes – meaningful direct perception of the environment will occur when such information is detected. The role of explicit knowledge, and the processes that make knowledge explicit, is not to *create* knowledge out of merely potentially meaningful input, nor even to *select* meanings to assign to inputs. The role of indirect forms of cognition is to *make others aware*, to share knowledge. (This can be extended to a reflexive mode, as in reminding oneself, making oneself aware.)

James Gibson's ecological approach   183

Gibson's theory of information-based perception thus forces a rethinking of the nature of all forms of cognition. *For a cognitivist like Chomsky (1959, 1980) a spoken word is simply a stimulus, just as it is for a behaviourist like Skinner (1957)*. Neither theory has the concept of stimulus *information*, and both are therefore forced to treat utterances as mere verbal stimuli. Chomsky rightly pointed out that any reduction of a language to a system of associative labellings is untenable, for the very production of speech is '*creative*'. One produces that which one has *not* heard (as well as what one has heard) more or less according to the rules of the language. The child's language may mirror that of its parents, but it is also much more than a mirror, as the child learns to ask questions, say what it wants and what it thinks and, in general, produce utterances never before spoken. Whereas for Skinner the contingencies of reinforcement are sufficient to explain learning, for Chomsky they are inadequate, and it is from this inadequacy that Chomsky argues for an 'innate universal grammar' – an inborn ability to make sense out of not completely meaningful stimuli. Each human child must be born with such knowledge, Chomsky asserts, to explain how, given mere verbal stimuli, he or she comes to know how to speak their language properly. An ecological approach to cognition calls this awkward hypothesis into question.

When children learn to produce language creatively, as when they invent grammatically regular constructions that happen not to exist in a language ('I goed to my friend's house'), this is sometimes called 'active learning' to distinguish it from mere passive learning or mirroring (De Villiers and De Villiers, 1978). What is striking about the theory of direct perception is that it accounts for such active learning as a kind of *perceptual* learning based on *information*, not a change of representation based on inputs and experience. There is now abundant evidence that infants actively learn about their world through visual perception: experience with objects, events and actions (such as reaching, grasping or sucking) leads to a kind of active learning of the properties of things (E.J. Gibson, 1984, 1988). For example, experience with the differences between certain rigid and non-rigid optical motions provides even a five-month-old with the knowledge that enables it to distinguish previously unseen kinds of motions (E.J. Gibson *et al.*, 1978). If perception is based on information, and not on stimulus inputs, then – James and Eleanor Gibson have argued – the debate between the cognitivists and the behaviourists over language learning is simply misguided. The problem is *not* how to explain the active learning of language based on the paucity of the verbal stimuli. Rather, the problem concerns *information*, and specifically the use of the *dual* information in speech: how can children learn to hear not only the utterance, but also what it denotes? According to Gibson (SCAPS, p. 281):

For the child who is learning to use language and at the same time learning to perceive the world, words are *not* simply auditory stimuli or vocal responses. They embody stimulus information, especially invariant information about the regularities of the environment. They consolidate the growing ability of the child to detect and abstract the invariants. They cut across the perceptual systems or 'sense modalities'. The words are like the invariants in that they are capable of being auditory or visual. . . . They even cut across the stimulus-response dichotomy, for they can be vocal-motor or manual-motor. Hence, the learning of language by the child is not simply the associative naming or labelling of impressions from the world. It is also, and more importantly, an expression of the distinctions, abstractions, and recognitions that the child is coming to achieve in perceiving.

The newborn infant exposed to speech gets information about the sounds being made, but little or no information about their meanings, and must learn about its world directly. As the infant develops, two kinds of language learning then take place the 'learning of the language code as a vocabulary' and 'learning to consolidate . . . knowledge by predication' (SCAPS, p. 282). The first involves the learning of complex associations, of words as labels for objects, places, events and actions that the child perceives. This is not behaviouristic learning by associating stimuli with responses, it is instead the learning *of* associations between ecological information and verbal information. Gibson (1975?, 5–52) contrasts his own list of meanings thus learned with those of Brown (1973) and Schlesinger (1974) (see Table 10.1). Each of Gibson's categories is based on optical information analyzed in EAVP, with the exception of negation (for which see below). Although these meanings are *derived* from ecological information, they are still *attached* meanings, as opposed to affordance meanings (Gibson, 1980). That is, they are not intrinsic to the words. 'Words, written or spoken, are like arbitrary signs . . . in having *reference to something else*. The meaning is attached and can therefore be detached. Affordances of things, however, have not been attached and cannot be *detached* (not added, associated, remembered)' (Gibson, 1975?, 5–52).

The second kind of language learning involves the consolidation of direct perceptions and attached meanings through predication. A mere list of labels can serve only the needs of categorizing and pointing (ostension). The fact that these labels can be *systematized* into stating facts, questions, commands, etc., removes the limits of mere association. This discovery of the predication of environmental facts was one of the greatest of human discoveries, celebrated by Chomsky and many others as implying a uniquely human cognitive skill. It is predication that allows the knowledge of the environment gained via perception to be made explicit and shared:

Perceiving helps talking, and talking fixes the gains of perceiving. It is true that

James Gibson's ecological approach 185

the adult who talks to a child can educate his attention to certain differences instead of others. It is true that when a child talks to himself he may enhance the tuning of his perception to certain differences rather than others. The range of possible discriminations is unlimited. Selection is inevitable. But this does not imply that the verbal fixing of information distorts the perception of the world. The curious observer can always observe more properties of the world than he can describe. (SCAPS, p. 282)

Table 10.1 'Structural meanings' in early utterances

Brown's Classification

I. OPERATIONS OF REFERENCE
Nominations: e.g. 'that book'
Notice: 'Hi children'
Recurrence: 'More meat, 'nother raisin'
Nonexistence: 'Allgone juice', 'no more dog'

II. RELATIONS
Attributive: Ad. + N (big train)
Possessive: N + M (Mommy lunch)
Locative: N + N (sweater chair)
Locative: V + N (go store)
Agent–action: N + V (Adam write)
Agent–object: N + N (Mommy sock)
Action–object: V + N (Ate meat)

Schlesinger's Classification of Relations

Agent–action: N + V
Action–object: V + N
Agent–object: N + N
Modifiers
Negation
Datives ('throw Daddy')
Ostension (Here, there, see)
Locatives

Gibson: Pick-up of structure or relations (meaning)

Appearance
Disappearance
   occlusion v. 'going out of existence' (allgone, no more)
Reappearance
   recurrence or return
Attribution
   of a property, e.g. size, colour
Possession
Location
Causality
Temporal relations
   before, after, yesterday, etc.
Negation?

Whereas cognitivists see language learning as the child's construction of a meaningful world out of stored 'rules' for the interpretation of not yet meaningful inputs, Gibson saw language as a process of stabilizing, making explicit and sharing a portion of the meaningful information we all use in our direct perception of the world. Direct perception is thus our basic mode of cognitive contact with the environment, and indirect modes of awareness extend and reorganize this cognitive contact, but do not alter it. As opposed to the theory of a mental construction of a meaningful environment, Gibson proposed a process of discovery: meanings and values are available to observers in their environment. There is always more meaning implicit in perception than has been made explicit by words, pictures, maps or other symbols. The key difficulty with any theory of meaning as based on discovery is to show that sufficient meaningful information is available to be discovered. Gibson began to do just this with his theory of ecological information for vision, but he also recognized specific problems in attempting to extend his account from perception into language. One fundamental problem is to explain the source of information for negation, as Gibson (1974, 5–42) pointed out:

> Information in the form of predication can be a *truth* or a *falsehood*. A person can misinform in the sense of *lie* (not to be confused with fiction). Information in the form of *stimulation* (a flowing *array* of energy) *cannot lie* – cannot be false in this sense (see below). The light and sound from the environment do not say untruths about the environment, only men do that. Information in the form of a *picture* can be *contradictory* or *equivocal* (e.g. goblet-face . . .) but cannot be *false* in the above sense. Pictures do not *predicate* or state an *equation* ([as in] logic or mathematics) and cannot lie (e.g., all swans are black; 2 + 2 = 5).

Negation requires a system of information in which statements are made about the way the world is, in which properties are ascribed to things. In direct perception, the use of information is not to make statements – the world does not communicate to us – but to facilitate awareness and action. In direct perception the difference between real and imaginary or illusory can be tested for, by means of tacit processes. Of these, Gibson singled out:

> the most decisive test for reality is whether you can discover new features and details by the act of scrutiny. Can you obtain new stimulation and extract new information from it. Is the information inexhaustible? Is there more to be seen? The imaginary scrutiny of an imaginary entity cannot pass this test (EAVP, p. 257)

Whereas a *display* itself is real (one can scrutinize the surface of a picture and discover ever-finer details) the *information captured* in a display is finite (as one approaches a photographic portrait ever closer, or blows

James Gibson's ecological approach

it up with a magnifier, eventually all one can see is the graininess of the surface; when one approaches a person ever closer, one can discover more and more details about their skin, etc.). The tests for reality of representations thus extend beyond the individual scrutiny of the displays and include social norms for the use of the displays, norms for the *sharing* of information. An individual alone can test for the difference between real and imaginary in direct perception, but in indirect perception, where the information has been sampled and selected,

> the difference between the factual and the fictional depends on the social system of communication and brings in complicated questions. Verbal descriptions can be true or false as predications. Visual depictions can be correct or incorrect in a wholly different way. A picture cannot be true in the way that a proposition is true, but it may or may not be true to life (EAVP, pp. 261–2)

Because indirect modes of cognition serve to help share knowledge, many of these modes of awareness have evolved into socially specific systems of representation. The most obvious example is language, each particular language being specific to a certain historico-cultural community (SCAPS, p. 91). But social conventions exist for a wide variety of representation systems: picturing, time measurement, numbering and mensuration, mapping, etc. When awareness becomes socialized, the learning process also becomes socialized, marking a significant difference between direct and indirect perception. 'I say', Gibson wrote in a short essay tucked into his copy of Arnheim's (1969) *Visual Thinking*,

> that perceiving does not involve the 'assimilating' of new impressions to prior knowledge as traditional theory maintains (Kant). It only involves an increasing sensitivity to available information. But learning in the sense of being told or being taught, learning by communication, depends on *learning the language*. You have to know the language before you can know the world mediated by language. But if you look and listen and feel for yourself you don't *need* any words, concepts, schemas, or preperceptions.

To understand fully indirect apprehension, one needs to go beyond the process of learning inherent in individuals' perceptual systems and investigate the process of socialized learning, or learning about the world via a community's representation systems.

From perceptual systems to representation systems

The primary act of animal cognition is direct perception of the objects, events and places around one, but among these objects there are other animals who are also perceiving the environment. When one observer perceives another, what is perceived is not merely an object in some place, but an observer who is situated at a point of view and aware of the surrounding habitat and what it contains (Gibson and Pick, 1963; Reed, 1988b). The perceived environment is an animate and social environment:

> The child begins, no doubt, by perceiving the affordances of things for her, for her own personal behavior. She walks and sits and grasps relative to her own legs and body and hands. But she must learn to perceive the affordances of things for other observers as well as for herself. An affordance is often valid for all the animals of a species, as when it is part of a niche. I have described the invariants that enable a child to perceive the same solid shape at different points of observation and that likewise enable two or more children to perceive the same shape at different points of observation. These are the invariants that enable two children to perceive the common affordance of the solid shape despite the different perspectives. . . . Only when each child perceives the values of things for others as well as for herself does she begin to be socialized. (EAVP, p. 141)

Two or more animals sharing their environment can share their awarenesses as well. Animals can gesture so as to communicate, either about their own state or about environmental states of affairs. A predator may move so as to appear non-threatening, and a harmless creature may attempt to look fierce. One member of a group may vocalize or gesture so as to warn another of danger; a parent may make comforting noises or gestures to its child; mates make alluring gestures and poses to one another. In all such cases, where the function of the act is truly communication, one animal is making a display (optical, acoustical, chemical, mechanical or otherwise) so as to provide information to another. This provided information is the basis of all mediated knowledge. Your agitated vocalization 'Fire!', may inform me directly of your nervous state, but it also may warn me *indirectly* of my imminent danger. My direct perception of your emotional state is based on an individual process of information pick-up. My indirect awareness of the danger is based on a group process of selecting and displaying information to be picked up, a social process of representing the environment. Gesturers must make movements that are not merely perceptible by observers in their group; their gestures must somehow effectively *indicate* environmental facts. There is considerable evidence that there is strong selection pressure for such movements to become differentiated into clearly categorizable patterns (Daanje, 1950; Darwin, 1872; Mayr, 1972) and some evidence that such communicative categories are learned, at least among primates.

At some point in human evolution – quite possibly as recently as 40,000 years ago, according to Lieberman (1984) – humans began to create vocalizations that indicated environmental facts independently of the state of the speaker or listener. Human vocalization thus evolved into *verbalization*, sounds that contained symbols which carry the meanings of things in the common environment of *all* individuals. These enable men to think of the same things, to have concepts in common, and to verify their concepts jointly. The cry 'wolf' has an entirely different function from either the cry of alarm at seeing a wolf or the howling of the wolf itself. (SCAPS, pp. 90–1)

The optical or acoustic information specifying a wolf, or even specifying a dangerous animal, is embodied in ecological laws of specificity (Turvey *et al.*, 1981). But the exact optical or acoustic properties of the word for wolf 'depend on a *linguistic community*, which is a unique invention of the human species' (SCAPS, p. 91). The laws of ecological information have emerged from general evolutionary processes operating throughout the ecosystem – there is selection pressure on most animals to adapt to this information (Reed, 1985). But the traditions of a community's symbolizations have emerged from particular evolutionary or historical lines, and the ability to use those symbols is correspondingly limited.

In contrast to perceptual systems, then, representation or symbol systems involve *cultural* and *historical* as well as individual psychological processes. In humans, the cultural and the individual ('natural') processes are thoroughly mixed, 'mediated apprehension gets *combined* and *fused* with direct apprehension' (Gibson, 1976?, 5–75). We use words to guide our perception and we use perception to guide our sharing of knowledge. 'Look at the —' is a fundamental fact of human childhood, and it conveniently illustrates how thoroughly intermingled is our tacit knowledge of the world and our explicit knowledge about it. The more explicit the knowledge is made, the more it requires a process of socialization or acculturation to be learned:

> The various affordances of surfaces, substances, layouts, and events get perceived in the course of development of the young animal by maturation and learning taken together, by *encountering* the surfaces in the habitat, without schooling. On the other hand, the referential meanings of marks on a surface get apprehended by children in ways that differ from the preceding, and also differ from one another. They are different for pictures, drawings, plots, signs, and letters of the alphabet. At one extreme, photographs are independent of cultural conventions. Drawings and diagrams are at least somewhat conventional. Alphabetic writing is wholly conventional. But however different the learning of pictorial reference may be from the learning of linguistic reference (and they *are* very different), they are even more radically different from the learning of what surfaces afford. Encountering these marks is not enough, and the more they vary with the culture to which the growing child belongs, the more this holds true. (Gibson, 1980, p. xiii)

Whereas picture perception requires a process of *perceptual* learning –

and in addition a socialized process in the case of diagrams, maps, X-rays and other pictorial material – language learning inherently involves more than a perceptual learning process, a process of explicit interpersonal teaching. Perceptual learning can (though it need not) occur 'out of school', but the scribe, accountant or writer must be taught.

The human self is *both* a natural individual and a member of a culture. In directly perceiving the environment there is always a co-perception of the self (EAVP, pp. 182 f.). In mediated awareness there is an awareness of the self as part of the symbolizing community, a group that shares knowledge, techniques and taboos. In addition to direct knowledge of ourselves through perception, we also know ourselves through sharing representation systems with others. The human discovery of writing combined the capacity for shared predication with permanence, so that the social group involved in sharing knowledge could be expanded: 'Social interaction became possible without a face-to-face meeting. Messages could be sent over great distances. Knowledge could be accumulated in storehouses. The young could be taught by the wisest teachers, living or dead. History and civilization began' (SCAPS, p. 242). As the child grows and develops in her use of language, numbers, pictures and other representations, she is more and more enabled to take advantage of explicit, socially gathered knowledge, as well as of socially developed customs. Socialization is not just a channelling of the self into pre-existing social norms, it is also an opportunity to develop and enlarge the self, through the use of explicit knowledge and socially developed techniques. The socialized child not only knows how to act properly, but also knows more about the world and may even make a contribution to civilization. Representation systems increase the possibilities for self-development almost limitlessly.

Human cognition does not differ from animal cognition because we can 'internalize' ideas, or visualize, or even plan actions. Evidence of these abilities is difficult to evaluate, but animals probably have at least some such 'internalization' capacities (Ingold, 1983). It is not the *fact* of visualizing, imagining or planning that sets us apart cognitively from other animals, but *with what* we can 'internalize' our thoughts. We can use words, alphabets, measuring systems, etc., all of which help both to consolidate and to extend our knowledge and planning abilities. For example, the existence of the alphabet helps us to remember or plan events according to a very complex (but conventional) order (Goody, 1983). The alphabet can be used to consolidate memories into retrievable lists of about two dozen categories, hierarchically organizing any pattern into a nested grouping of sub-categories, each of which can also be categorized similarly, and so on. Rhyming, metre, assonance-structure, numbering and other linguistic methods work in similar ways to fix and consolidate our cognitive skills. Human memory cannot have a 'fixed capacity' precisely because civilized humans have continued to invent and improve our 'tools of the intellect' (Goody, 1983, p. 84).

Indirect knowledge is 'culturally transmitted knowledge' that is embodied in 'toys, pictures and words' which enable adults to help make their children aware of the environment in addition to their own perception. These mediators

> transmit to the next generation the tricks of the human trade. The labors of the first perceivers are spared their descendants. The extracting and abstracting of invariants that specify the environment are made vastly easier with these aids to comprehension. But they are not themselves knowledge, as we are tempted to think. All they can do is to facilitate knowing by the young. (EAVP, p. 258)

Knowing is the process of using information. It may be guided by words, pictures, models or tools, but the mere possession of these aids in no way guarantees that knowing will occur. Further, perceiving and knowing are self-motivating; they are desirable in their own right. Children are inquisitive and will make the effort to know regardless of what information and representations are available. These efforts towards cognition are not cognition themselves, but visualizing, daydreaming, planning, and so on are excellent ways of developing and tuning the various processes of cognition. Whatever we know tacitly about the world is based on information. Whatever we know explicitly about the world is based on descriptions, depictions, indices, etc., that help to consolidate the available information and processes of using that information. The re-calling or re-presenting of mediators to our minds may *accompany* the effort to know, but it is not the process itself. The great ballad singers of the world, who can recite Homeric-length epics, do not recall the words but the story: they re-create the words in retelling the story each time (Lord, 1960; Wallace and Rubin, 1988). Goody (1977) claims that it is only literate cultures that consider memory to be analogous to the recalling of items from a text or list. The symbols of language are not mere reflections of our mental achievements, they themselves *are* achievements. 'In oral memory the many failures tend to get forgotten in favour of the occasional hits. It is the systematic recording (or even the possibility of so doing) rather than an attitude of mind' that allows for the kind of self-improvement possible only through critical thought. 'Writing renders contradiction and proof explicit – the ideas themselves are certainly present in oral societies – it not only makes possible a particular type of formalised proof (e.g. *modus tollens*), it also accumulates and records these proofs

192 Against Cognitivism

for future generations and for further operations' (Goody, 1983, pp. 91, 96).

Conclusion: the ecology of symbolizing

The tendency to separate symbols from their symbolizers, to hypothesize a mental realm that guides our action in the physical environment, is an ancient and pervasive fallacy in Western thought. However, once one gets stuck in this realm of the ideal, no one has ever figured how to get back out to the real world (Fodor, 1980). The problem of meaning and cognition cannot be solved by considering human behaviour physically, as responses to stimuli. But it is equally true that the hypothesis of an ideal realm of meaningful symbols does not further our understanding of cognition considered as knowledge of the environment. The correct question to be asked is how people come to know the meaningful environment, not how they respond to stimuli, nor how they become aware of inner ideas. No one has stated this better than Gibson (SCAPS, p. 26):

> In the study of anthropology and ecology, the 'natural' environment is often distinguished from the 'cultural' environment. As described here, there is no sharp division between them. Culture evolved out of natural opportunities. The cultural environment, however, is often divided into two parts, 'material' culture and 'non-material' culture. This is a seriously misleading distinction, for it seems to imply that language, tradition, art, music, law, and religion are immaterial, insubstantial, or intangible, whereas tools, shelters, clothing, vehicles and books are not. Symbols are taken to be profoundly different from things. But let us be clear about this. There have to be modes of stimulation, or ways of conveying information, for any individual to perceive anything, however abstract. He must be sensitive to [stimulus information] no matter how universal or fine-spun the thing he apprehends. No symbol exists except as it is realised in sound, projected light, mechanical contact, or the like. All knowledge rests on sensitivity.

The process of direct perception has been differentiated and refined in a vast number of ways by human societies and civilizations (see Marshack, 1989 for a review of the prehistoric evidence for cultural variations in symbolizing). A tentative list of some of these peculiarly human modes of indirect cognition is given in Table 10.2. Note that each mode of indirect awareness has its roots in ecological information. Note also that each mode is *standardized* and embodied in culturally developed *representation systems*. These cultural-historical entities are preserved, modified and used in communication and teaching. They are

Table 10.2 Human modes of indirect cognition

Ecological Information		Cultural Institutions
For objects and events	Picture-making	Drawing systems
For orientation	Body-scaled measure	Standardized measuring
For paths through the environment	Maps	Cartography
For speech	Pre-alphabetic scripts	Alphabetic writing
For affordances for oneself and others	Exchange of goods	Systems of exchange and storage of values (money)
For events	Time measurement	Clocks and calendars

Note: Each representation is a cultural institution that has evolved from a basis in direct perception, through a process of consolidation via indirect cognition. On the left is listed the information basis of the systems in direct perception. In the middle is the kind of variable, individualistic indirect perception that different cultures have developed out of the direct form. On the right are the culturally stabilized institutional forms of the consolidated cognition.

Sources of material for the study of culturally specific representation systems are as follows: Pictures (Hagen, 1986); measurement (Dilke, 1987; Kula, 1985); mapping (Crone, 1956; Hartley and Woodward, 1987); the alphabet (DeFrancis, 1988; Diringer, 1962; Gelb, 1963); exchange and money (Marx, 1973; Polanyi, 1957); time (Landes, 1983; Zerubavel, 1985).

One further system, the number system, is not illustrated. This is because it apparently evolved from a consolidation of several modes of indirect cognition, or even from all other modes (see Ifrah, 1985; Menninger, 1969).

the fundamental tools of cognition. It is about time that cognitive science broke out from the stale metaphors of computerese into the rich field of human history and comparative culture, so that we can begin to investigate these marvellous and diverse ways of apprehending reality, and of sharing our knowledge with others. True, cognition can and does proceed without materially produced writing, pictures, etc., but without these it is seriously curtailed, and education becomes exceedingly awkward and ritualized, instead of facile and available to individuals on their own. These aids to cognition, these tools of the intellect, have now become cultural institutions, in which all participate. The study of these institutions is the province of sociology, anthropology and history. But to understand the basic function of these modes of cognition is the job of psychologists (Reed, 1990, forthcoming). What enables these systems to be used for sharing awarenesses? How is the information coded, the tacit knowledge made explicit? What about historical and cultural variation and the cultural specificity of representation systems? These are important questions that cognitive psychology can ignore only at the peril of becoming irrelevant to human concerns.

Note

1. Citations from Gibson in the form of a date followed by a number are to unpublished material in the James J. Gibson archives, Accession no.14/23/ 1932 of the Department of Manuscripts and Archives, Olin Library, Cornell University. A question mark indicates that the date is uncertain. I acknowledge the assistance of the staff at the Manuscript Department with gratitude. For more information on this collection and Gibson's unpublished work, see Reed (1988a).

References

Arnheim, R. (1969), *Visual Thinking*, Berkeley, CA: University of California Press.
Bassett, M.F. and Warne, C.J. (1919), 'On lapse of verbal meaning with repetition', *American Journal of Psychology*, 30, 415–18.
Brown, R. (1973), *A first language: The early stage*, Cambridge, MA: Harvard University Press.
Chomsky, N. (1959), Review of B.F. Skinner's *Verbal Behaviour*, *Language*, 35, 26–58.
Chomsky, N. (1980), *Rules and Representations*, New York: Columbia University Press.
Crone, G.R. (1966), *Maps and their Makers: An introduction to the history of cartography* (3rd edn), London: Hutchinson.
Daanje, A. (1950), 'On the locomotory movements in birds and the intention movements derived from them', *Behaviour*, 3, 48–98.
Darwin, C. (1872), *The Expressions of the Emotions in Man and Animals*, London: John Murray.
DeFrancis, D. (1988), *Visible Speech*, Honolulu: University of Hawaii Press.
De Villiers, J. and De Villiers, P.A. (1978) *Language Acquisition*, Cambridge MA: Harvard University Press.
Dilke, O.A.W. (1987), *Mathematics and measurement in the Ancient World*, Berkeley and Los Angeles, CA: University of California Press.
Diringer, D. (1962), *Writing*, London: Thames & Hudson.
Don, V.J. and Weld, H.P. (1924), 'Lapse of meaning with visual fixation', *American Journal of Psychology*, 35, 446–50.
Fodor, J.A. (1975), *The Language of Thought*, New York: Crowell.
Fodor, J.A. (1980), 'Methodological solipsism considered as a research strategy in cognitive psychology', *Behavioral and Brain Sciences*, 3, 63–109.
Fodor, J.A. (1985), Precis of *The Modularity of Mind*, *Behavioral and Brain Sciences*, 8, 1–5.
Gallistel, C.R. (1980), *The Organization of Action*, Hillsdale, NJ: Erlbaum.
Gelb, I.J. (1963), *The Study of Writing*, Chicago: University of Chicago Press.
Gibson, E.J. (1953), 'Improvement in perceptual judgements as a function of controlled practice or training', *Psychological Bulletin*, 50, 401–31.
Gibson, E.J. (1969), *Principles of Perceptual Learning and Development*, New York: Appleton-Century-Crofts.
Gibson, E.J. (1982), 'The concept of affordances in development: The renascence of functionalism', in W.A. Collins (ed.), *The Concept of Development*, Hillsdale, NJ: Erlbaum.
Gibson, E.J. (1984), 'Perceptual development from the ecological approach',

in M. Lamb, A. Brown and B. Rogoff (eds), *Advances in Developmental Psychology*, vol. 3, Hillsdale, NJ: Erlbaum.
Gibson, E.J. (1988), 'Exploratory behaviour in the development of perceiving, acting and the acquiring of knowledge', *Annual Review of Psychology*, **39**, 1–41.
Gibson, E.J., Owsley, C.J. and Johnston, J. (1978), 'Perception of invariants by 5-month-old infants: Differentiation of two types of motion', *Developmental Psychology*, **14**, 407–15.
Gibson, J.J. (1933), 'Adaptation, after-effect and contrast in the perception of curved lines', *Journal of Experimental Psychology*, **16**, 1–31.
Gibson, J.J. (1937) 'Adaptation with negative after-effect', *Psychological Review*, **44**, 222–44.
Gibson, J.J. (1939), 'The Aryan myth', *Journal of Educational Sociology*, **13**, 164–71.
Gibson, J.J. (1950), *The Perception of the Visual World*, Boston, MA: Houghton-Mifflin.
Gibson, J.J. (1958), 'The registering of objective facts: An interpretation of Woodworth's theory of perceiving', in G. Seward and J. Seward (eds), *Current Psychological Issues: Essays in honour of Robert S. Woodworth*, New York: Holt, Rinehart & Winston.
Gibson, J.J. (1966), *The Senses Considered as Perceptual Systems*, Boston, MA: Houghton Mifflin.
Gibson, J.J. (1979), *The Ecological Approach to Visual Perception*, Boston, MA: Houghton Mifflin.
Gibson, J.J. (1980), 'Foreword. A prefatory essay on the perception of surfaces versus the perception of markings on a surface', in M.A. Hagen (ed.), *The Perception of Pictures*, vol. 1, New York: Academic Press.
Gibson, J.J. (1982), *Reasons for Realism: Selected essays of James J. Gibson*, (eds) E. Reed and R. Jones, Hillsdale, NJ: Erlbaum.
Gibson, J.J. and Pick, A.D. (1963), 'Perception of another person's looking behavior', *American Journal of Psychology*, **76**, 386–94.
Gibson, J.J., Smith, O.W., Steinshneider, A. and Johnson, C.W. (1958), 'The relative accuracy of visual perception of motion during fixation and pursuit', *American Journal of Psychology*, **70**, 64–8.
Goody, J. (1977), *The Domestication of the Savage Mind*, Cambridge: Cambridge University Press.
Goody, J. (1983), 'Literacy and achievement in the ancient world', in F. Coulmas and K. Ehrlich (eds), *Writing in Focus* New York: Mouton.
Hagen, M.A. (1986), *Varieties of Realism: Geometries of representational art*, Cambridge: Cambridge University Press.
Hartley, J.B. and Woodward, D. (eds) (1987), *History of Cartography*, vol. 1, Chicago: University of Chicago Press.
Heil, J. (1979), 'The gap in the ecological approach', *Journal for the Theory of Social Behaviour*, **9**, 265–96.
Holt, E.B. (1915), *The Freudian Wish and its Place in Ethics*, New York: Holt.
Ifrah, G. (1985), *From One to Zero: A history of numbers*, New York: Viking.
Ingold, T. (1983), 'The architect and the bee: Reflections on the work of animals and men', *Man* (N.S.), **18**, 1–20.
Johnson-Laird, P.N. (1983), *Mental Models*, Cambridge: Cambridge University Press.
Kula, W. (1985), *Measures and Men*, Princeton, NJ: Princeton University Press.

Landes, D.S. (1983), *Revolution in Time: Clocks and the making of the modern world*, Cambridge, MA: Harvard University Press (paperback edn 1985).
Lieberman, P. (1984), *The Biology and Evolution of Language*, Cambridge, MA: Harvard University Press.
Lord, A.B. (1960), *The Singers of Tales*, Cambridge, MA: Harvard University Press.
Luria, A.R. (1973), *Working Brain*, New York: Basic Books.
Luria, A.R. (1978), 'The development of writing', in M. Cole (ed.), *The Selected Writings of A.R. Luria*, New York: M.E. Sharpe; first published 1929.
Marr, D. (1982), *Vision: A computational investigation into the human representation and processing of visual information*, San Francisco: W.H. Freeman.
Marshack, A. (1989), 'Evolution of the human capacity: The symbolic evidence', *Yearbook of Physical Anthropology*, 32, 1–34.
Marx, K. (1973) *Grundrisse*, Harmondsworth: Penguin.
Mayr, E. (1972), *Population, Species and Evolution*, Cambridge, MA: Harvard University Press.
Menninger, K. (1969), *Number Words and Number Symbols: A cultural history of numbers*, Cambridge, MA: MIT.
Michaels, C.F. and Carello, C. (1981), *Direct Perception*, Englewood Cliffs, NJ: Prentice-Hall.
Miller, G.A., Galanter, E. and Pribram, K. (1960), *Plans and the Structure of Behavior*, New York: Holt, Rinehart & Winston.
Neisser, U. (1967), *Cognitive Psychology*, New York: Appleton-Century-Crofts.
Neisser, U. (1976), *Cognition and Reality*, San Francisco: W.H. Freeman.
Pinker, S. (ed.) (1985), *Visual Cognition*, Cambridge: MA: MIT.
Polanyi, K. (1967), *The Great Transformation*, Boston, MA: Beacon Press.
Pylyshyn, Z.W. (1984), *Computation and Cognition*, Cambridge, MA: MIT.
Reed, E.S. (1980), 'Information pickup is the activity of perceiving', *Behavioral and Brain Sciences*, 3, 397–8.
Reed, E.S. (1985), 'An ecological approach to the evolution of behavior', in T.D. Johnston and A.T. Pietrewitcz (eds), *Issues in the Ecological Study of Learning*, Hillsdale, NJ: Erlbaum.
Reed, E.S. (1986a), 'James J. Gibson's revolution in perceptual psychology: A case study of the transformation of scientific ideas', *Studies in the History and Philosophy of Science*, 17, 65–98.
Reed, E.S. (1986b), Review of Howard Gardner, *The Mind's New Science*, *Isis*, 77, 530–2.
Reed, E.S. (1988a), *James J. Gibson and the Psychology of Perception*, New Haven, CT: Yale University Press.
Reed, E.S. (1988b), 'The affordances of the animate environment: Social science from an ecological point of view', in T. Ingold (ed.), *What is an Animal?*, London: Unwin & Hyman.
Reed, E.S. (1989a), Theory, concept and experiment in the history of psychology: An old tradition behind a "young" science', *History of the Human Sciences*, 2, 333–56.
Reed, E.S. (1989b), 'The neural regulation of adaptive behavior: An essay on Gerald Edelman's *Neural Darwinism*', *Ecological Psychology*, 1, 97–117.
Reed, E.S. (1990), 'The intention to use a specific affordance: A framework for psychology', in R. Wozniak and K. Fischer (eds), *Cognitive Development in Specific Environments*, Hillsdale, NJ: Erlbaum.

Reed, E.S. (1991), 'Cognition as the cooperative appropriation of affordances', *Ecological Psychology*, **3**, 135–58.
Reed, E.S. and Jones, R.K. (1981), 'Is perception blind? A reply to Heil', *Journal for the Theory of Social Behaviour*, **11**, 87–91.
Requin, J., Semjen, A. and Bonnet, M. (1984), 'Bernstein's purposeful brain', in H.T.A. Whiting (ed.), *Human Motor Actions: Bernstein reassessed*, North-Holland: Elsevier.
Schlesinger, I.M. (1974), 'Relational concepts underlying language', in R.L. Schiefelbusche and L.L. Lloyd (eds), *Language Perspectives: Acquisition, retardation and intervention*, Baltimore, MD: University Park Press.
Schmandt-Besserat, D. (1980), 'The envelopes that bear the first writing', *Technology and Culture*, **21**, 357–85.
Severance, E. and Washburn, M.F. (1907), 'The loss of associative power in words after long fixation', *American Journal of Psychology*, **18**, 182–6.
Skinner, B.F. (1957), *Verbal Behavior*, New York: Appleton-Century-Crofts.
Turvey, M.T., Shaw, R.E., Reed, E.S. and Mace, W.M. (1981), 'Ecological laws of perceiving and acting: A reply to Fodor and Pylyshyn', *Cognition*, **9**, 237–304.
Ullman, S. (1980), 'Against direct perception', *The Behavioral and Brain Sciences*, **3**, 373–415.
Vygotsky, L.S. (1978), *Mind in Society: The development of the higher psychological processes*, M. Cole, V. John-Steiner, S. Scribner and E. Souberman (eds), Cambridge, MA: Harvard University Press.
Wallace, W. and Rubin, D. (1988), 'Memory of a ballad singer', in M. Gruneberg, P. Morris and R. Sykes (eds), *Practical Aspects of Memory: Current research and issues*, New York: Wiley.
Woodworth, R.S. (1947), 'Reinforcement of perception', *American Journal of Psychology*, **60**, 119–24.
Zerubavel, E. (1985), *Hidden Rhythms: Schedules and calendars in social life*, Berkeley, CA: University of California Press.

11
Ecological realism and the fallacy of 'objectification'*

William Noble

Editors' introduction

An important criticism of cognitive psychology is that it treats historically contingent practices as though they were 'natural' and universal. Yet the critics themselves – in their attempts to define more fundamental forms of relation between organisms and environments *from which* derivative, social forms might develop – can appear to be involved in their own kind of biological reductionism.

As Reed has explained in Chapter 10, Gibson's theory of direct perception should be regarded as a preliminary to a sociohistorical account of human cognition. The following chapter is based on an important discussion of Gibson's work first published by William Noble in 1981. Noble argues that there are two problems within Gibson's own account of perception that will need to be resolved before the wider project could be realized. The first problem is Gibson's vacillation between a 'static' realism that treats the environment as 'given', and a pragmatist account of the organism and environment as interdependent (see also Katz, 1987). The second, related problem is Gibson's failure to explore the fundamental difference that language makes to the way humans relate to their world.

References

Katz, S. (1987), 'Is Gibson a relativist?' in Costall, A.P. and Still, A.W. (eds), *Cognitive Psychology in Question*, Hemel Hempstead: Harvester Wheatsheaf.

* * *

* I am indebted to Bronwyn Davies, whose reading of a draft of the original version of this chapter helped remove some of its more distressing ambiguities and opacities. I also thank the reviewers of the original paper, and Alan Costall in his review of the present version; his comments obliged me to develop certain arguments more distinctly. This chapter is a revised and expanded version of a paper which appeared in *Journal for the Theory of Social Behaviour*, 1981.

Prefatory remarks

The main aims of this chapter are (1) to specify the nature of the problem of 'objectification' in Gibson's ecological theory of perception, and (2) to introduce pragmatist and symbolic-interactionist perspectives deriving from the work of George Herbert Mead as they bear upon the problem of 'objectification' and on the related issue of the nature of human perceptual awareness. I see a symbolic-interactionist or similar social-interactionist perspective as the only sort to provide any hope of supplying the means to account for the self-consciousness of human perceiving, without threat of a return to mind–body dualism.

The self-consciousness of human perceiving is not dealt with in ecological theory, but it needs to be, because the theory seeks to cover the realities of perceiving exhaustively. Human activity is 'minded', but the conceptual tools of traditional psychology can make nothing of what it means for action to have this 'minded' (self-conscious) character, outside of a Cartesian construction of 'mind' (as immaterial entity). The ecological approach seeks to avoid this species of 'mentalism', but in so doing ducks the issue of self-consciousness. A symbolic-interactionist position is congenial to the anti-mentalist commitment of ecological theory, for it holds that knowledge deriving from the social life of language-using agents affords the 'mindedness' of human agency.

Thus, at the heart of an explanation of the reality of human perceiving as self-conscious is language as a fact of human life; it is through language used to represent reality in symbolic form that humans become aware *that* they perceive and *of what* they perceive (Noble, 1987). There is reference in passing to Mead's form of the argument towards the end of the present chapter.

Language is identified as the key to an understanding of human awareness. The particular aspect of the use of language so identified is its referential function – its use by people in communicative settings, by means of arbitrary symbols with conventional meanings, to represent states of affairs, to engage in acts of description, to provide accounts of what is afoot. Typical human communicatve settings are, initially, closely interpersonal. As can be observed in the cognitive development of young children (e.g. Lock, 1980), it is through the guided use of symbols referentially that the child structures its perceptions, becomes increasingly aware of the fact of a perceptible world and becomes aware of its perception of that world. Further observations on language and perceiving are made in an 'afterword' to the present chapter.

Introduction

Gibson's theory of perception has been called 'radical' (Neisser, 1976) and even 'revolutionary' (Reed and Jones, 1979) in its challenges – on the one hand to the mind–body dualism (or 'mentalism') that continues as a snare for contemporary cognitive psychology; and on the other to the mechanistic environmentalist doctrines of behaviourism.[1] These challenges are forceful, and the theory is unorthodox. But I contend that the theory is not radical enough, and in his vestigial adherence to certain customs of traditional psychological outlook Gibson has retained troublesome elements in his account of perception.

I assume a familiarity on the reader's part with Gibson's theory (e.g. 1950, 1966, 1979), or at least with reliable synopses of it now appearing in secondary literature (e.g. Ben-Zeev, 1981; Costall, 1981; Mace, 1985; Michaels and Carello, 1981, Chs 1 and 2). But I will begin by giving an account of those features of Gibsonian theorizing that seem to me most powerful, and will then argue that there are two problems in the theory that need attention. I will further argue that the means for release from these problems lie in aspects of the pragmatist theoretical perspective, particularly in the work of Mead, but heralded in the earlier work of Dewey.

The value of adverting to pragmatism lies in the concordance of orientation between that perspective and Gibson's. To illustrate this I will preface introduction of Mead's analyses by showing the parallel between Gibson's and Dewey's theoretical outlooks. I believe Mead would have delighted in Gibson's final work (1979), because of the complementary solutions it provides to aspects of the puzzles he confronted (1938).

Gibson (1967a) once described his early career as influenced in part by 'a taste for pragmatism', but he was impatient with philosophy, impressed by behaviourism, and once he came under the influence of Koffka his theoretical effort (while never assimilating Gestaltist views of mind) turned towards the question of structure, in Gibson's case to the structure of the 'stimulus'. That is why it is accurate to say that Gibson neglected (rather than overlooked) the pragmatist perspective. In the last analysis I think it would be best to say that Gibson's 'pragmatic taste' is *tacit* (to invoke Polanyi's [1967] admirable term). It is not *reflexive*. For sure, he is *pragmatic* (and not idealistic). He is *for* the real world of experience, but he is not 'a pragmatist' in his theorizing. He attends *from* a pragmatic outlook *to* a naively realistic theory of the perceived world. He does not attend *to* the very pragmatist perspective that can account for one's interactions with the world, and for one's casual or deliberate theorizings about those interactions.

A brief account of Gibson's theory

To paraphrase an image I have used with students (cleaned up for this occasion): A critic of Gibson, like Gregory (1974), may be right to

202 Against Cognitivism

dismiss his ecological account of perception because it seemingly fails to address the contrivances of the laboratory illusionist. But vital components of the same critic's *actions* (e.g. in looking around to find pen and ink with which to record such negatives) are best accounted for by the to-be-dismissed theory. In other words, while much contemporary theorizing in perception can be bent to the issue of, say, why the moon looks bigger straight ahead than straight up, most such theory has no success in accounting for how we can get off our chairs and through the door without mishap.

From the earliest formulations (Gibson and Crooks, 1938), through the war years (Gibson, 1947) and beyond (Gibson, 1950, 1966), and culminating in his final work (1979), Gibson has consistently centred his attention on aspects of the world of lived experience, and attempted to derive a description of that world, as experienced, which will allow an account of how we perceive what we do. In his final work I believe he has cracked open many problems of perception, and I take this work as definitive.

To begin with, a description of the world for an experiencing organism is constrained by the sort of *organism* for which the world is an *environment*:

[T]he words *animal* and *environment* make an inseparable pair. Each term implies the other. No animal could exist without an environment surrounding it. Equally, an environment implies an animal (or at least an organism) to be surrounded. [M]illions of years ago . . . [t]he earth was a physical reality . . . [i]t was a potential environment, prerequisite to the evolution of life on this planet. We might agree to call it a world, but it was not an environment. (Gibson, 1979, p. 8)[2]

What constitutes environment thus varies according to the kind of organism (be it fish, mammal or bird) whose world we set ourselves to describe. Limiting our account to organisms that experience the environment in virtue of systems sensitive to patterns of energy, three fundamental properties can be delineated: medium, substance and surface. A relatively homogeneous medium like air or water allows the propagation of electromagnetic, mechanical and chemical energy in ways governed by the medium's own physical and chemical composition. A substance like 'the ground' is relatively heterogeneous and differentially affects the propagation of energy – reflecting and absorbing it according to its physical and chemical properties and (allied with these) the layout of its surface. Bringing attention to bear on just one form of energy – electromagnetic – we can recognize that all substantial elements in a medium, by definition, have surfaces (though some substances, like smoke or clouds, are nascent and evanescent continually). Electromagnetic energy is affected peculiarly by the layout of the surface of a substance, and by its composition. To get to specifics – what humans designate as 'a large round grey rock' affects the propagation and reflection of electromagnetic energy differently from 'a small square red brick'.

A proportion of reflected electromagnetic energy from the surfaces of the world (and the particles of an aerial medium) becomes describable as *ambient light* when it 'environs' – when it fills a medium that is part of the habitable world of an organism sensitive to the patterning (or optical structure) of such reflected energy. 'Visual perception' is the pick-up of information specifying environmental features, within a continuous flowing sample of the optical structure, by organisms which move across, around and under the surfaces of substances of their environments. The character of the sample is given by the *modus vivendi* and *modus operandi* of the organism,[3] and by the tuning properties of its nervous system. But that it is a flowing (or oscillating, or at any rate dynamic) sample is evident when one considers that biological systems with exteroceptive sensitivity are typically motionless only when asleep (one would also except those occasions when organisms with the capacity to 'freeze' do so to avoid detection). All organisms are fairly constantly on the move in search of food, shelter or inter-organism contact.

By a series of fairly complex yet elegant analyses and demonstrations it is possible to show that the physical features and properties of substances are completely specified within the invariant patterns of energetic structural modulation that are the unavoidable accompaniments of movement through the environment. And, most critically, for a human observer (but not exclusively), part of the structure of the array of ambient light specifies that observer *per se*. The limits of that array are bounded in humans by the observer's body and head (our eyes are not out in front of us); hence at all times of human visual activity the observing self is contained in the field of view: 'self-perception and environment perception go together' (Gibson, 1979, p. 116). The co-perception of environment and self allows the pick-up of information simultaneously about one's destination (and its imminence), and about oneself in imminent contact with it. This may be why, though we shrink back to some extent in a movie theatre when a film depicting imminent contact is run, we none the less remain in our seats, because the limit of the field of view is not ourselves but the edge of the screen. A flight simulator, however, in completely filling the field of view, can make us airsick.

Again, for human and anthropoid observers, a vital component of the field of view is the organism's own hands and arms that extend from close to the lateral limits of the field and can be monitored and guided in their various complex actions with respect to the surfaces of substances in the environment. That sort of description of our own appendages feels too remote, and of course it is incomplete because we are also sensitive to the correlated mechanical energy generated by our own bodily and haptic activity. But the pup or kitten which chases its own tail may need to effect a few 'self-inflicted' wounds before the invariance of this particular visual and kinaesthetic event is discovered. And the experience of a 'dead' arm, during paralysis or anaesthesia, is enough to make you perceive your own body parts as mere objects stuck upon you like the old sailor's albatross. There is nothing *necessarily* integral about the experienced body. For the most part it is experienced as a unified system because of the maintenance of sensitivity to invariant energy patterns.

As Polanyi (1967) observes, perceiving is *tacit*; we attend *from* our bodies to the environment (or, in the case of self-exploration, *from* our heads and/or hands *to* the remainder of our bodies). Such a construct can be recruited, I believe, to settle a problem that Hamlyn (1977) raises in respect of Gibsonian theory. Hamlyn points to the distinctive, sensed quality of 'visualness' as contrasted with the quality of 'tangibleness', and asserts that these qualities remain unaccounted for in Gibsonian theory. The experiences that Hamlyn notes, about 'visualness' and 'tangibleness', can be considered as resulting from an unusual activity (for most people – not, however, for philosophers or theorists of perception): contemplation of one's sensory surfaces themselves. Part of our self-conscious knowledge is that we possess distinguishable bodily features differentially sensitive to the environment. To say that there is some 'visual quality' about visual perception that is distinguishable from the 'tangible quality' of touch is to draw attention to what we normally perceive *from*. When adopting a self-conscious attitude we can become aware of the fact that we can attend to the world with our hands separately from our eyes.[4] In actual perceiving this distinction is non-operative except in circumstances where we are prevented from simultaneously attending to the world from our 'head-and-hands'. Tasks like putting a phonograph record (disc) on a turntable, or inserting a light bulb, entail the momentary disconnection of visual and haptic modes of attention; typically, attention *from* these modes is correlated and the flow of information available for both can be conceptualized as a 'higher order' of invariance.

Two problems

The objectification of the world and the lodging of the 'affordances' (utilities) of objects in that objectivated world are two troublesome features of Gibson's ecological theory. These problems exist, respectively, because Gibson's treatment of the 'act' is less than adequate; and because he overlooks important functions of language (and hence of the 'social' dimension) in everyday perception.

Regarding the problem of objectification: the success in accounting for the phenomena of perceptual experience by detailed analysis of the structure of energy specifying various features of surfaces has led this theorist to advance the cause of 'realism' (Gibson, 1967b). In a paper devoted to analyzing this position of Gibson's, Henle (1974) asks how it comes about that some components rather than others in the structure of the optic array (the nested set of solid visual angles) get aggregated as they do. And the only sort of answer she can obtain from Gibson's work is to do with the objective structure of the world (Gibson, consistent with his flight from mentalism, is wary of 'organizing principles' of the sort advocated by Gestalt theorists): 'The array of contrasts and visual solid angles is discontinuous, since it is defined by abrupt steps of intensity or borders that constitute "forms"' (Gibson, 1972, p. 1, quoted in Henle, 1974, p. 46). Now, Gibson's use of quotation marks round the word 'forms' is no doubt intended to signal his dissatisfaction with that term as failing to capture the ecological facts of the matter (see Gibson, 1951, 1979, p. 247; Gibson and Gibson, 1957).

It is my contention, however, that a larger problem lies behind a construct like 'form' (or 'formless invariant'). In the passage quoted above, and in the opening section of Chapter 3 of the 1979 work (pp. 33–6), we witness Gibson attributing perceived structure directly and non-inferentially (i.e. naively) to the structure of the world. But the very use of quotation marks round the word 'forms' reminds us of Gibson's insistence on the mobility and activity of perceivers. There are no canonical 'forms' of things, though there may be typical appearances due to the routinizing of places and paths of observation relative to them.[5] This example serves as a reminder that the concept of *environment* is a relational one, the word 'world' being held as non-relational, i.e. independent of any organism (see earlier quote). 'Forms' or 'formless invariants' are essentially environmental; they entail particular kinds of organisms living and operating in particular kinds of ways. I develop this point later through the writing of Mead.

Let us be clear that Gibson recognizes – but only in general terms – this organismic side to the equation at the biological-behavioural level;

The environment of any animal (and of all animals) contains substances, surfaces and their layout, enclosures, objects, places, events, and the other animals. This description is very general; it holds true for insects, birds, mammals, and men. Let us now attempt a more particular description, selecting those surfaces, layouts, objects, and events that are of special concern to animals that behave more or less as we do. The total environment is too vast for description even by the ecologist, and we should select those features of it that are perceptible by animals like ourselves. (Gibson, 1979, p. 36)

In my view Gibson does not represent the relational character of 'environment' adequately. He acknowledges it, then inclines to abandon it in favour of the 'naive realist' position that allows objects, 'forms', the surface of support, and other (essentially *environmental*) features to inhere independently in 'the world'. In the quote above, the term 'environment' is taken in a general way – to apply logically to all animals. But a closer adherence to the relational character of the term would immediately force the point that the very concept is as perceived and talked about from a human observer's viewpoint.

Gibson's whole theoretical programme has derived much of its power from insistence on the organism as an active investigator of its environment, and his account of co-perception of organism and environment brings him to the brink of a thoroughgoing 'objective relativism' (to borrow from Mead). But his distaste for idealism makes him overlook the pragmatic nature of the act (as defined by Mead) in the production of an organism's perceptual world. He can see that organismic activity is vital in any valid account of perceptual experience, but he cannot see that the act itself – what the organism is doing, is on its way to doing,[6] can do and cannot – is, as I will show through Mead's analysis, bound up in the generation of its perceptually experienced world.

In Gibson's view, limitations in information extraction, *inter alia*, are to do with limitations in neural structure – but an affordance is an affordance is an affordance.

I speculate that Gibson's neglect of the pragmatist tradition (explicable by the fact that his background is thoroughly psychological) has meant a lack of access to non-mentalistic concepts of 'the organism's role' in the creation of its experience. Notions such as 'purposeful action', for a psychologist, belong to 'motivation'; and for Gibson, I suspect, that would be classed as part of the baggage of mentalism and put to one side.[7]

The foregoing is a statement of the problem of objectification in Gibsonian theory. The lodging of affordances wholly within that objectivated structure is the second problem; and of course it flows from the first. As regards the objectification issue I will endeavour presently to point to a more adequate representation of the organism–environment relation, but I prefer to leave the issue there, to take up the question of affordance, and return to a fresh look at both after giving an account of pragmatist thinking as it bears upon perceiving.

Ecological realism   207

The problem of affordance is best pointed up by reference to what I have dubbed 'the muddle of the mailbox' (Gibsonians will recognize that style of phrasing). At the biological-behavioural level of 'activity' it is quite feasible to argue for the direct availability of the affordances of surfaces (for sitting on, crawling under, picking up, and so forth) in the structure of the ambient array. The principle of co-perception of environment and organism can readily be invoked to account for one's detection of utility directly. In discussion of an object like a mailbox (postbox), Gibson contrasts the Gestaltist position with his own by stating:

> For Koffka it was the *phenomenal* postbox that invited letter-mailing, not the physical postbox. But this duality is pernicious. I prefer to say that the real postbox (the *only* one) affords letter-mailing to a letter-writing human in a community with a postal system. This fact is perceived when the postbox is identified as such, and it is apprehended whether the postbox is in sight or out of sight. To feel a special attraction to it when one has a letter to mail is not surprising, but the main fact is that it is perceived as part of the environment – as an item of the neighbourhood in which we live. Everyone above the age of six knows what it is for and where the nearest one is. The perception of its affordance should therefore not be confused with the temporary special attraction it may have. (Gibson, 1979, p. 139)

This account circumvents the Gestalist notion of 'demand character' by making that an occasional feature of this aspect of the landscape (i.e. the 'demand character' of a mailbox has saliency only when one actually wants to mail a letter). An object's 'affordance', then, remains as a persistent quality given in (offered in) the structure of the optic array.

Now, if we summon up a cognitivist, a vulgar form of their opposition to this seemingly outlandish claim would probably be to say: there is nothing in the structure of the array, when an object labelled 'mailbox' comes into awareness, to inform one about the complex social organization known as 'the postal system'. On the contrary, that information is in one's head, and the meaning of the mailbox is 'completed' only when I (the cognitivist), as one who knows about its function, am brought into the picture. If you stood someone quite foreign to Western-style culture alongside me and the pair of us gazed at this mailbox object, I'll grant you (being a generous cognitivist) the argument that its affordance of 'containment-of-small-objects' might be directly accessible to each of us in the structure of the optic array, but that it is a *mailbox* is an item of cultural knowledge that only I possess, and has nothing to do with the structure of light. On the contrary, it is to do with the structure (or the 'content') of my brain (or 'memory').

Gibson, in reply, would simply emphasize that he has not omitted to refer to the background conditions for perceiving the affordance (the postbox 'affords letter-mailing to a letter-writing human in a community with a postal system'). But I (the present writer) don't think that gets us out of trouble. What I *can* say (and Gibson might) to the vulgar cognitivist is that the affordance of the object as a special kind of container is directly given in the structure of the array because we (Gibson, the cognitivist, and I), being aware members of our culture, co-perceive ourselves in relation to the mailbox, and we are components of the ambient array just as the mailbox is. The completion of the meaning of the mailbox indeed entails someone with a particular awareness, but such a one is part of the array – hence the affordance of mailing is all there in the array. The 'non-Westerner' has access to only the 'containership' affordance of the box; a process of further exploration is required in order that such a person comes to discriminate 'containership' in general from the special form of containership that this item affords.

But now what happens when there is a mail strike and one doesn't know about it? There is nothing in the structure of ambient light to tell one about the temporary dissolution of the affordance of mailing. Gibson would duck under this by saying that things can be misperceived and sometimes we have to learn (or relearn) what things really are. I (the writer; we have now dismissed the cognitivist) will accept this, but would contend that we have reached a major difficulty. We are no longer dealing with the world of directly accessible affordances because we are dealing with objects (like mailboxes) that are socially sustained. We have now to lay down *prerequisites* for the perceiving of affordances, and these prerequisites have to do with the co-operative linguistic community that symbolically invests and sustains objects and their affordances. The mailbox's affordance as a container is perhaps given in the structure of the array, but social organization and the 'co-operation-at-a-distance' that language permits is entailed in the investment of this container as a special device that has one special function *and no other*. When we come to 'social' objects, we leave the realm of the purely biological-behavioural and enter the world of cultural rules and roles. In the human community there just is a vast proportion of perceptual experience that is sustained by cultural rule-given prerequisites. It is naive – not to say one-eyed – for Gibson to pass lightly from the natural environment to the socially sustained environment yet go on describing the objects of the latter as no different to the objects of the former, thereby failing to see the enlarging fact that the relationship between persons and objects is now complexly mediated by a normative structure that is not connected with the visible affordances of objects *per se*.[8]

Now there is an obvious sense in which language mediates perception, and of this sense Gibson is quite aware. When he refers in the quote about the mailbox, to everyone above the age of six *knowing* what it is for, he is recruiting, implicitly, knowledge based on instruction. Language here is being used in its 'informative' mode, and as such it substitutes for direct discovery of an object's affordance. Elsewhere Gibson discusses this feature of language (1966, p. 235, pp. 280–2; 1979, pp. 260–1).[9]

But it is the *normative* quality of such perceptions that is bound in with language, and with the meanings of objects. To perceive the mailbox's affordance 'correctly' is to assent to a set of social rules about uses and abuses of a mailbox. We are doing more, when we map into the meanings of social objects, than successfully identifying their affordances; we are *going along with* culturally sanctioned ways of perceiving such objects. If I, as an urban guerrilla, perceive the mailbox as a symbol of the power of an oppressive bureaucracy that regulates my ways of making contact with the world (prohibiting the use of the mailbox as a receptacle for a bomb – and even certain kinds of literature), then I am in no wise assenting to its meaning for the culture, and hence the 'correct' perception of it as a cultural object. The perception of all socially (linguistically) sustained objects has this normative character. In perceiving a (culturally valued) thing as an 'X' I automatically exclude perceptions of it as a 'Y' or a 'Z'. This is the underlying thrust of any theory of linguistic relativity. The name of a thing, in and of itself, does not *cause* it to be perceived in one way or another. Rather, in mapping into socially sustained meanings we act cooperatively in civil life and perceive the culture's objects in culturally defined ways.

Gibson 'goes along' with this tacit dimension of perception, in the real sense that he takes it for granted. He is, then, for 'law and order' in the way cultural objects are used, hence perceived. (So am I, more or less, but that's not the point. The point is *he* doesn't show any signs of realizing that fact.) This is an example of our 'pragmatic' theorist failing to reflect on the pragmatistics of his own theorizing. The failure continues in Reed's (1987) attempt to neutralize the foregoing argument about affordances being relational by saying that it reduces affordance to a species of Lewinian 'valence', hence bound in with individuals' needs, rather than being a public property of the object, as with an affordance. Reed cites Gibson as saying (1979, p. 139), 'The object offers what it does because it is what it is.' This misses my point in two ways: first, the relational character of affordances occurs at the level of the organism's capacities. An object can display the affordance of, for example, 'usability as a rake' only in virtue of there being organisms with the capacity to so use it. This relation is quite independent of any issue of momentary need or here-and-now use. Secondly, the assertion that an object offers what it does because of what it 'is' also ignores the fact that what an object *is*, for an encultured species, depends on how it is socially defined.

The foregoing is a statement of two problems that arguably obtain in Gibson's ecological theory. It is my contention that these problems can be overcome by incorporation of understandings that were developed within the pragmatist approach to human conduct.

Pragmatism and perception

C.S. Peirce is generally acknowledged as having laid the foundation of pragmatism (Scheffler, 1974), but the theorists I wish to rely upon are Dewey and Mead, since they addressed the issue of perception as bound in with action, whereas Peirce adopted a more idealist stance (Tibbetts, 1975–6). I seek to show, by reference to Dewey (1896), the concordance between pragmatist theorizing and Gibsonian theorizing so as to establish the relevance of this perspective for the issues being tried in the present chapter. Thereafter the focus is on Mead, who engaged himself in analyses that bear directly on the two problems I have identified in the foregoing section.

Dewey is concerned to clarify a problem that he perceived in the psychology of his day – namely, that the bugbear of 'mind–body' dualism had not been eradicated, but rather was being replicated in the 'stimulus–response' construction of the reflex arc. This led to a conception of organismic function as essentially disjointed. Dewey gives an example of the way a reflexological account (of a child grasping for a lighted candle) breaks up the co-ordination of an act into a set of 'unallied processes'.

> The ordinary interpretation[10] would say the sensation of light is a stimulus to the grasping as a response, the burn resulting is a stimulus to withdrawing the hand as response and so on. There is, of course, no doubt that is a rough practical way of representing the process. But when we ask for its psychological[11] adequacy, the case is quite different. Upon analysis, we find that we begin not with a sensory stimulus, but with a sensori–motor coordination, the optical–ocular, and that in a certain sense it is the movement which is primary, and the sensation which is secondary, the movement of body, head and eye muscles determining the quality of what is experienced. In other words, the real beginning is with the act of seeing; it is looking, and not a sensation of light. (Dewey, 1896, pp. 358–9)

Gibson predicates his theoretic upon precisely the same point. What we do determines what we perceive. We obtain stimulation, it is not (typically) imposed upon us (Gibson, 1966, pp. 31–3). This for him is the significance of the concept of activity.

Dewey goes on to state that the initiating action (looking at the light) stimulates the next action – reaching out towards it; and this, he says, is simply because visual and haptic inspection are each, 'practically a subordinate member of a bigger coordination' (p. 359). Looking and grasping are not separable elements of behaviour for the reason that we look *for* objects every bit as much as we look *at* surfaces. 'In other words, we now have an enlarged and transformed coordination; the act is seeing no less than before, but it is now seeing-for-reaching purposes' (Dewey, 1896, p. 359). '. . . the visual control of the hands is inseparably connected with the visual perception of objects. . . . The transporting of things is part and parcel of seeing them as portable or not' (Gibson, 1979, p. 235).

Dewey then asserts that if the child burns its hand by reaching too close to the flame, this represents the completion of the overall action and is part of the original and ongoing act of looking. 'The burn is the original seeing, the original optical-ocular experience enlarged and transformed in its value. It is no longer mere seeing; it is seeing-of-a-light-that-means-pain-when-contact-occurs' (pp. 359–60). Gibson would use the term 'detection of invariance' to describe the above perceptual occurrence.

Dewey proceeds from this point to a detailed consideration of stimulus and response from the standpoint of action, and argues that a mere sensation cannot constitute a stimulus, a mere movement cannot constitute a response. The occurrence of a sensation means the *lack* of a stimulus and the possibility for setting in train an action to constitute (discover, bring into focus) the actual stimulus. If I hear an odd sound, I act to constitute that sound as an objective stimulus. My moving around to obtain this stimulus cannot be taken as a response thereto; a response is again an act *vis-à-vis* an objective and correctly perceived stimulus. The reflex arc, Dewey concludes, is not a thing in itself; it is part of a *circle* – the act – whose closure is the 'constitution of a stimulus'. Gibson (1967b) states:

> The sensitivity of the retina, the cochlea, the skin . . . can be studied by . . . classical psychophysics but the shifting patterns of nervous input when the eyes move, the head turns, the hand gropes . . . are only half of an input–output circle, and this circular act of attention has an entirely different order of sensitivity. It focuses not on stimulation but on stimulus information. (p. 163)

While Dewey's (1896) style is, of course, a mite archaic for the present-day reader, the argument is clear enough and, as is also clear from the foregoing, shows a striking parallel with Gibsonian theorizing.[12] Dewey concentrates, however, on the 'act' in bringing to realization the stimulus (and the response), whereas Gibson, though acknowledging action in a general sense, concentrates instead on pre-existing structure to be discovered through 'organism movement'. From Dewey's writing we have a strong sense of persons carrying out actions intentionally, i.e. teleologically; in Gibson's case we come away, rather, with a strong sense of environment in which action may or may not go on.

Gibson's objectification of environment

This brings us face to face with the first of our two problems, that of objectification, which I believe permeates Gibson's theory. In a pragmatic account, meaning is realized in practice: an object's affordance, therefore – indeed, its existence – is in relation to its use (to its being addressed, or noticed, or employed) by organisms. Gibson, frankly, would reject that view as being in some way 'mentalistic'. The reason behind his objection again reveals his neglect of pragmatism, for the only model of 'action' he knows is Piaget's, and of course Piaget (like Neisser, 1976) calls upon a 'mentalistic' construct like 'schema' to explain such matters as intention, or the so-called 'intelligent' use of objects (tools, for example):

> Piaget . . . sometimes seems to imply that the hands are tools of a child's intelligence. But this is like saying that the hand is a tool of an inner child in more or less the same way that an object is a tool for a child with hands. This is surely an error. (Gibson, 1979, p. 235)

Turning to Mead, we find concordance with Gibsonian thinking at several points, but I believe we also find the necessary means for telling the story more accurately as regards the nature of 'objects' and their affordances.

This chapter is not the place to expatiate on the work of G.H. Mead, a philosopher whose contribution to psychology is often taken to begin and end with his course on 'Social Psychology' which was published posthumously under the title *Mind, Self, and Society* (1934). Mead has always enjoyed a special following, usually among humanistic sociologists and pragmatist philosophers, but his work is coming increasingly to the attention of those psychologists seeking an alternative to both behaviourism and cognitivism.[13] One philosopher who has recognized the relevance – particularly of Mead, but of pragmatism in general – to the empirical study of human perception is Tibbetts (e.g. 1972, 1974, 1975–6). Tibbetts has preferred to connect pragmatism with the direct descendant of functionalism in perception psychology – namely, the transactional functionalism of Ames, Kilpatrick, Ittelson, and others. While such a linkage is entirely feasible, it takes us in the wrong direction with respect to Gibsonian theorizing (Mead's perspective is open, I think, to being taken in both directions, depending on what is given emphasis in his writing). Neither is this chapter the place to engage in discourse upon Tibbetts's work. The point is that a reading of Tibbetts allows an appreciation of the relevance of pragmatism to current theorizing in perception psychology and, more specifically, allows one to note the breadth of Mead's concerns, to realize that he was involved in a great deal besides 'social psychology' as ordinarily understood. I will, necessarily, pick my own path through Mead's writings, rather than follow Tibbetts, for the obvious reason that I am interested in arriving at Gibsonian theory, and (less obviously) I am not at all interested in arriving at transactional functionalism.

Gibson's interest is in the analysis of optical structure as this is available to human observers, with a view to defining and describing the features of that structure that allow the detection and discrimination of affordances. While Mead centres his focus on the perceiving organism – the agent of perception – and has nothing specific to say about optical structure, he is consistently aware of the fact that affordances 'point both ways': to the observer, and to the environment. However, he establishes the observer's role within the organism–environment relation more firmly than Gibson does, while presenting an account of perception not essentially different to Gibson's.[14]

In a paper from 1907, Mead questions the empiricist assumption that the storing up of memories of previous experience somehow marks the process of learning about the affordances of the world. He takes the case of a chicken ('chick' is his word) that pecks at a cinnabar caterpillar, only to discover its unpleasant taste. Mead asserts that from a purely logical point of view an explanation of the chicken's avoidance of this object in future, by reference to a mental sequence of experiences in the past, is inadequate:

> The mere reintegration of the experience would not protect the chick. Either the chick would peck again, since presumably the same bad taste and same rejection would follow, simply reinforced by the revival of the past experience, and this would bring about no improvement in adaptation; or else the past experience would be revived with the appearance of the old stimulus. This stimulus was not a caterpillar with certain markings, but a moving object within reach. The revival of the experience with this generalized stimulus ... would lead to the rejection, not of cinnabar caterpillars alone, but of all moving objects within reach. The ability to distinguish between stimuli which had been identical in their value before, arises together with the new reaction, that of rejection. (Mead, 1907, p. 385)

And a bit further on, he observes:

A dog's shrinking from the sight of the whip involves not simply the revival of the painful experience of the flogging; it involves his reacting to characteristics in the sight of the whip which led to no reaction at first. It is not then so much the association of an old visual or olfactory experience with the impulse, as the arising of a new visual or olfactory experience which now becomes the stimulus for the particular impulse or reaction. (p. 386)

These illustrations and arguments are entirely consonant with a view, such as Gibson's, that we discover the properties of things in the structure that exists 'persistently' in the environment; that we proceed in life by differentiating the qualities of the environment, rather than by constructing a store of memory images that get 'consulted' by an inner eye during our interactions with the environment (Gibson and Gibson, 1955).

Mead does go on to make an analysis of the process of differentiation in terms of the appearance of a new stimulus for the elicitation of a pre-existing response (that of an instinctive capacity to orally eject uningestible matter, in the case of the chicken). Gibson would no doubt quarrel with such a construction and prefer to speak of the detection of an invariant relation in the environment. However, Mead, it seems to me, has drawn attention to what the chicken is *doing* as well as what the environment affords. The invariance in question – the inedibility of that species for this one – *entails* the chicken. It is the chicken for which this is an invariance; furthermore, it is in virtue of the chicken's *modus operandi* (pecking at moving objects) and its *modus vivendi* (inability to consume certain objects) that the affordance comes to light.

Mead expresses this point elsewhere (1934) when he remarks:

It is a difficult matter to state just what we mean by dividing up a certain situation between the organism and its environment. Certain objects come to exist for us because of the character of the organism. Take the case of food. If an animal that can digest grass, such as an ox, comes into the world, then grass becomes food. That object did not exist before, that is, grass as food. The advent of the ox brings in a new object. In that sense, organisms are responsible for the appearance of whole sets of objects that did not exist before. (p. 129)

This kind of viewpoint helps to settle a puzzle of Gibsonian theory that is not central to our present purpose, but bears directly upon it: Gibson's constant reference to 'information pickup'. The question – and it is one that Hamlyn seems to ask (1969, 1977) – is: information *for what*? Mead would reply that information, as far as the chicken (or the ox) is concerned, is *for* survival, nourishment, reproduction – in other words, *for* continued action.

Much more to the point, information for continued action is generated *in* action, and its nature is limited by the kinds of actions the organism

Ecological realism 215

is capable of physically (pecking as against chewing), and in turn by the kinds of physiological processes (protein v. cellulose breakdown) that govern its continuation as an organic system (Mead, 1936, pp. 164–5). Thus – returning to the present problem, the objectification of environment in Gibsonian theory – we find in Mead (1907) the following point, which has vital significance:

> To assume that a chick can find in the contact of its bill together with those of its feet the materials that answer to the perception of a physical thing is almost inconceivable. Even the cat and the dog must find in their paws or mouths, fashioned seemingly for the purposes, not of 'feeling things', but of locomotion or tearing and masticating, but a minimum of that material which goes into the structure of our perceptions. (1907, p. 389)

Objects are *realized*, they do not pre-exist. Their being taken for granted as independent features of the (human) environment in no way counteracts this point. Objects – to turn to a favourite phrase of Mead's – are 'collapsed acts'; their forms and identities are taken teleologically in the course of our actions in relation to them. They do not exist in their own right, but rather become existents in virtue of organismic agency in relation to them. It is the human and anthropoid capacity to handle, transport and transform that engenders objects out of the material environment. Without the means to transport and manipulate, 'objects' are scarcely a feature of the perceptible habitat at all.

There is a further, peculiarly human capacity – namely, to 'objectivate' portable/manipulable environmental items. By 'objectivation' here I mean the human capacity to conceive of such items as *being* 'objects', as having identity, as belonging to such-and-such a category or class. Humans are aware of these items as objects in virtue of the linguistic community's investing the perceivable with the conceptual. Chickens barely live in a world of 'objects' considered as manipulanda, and are not at all in the realm of 'objects' at a conceptual level. It is, incidentally, through the human conceptual capacity to 'objectivate' that the practice of 'objectification' emerges in the discourse of ecological theory.

The assertions about affordances' dependencies on capacities stand in opposition to Gibson's general view that affordances of the environment reside there persistently. Instead we have a surer balance, when using the term environment *relationally*, between the structure of the world and the structure and function of organisms (see Heft, 1989). In Henle's (1974) account of Gibson's notion of aggregation of components of the optic array we are offered a description of its structure that is supposedly independent of organisms (but is in fact derived from how human organisms tap into that structure). In an account derived from Mead's analyses we come to a point where the components of the array are aggregated in direct relation to the actions that organisms can undertake. The balance of the relationship implied in the concept 'ecological' is restored by this latter account, and while the structure of the world necessarily becomes thereby *ineffable* in the absence of organisms self-consciously aware of it, we also avoid the covert anthropocentrism that must adhere to any environmental description that implies objectification. Our safest conclusion, then, is that things are not distinguished that afford no distinction in practice, and physical-physiological limitations on practice ensure that aspects of the structure of light are unaggregated for some species, aggregated for others.

The escape from an objectification that is implicit in Gibsonian theory – and hence from naive realism – into what might be called 'sophisticated' or interactive realism (or 'objective relativism', to use Mead's term) is allowed by pragmatist discourse; hence we skirt the pitfalls of a more cognitivist route. I believe Gibson would have given houseroom to the foregoing observations in that the restoration of 'environment' as a truly relational term does not entail a return to dualism.

Affordances of social objects

Any attempt to do justice to Mead's treatment of the self in social interaction would require a separate (and non-brief) treatise. I have already anticipated, in earlier remarks in this chapter, the significant feature of social objects: the fact that they are sustained by language. Here I will try to produce images derived from Mead's development of ideas about mind and self, as a way of giving substance to those earlier remarks.

Mind, for Mead, is the awareness of co-perception of self and environment (cf. Gibson, 1979). It originates in response to the resistances offered by the people and objects of the environment. Humans do not exhibit a 'pre-programmed' repertoire of adjustments to the environment in the way that other animals do. Human interaction with the environment cannot be predicted, in the way that the routines of other, even highly developed, creatures can. A beaver or a trapdoor spider may exhibit elaborate forms of behaviour in respect to damming or nest-building, but these adjustments cannot be taken as marks of intentionality (as I earlier defined that term – see Note 6) because such creatures are bound, in evolutionary terms, by sequences of 'gestures' from which they do not deviate.[15]

Humans, by contrast, exhibit experimental forms of interaction with the world because their actions, from birth, are invested with meaning and consequence by others of the social group. The achievement of co-perception of the human self in interaction with the environment is engendered by the actions of others who are interested in our actions from birth. In being an object of another's regard and remark one acquires selfhood (taking oneself as one's own object – perceiving oneself in one's own acts). Language is the means whereby one's actions are designated (named, pointed out, interpreted) by others and by oneself, and hence 'arrested', made known to the organism – made, themselves, objects of regard for others and oneself. Mind, then, can be considered as consciousness of self, in action or contemplation, and it is teleological: it achieves its goal as a prerequisite to the initiation of action. In undertaking any act its completion is already perceived, because we designate objectives to ourselves, just as we take ourselves as objects of our own regard – and the means of designating is language (used representationally). All this lies at base in the peculiarly human capacity to initiate and modify action, to experiment (and, incidentally, to think about our own processes of perception, Gibson's thoughts included).

Mead has proposed the radical view that all environmental interaction is social, in the sense that even when we act upon inanimate objects, we perceive our own organism as a self in co-operative relation with those objects. In elaborating that thought, Mead provides a key point that brings us to the position I outlined earlier in this chapter:

> All objects are originally social objects, but in the case of inanimate things we have abstracted from all content except the resistance which is the stuff of perceptual things, ourselves or other things. They are all in some sense hypothetical until we get them into the manipulatory field and complete the act which the distance experience initiates. *While in a perceptual world the ultimate test is the handling of what we see, we stop far short of this in most tests of the reality of things. We depend upon the substantive meanings of what we see, that is, upon the universalized social responses* which implicate experimental[16] data but do not demand them. There is the familiar illustration of the bank [mailbox] that remains solvent [goes on affording mailing] when its gold reserve is stolen [when the mail-deliverers are on strike] as long as the theft remains undiscovered [provided one doesn't know that]. (Mead, 1938, p. 151; emphasis added)

The dependence on substantive meanings specifies the nature of one's relation with *visibly* social objects like mailboxes. (It would take our theme too far astray to raise discussion of Mead's more far-reaching claim; hence my use of the term 'visible' to designate those objects whose affordances are uncontroversially defined by social custom.) And Mead's image, in the final sentence, of the 'façade' of solidarity (realness) is, as I have interpolated, a way of expressing the idea that without the continued adherence by the social group to the conventionalized practices connected with such objects, their affordances disintegrate; they become historical rather than present objects.[17]

Summing up

Within the realm of perception psychology James Gibson's work has broken through the confusion produced by a mentalist tradition, and has allowed students of the subject to see the nature of ecological optics and its importance for any adequate account of organismic contact with the environment. Gibson's own 'secondary socialization' in the discipline of psychology has prevented him from seeing important links between his work and that of the pragmatist philosophers, and the profit in pointing out these links lies in the solutions to problems that arise in Gibsonian theory. I have identified two such problems; I am satisfied that their solution is to be found in the work of Mead, and to some degree in that of Dewey. I cannot be sure that I have laid out the case for connecting Gibsonian theory with pragmatism as fully or clearly as it could be, and it remains for others in the field of perceptual theory to 'look for themselves'.

Afterword

G.H. Mead set out the distinction between communicative gestures and significant symbols and argued for a recognition of the importance of the difference between them, despite the fact that they are obviously related to each other. Communicative gestures are abundantly found in many species of animate life. The use of significant symbols appears to be unique to human communication. Mead left that legacy, but theorists of cognitive evolution are still faced with the interesting puzzle of how to try to account for the evolutionary emergence of significant symbols.

A 'symbol' is defined (*Chambers Twentieth Century Dictionary*) as 'that which by custom or convention represents something else'. 'Symbols' are thus 'things that stand for other things'. My efforts in recent times (with archaeologist Iain Davidson) to account for the prehistoric occurrence of symbols has led first of all to our framing the problem as one of positing a scenario in which communicative gestures could yield up the emergence of signs used for representational purposes. This has led to the further argument (Davidson and Noble, 1989; Noble and Davidson, 1989) that the making of marks on surfaces whose basis is iconic gesture provides the occasion of that evolutionary emergence. Through their persistence in or on a surface such marks have a good chance of becoming themselves objects of perception, becoming noticed. Because of their isomorphism with the iconic gesture that produced them, they also have a good chance of becoming noticed as 'things that stand for other things'. And because they are marks made by whoever prehistorically had the capacity to do so, their multiplication, transformation and transportation under the control of the mark-maker could readily follow their initial production.

By whatever means symbols emerged, their 'invention' affords the *self-conscious* investiture of objects and events with meaning – self-conscious because the symbol-users are aware of both the 'sign' and the 'signified' (and aware that the 'sign' is their own product). Such invention is necessarily constrained by socially shared symbolic exchange. 'Custom and convention' figure in the definition of a 'symbol'. Meaningfulness cannot arise outside social settings, as Mead argued (1934), though once acquired in those settings, meanings can be applied by socialized individuals in isolated settings. This is also the essence of Vygotsky's (1981) sense of the 'interpsychological' preceding the 'intrapsychological'. New meanings can be created by individuals, through the manipulation and exploitation of whatever symbol resources are at their disposal. The realization of any individual creation none the less entails its incorporation in a socially shared repertoire of meanings. Wittgenstein (1958) argued that meaning, by its very nature, can arise only in particular occasions of communal action. Language is public, even though some occasions of its use may be isolated and private.

Gibson argued (e.g. 1979, p. 200) that perceiving is also public. What is available to be perceived by one observer is potentially available to be perceived by others. A power conferred on language-users, through their self-conscious awareness of what they perceive, is the development of rhetorics – explanations, fables, stories and theories (Noble, 1987). Gibson's theory is just one in the vast rhetorical array. An irony is that out of the communal, public resource of language – and probably because of its usability in isolated settings – there can arise theories claiming all cognition as the private possession of individual minds. This is the essence of Cartesian cognitivism, the position opposed by proponents of the ecological approach.

Notes

1. One can see implicit and explicit signs in more recent writing by Skinner (1977) of (unrecognized) *rapprochement* with the Gibsonian approach. This is not too surprising; Gibson is happy to acknowledge his behaviourist background yet, like Skinner, he is distinctly non-Watsonian. Indeed, taking a different perspective on what seems at first such an improbable convergence, it is clear from the same paper by Skinner (1977) that *he* inclines to pragmatism, as did Gibson. Both theorists would no doubt have embraced this epistemological position more consistently and intelligibly had they allowed themselves to be exposed (or acknowledged more explicitly being exposed?) to broader philosophical perspectives than the academic profession of psychology permits.

2. The distinction between 'world' and 'environment' implied here is that the former is an entity independent of organisms; the latter entails organisms to be environed. The importance of the distinction between these terms will occupy us presently.
3. But Gibson, as I will argue, does not embrace the full (pragmatic) implication of the organism's ways of subsisting and operating for the 'production' of what is perceptible.
4. It is this very ability that allowed the armchair empiricists to conceive of 'space perception' as the combining of independent visual and tactile sensations. Incidentally, the use of 'armchair' in that last sentence is not gratuitous. When contemplating the nature of perception we are often sitting down, engaging in (ecologically) purposeless explorations of the feeling of seeing and the feeling of touching. As I imply in the text after this note, perception as ongoing information pick-up in the real (purposive) world does not have this 'detached' character because it is not self-conscious in an 'armchair' sense (it is of course perpetually, but for the most part tacitly, self-inclusive).
5. Hence, perhaps, the curiosity value of familiar objects seen from unfamiliar angles.
6. In the original text I used the phrase 'intending to do' here. That usage is ambiguous and could be taken to imply that I assume all organisms 'have intentions' in the sense of 'having plans in mind'. All animals can be considered to act purposefully; only language-users can frame up those purposes as propositions or plans and hence 'have intentions' as a feature of their awareness.
7. Here, one suspects, Gibson might find sympathy with certain of Skinner's objections (e.g. 1988, pp. 344–5) to mental-term talk.
8. Actually, for humans, even the so-called 'natural environment' is increasingly 'socially sustained' (National Parks, protected species, etc.).
9. In his 1966 work (p. 235) Gibson draws on William James's distinction (1890, pp. 221–3) between 'knowledge of acquaintance' and 'knowledge about'. The former is personally experienced knowledge of the world; the latter is, essentially, knowledge picked up from others. Gibson comes over as never too impressed by the latter, and indeed it is arguably his *moral* purpose to encourage us all to make 'knowledge of acquaintance' paramount in our lives: 'This book is dedicated to all persons who want to look for themselves' (Gibson, 1966, p. 321). But moral injunctions and real-world practice are quite distinct. Gibson simply overlooks the fact that civil society depends upon 'knowledge about' for the maintenance of cultural objects. In the case of the mailbox it is just a fact that very few cultural members have actually achieved direct perception of the 'postal system' behind the mailbox; have 'looked for themselves' at the process from 'letter dispatch' to 'letter receipt'. We know about the mailbox's function because we believe what we are *told* in respect to how the postal system works (*that* it works is another issue; *how* it works is, for most of us, based upon stories and reports from others; upon information picked up in symbolic interaction, not directly picked up in perceptual interaction). And it is unavoidably the case that an expanding proportion of our perceptual experience has to be mediated in this fashion, or we would quite fail to undertake the transactions we perform in civil life.

This is more of a cavil, however, and not the statement of a real problem

Ecological realism 221

in Gibson's theory. I elaborate on the 'problem' in the text following this note.
10. By the term 'ordinary interpretation' Dewey means the reflexological account that he is trying to combat.
11. Dewey here is expressing the wish that psychology ought reasonably to oppose the 'ordinary interpretation' in favour of the account he proceeds to give. History shows that psychology has gone on with 'ordinary interpretations', however, and still balks at latter-day attempts, like Gibsonian theory, to see things otherwise.
12. Dewey's (1896) paper is regarded as having an important place in functionalist psychology as well as in pragmatist philosophy. Hence, given Gibson's alleged identification with the functionalist tradition (MacLeod, 1974), and his 'taste for pragmatism', its influence on his thinking is not a great surprise.
13. An objection to locating Mead in a different camp to behaviourism might be raised, inasmuch as Mead himself used the term 'social behaviourism' to describe his theorizing in social psychology. Cook (1977) has shown quite convincingly, however, the close links, to which Mead himself points, with functionalism (especially the 1896 paper by Dewey) and hence with pragmatism. Mead's use of the term 'behaviourism' is thus not intended to imply allegiance with Watsonian-style behaviourism, but rather to signal a rejection of idealism (rather like Skinner's use of the term).
14. The absence of a specific treatment by Mead of the structure of reflected light in no sense implies an absence of realization of its importance on his part. Numerous references are to be found in Mead (1938) to the notions of surface, medium, substance, occlusion, and ocular adjustments to reflected optical energy. What Mead lacked was the particular analytic skill, abundant in Gibson, for grasping the facts of *ecological* optics. That is why I said earlier that Mead would have been delighted by Gibson's theorizing.
15. This is not to imply that animals other than humans are locked into some set of mechanical routines that get repeated irrespective of environmental constraint. It simply means that spiders do not build dams and beavers do not spin webs.
16. The word 'experimental' as used here by Mead has a connotation of 'experiential' (consider the French term *expérience*, which covers both these meanings).
17. Alan Costall pointed out that the scene interpolated is not quite parallel to Mead's. In Mead's story the bank actually goes on 'working' despite absence of reserves. In my example the uninformed citizen takes it that the postal system is working when it actually isn't. I think the following remarks can adjust the cases into reasonable realignment.

   The bank can be said to 'go on functioning' in a way that the mailbox doesn't, inasmuch as customers, tellers, etc., act in relation to each other as though business could be carried on as normal – transactions are completed, money is deposited and withdrawn. For the moment, therefore, the bank works. But the mailbox, too, works (for the moment), inasmuch as mail items may still be deposited in it by the unsuspecting sender. The difference in the two cases is that the apparent functionality of the bank is sustained by interpersonal activity; that of the mailbox by purely intrapersonal. The façade of functionality in both cases is socially derived.

References

Ben-Zeev, A. (1981), 'J.J. Gibson and the ecological approach to perception', *Studies in the History and Philosophy of Science*, **12**, 107–39.
Cook, G.A.G.H. (1977), 'Mead's social behaviorism', *Journal of the History of the Behavioral Sciences*, **13**, 307–16.
Costall, A. (1981), 'On how so much information controls so much behaviour: James Gibson's theory of direct perception', in G. Butterworth (ed.), *Infancy and Epistemology*, Brighton: Harvester, pp. 30–51.
Davidson, I. and Noble, W. (1989), 'The archaeology of perception: Traces of depiction and language', *Current Anthropology*, **30**, 125–55.
Dewey, J. (1896), 'The reflex arc concept in psychology', *Psychological Review*, **3**, 357–70.
Gibson, J.J. (ed.) (1947), *Motion Picture Testing and Research*, AAF Aviation Psychology Research Report No. 7, Washington, DC: Government Printing Office.
Gibson, J.J. (1950), *The Perception of the Visual World*, Boston, MA: Houghton Mifflin.
Gibson, J.J. (1951), 'What is a form?', *Psychological Review*, **58**, 403–12.
Gibson, J.J. (1966), *The Senses Considered as Perceptual Systems*, Boston, MA: Houghton Mifflin.
Gibson, J.J. (1967a), 'James J. Gibson' in E.G. Boring and G. Lindzey (eds), *A History of Psychology in Autobiography*, vol. 5, New York: Appleton, pp. 125–43.
Gibson, J.J. (1967b), 'New reasons for realism', *Synthese*, **17**, 173–201.
Gibson, J.J. (1972) 'Two methods of describing ambient light', unpublished manuscript, February.
Gibson, J.J. (1979), *The Ecological Approach to Visual Perception*, Boston, MA: Houghton Mifflin.
Gibson, J.J. and Crooks, L.E. (1938), 'A theoretical field-analysis of automobile-driving', *American Journal of Psychology*, **51**, 453–71.
Gibson, J.J. and Gibson, E.J. (1955), 'Perceptual learning: Differentiation or enrichment?', *Psychological Review*, **62**, 32–41.
Gibson, J.J. and Gibson, E.J. (1957), 'Continuous perspective transformations and the perception of rigid motion', *Journal of Experimental Psychology*, **54**, 129–38.
Gregory, R.L. (1974), 'Choosing a paradigm for perception', in E.C. Carterette and M.P. Friedman (eds), *Handbook of Perception*, vol. 1, New York: Academic Press, pp. 255–83.
Hamlyn, D.W. (1969), *The Psychology of Perception* (2nd edn), London: Routledge.
Hamlyn, D.W. (1977), 'The concept of information in Gibson's theory of perception', *Journal for the Theory of Social Behaviour*, **7**, 5–16.
Heft, H. (1989), 'Affordances and the body: An intentional analysis of Gibson's ecological approach to visual perception', *Journal for the Theory of Social Behaviour*, **19**, 1–30.
Henle, M. (1974) 'On naive realism', in R.B. MacLeod and H.L. Pick, Jr (eds), *Perception: Essays in honor of James J. Gibson*, Ithaca, NY: Cornell University Press, pp. 40–56.
James, W. (1890), *Principles of Psychology*, vol. 1, New York: Holt.
Lock, A. (1980), *The Guided Reinvention of Language*, London: Academic Press.

Mace, W.M. (1985), 'J.J. Gibson's ecological theory of information pickup: Cognition from the ground up', in T. Knapp and L.C. Robertson (eds), *Approaches to Cognition: Contrasts and controversies*, Hillsdale, NJ: Erlbaum, pp. 137–57.
MacLeod, R.B. (1974), 'A tribute to James J. Gibson', in R.B. MacLeod and H.L. Pick, Jr (eds), *Perception: Essays in honor of James J. Gibson*, Ithaca, NY: Cornell University Press, pp. 11–13.
Mead, G.H. (1907), 'Concerning animal perception', *Psychological Review*, 14, 383–90.
Mead, G.H. (1934), *Mind, Self, and Society*, ed. C.W. Morris, Chicago: University of Chicago Press.
Mead, G.H. (1936), *Movements of Thought in the Nineteenth Century*, ed. M.H. Moore, Chicago: University of Chicago Press.
Mead, G.H. (1938), *The Philosophy of the Act*, ed. C.W. Morris, Chicago: University of Chicago Press.
Michaels, C.F. and Carello, C. (1981), *Direct Perception*, Englewood Cliffs, NJ: Prentice-Hall.
Neisser, U. (1976), *Cognition and Reality*, San Francisco: W.H. Freeman.
Noble, W. (1981), 'Gibsonian theory and the pragmatist perspective', *Journal for the Theory of Social Behaviour*, 11, 65–85.
Noble, W. (1987), 'Perception and language: Toward a complete ecological psychology', in A.P. Costall and A.W. Still (eds), *Cognitive Psychology in Question*, Hemel Hempstead: Harvester Wheatsheaf, pp. 128–41.
Noble, W. and Davidson, I. (1989), 'On depiction and language', *Current Anthropology*, 30, 337–42.
Polanyi, M. (1967), *The Tacit Dimension*, London: Routledge.
Reed, E.S. and Jones, R.K. (1979), 'James Gibson's ecological revolution in psychology', *Philosophy of the Social Sciences*, 9, 189–204.
Reed, E.S. (1987), 'Why do things look as they do? The implications of J.J. Gibson's *The ecological approach to visual perception*', in A.P. Costall and A.W. Still (eds), *Cognitive Psychology in Question*, Hemel Hempstead: Harvester Wheatsheaf, pp. 94–114.
Scheffler, I. (1974), *Four Pragmatists*, London: Routledge.
Skinner, B.F. (1977), 'Why I am not a cognitive psychologist', *Behaviorism*, 5, 1–10.
Skinner, B.F. (1988), 'Reply to Rey', in A.C. Catania and S. Harnad (eds), *The Selection of Behavior: The operant behaviorism of B.F. Skinner*, New York: Cambridge University Press, pp. 344–5.
Tibbetts, P. (1972), 'The transactional theory of human knowledge and action: Notes towards a "behavioral ecology"', *Man–Environment Systems*, 2, 37–59.
Tibbetts, P. (1974), 'Mead's theory of the act and perception: Some empirical confirmations', *The Personalist*, 55, 115–38.
Tibbetts, P. (1975–6), 'Peirce and Mead on perceptual immediacy and human action', *Philosophy and Phenomenological Research*, 36, 222–32.
Vygotsky, L.S. (1981), 'The genesis of higher mental functions', in J.V. Wertsch (ed.), *The Concept of Activity in Soviet Psychology*, Armonk, NY: M.E. Sharpe.
Wittgenstein, L. (1958), *Philosophical Investigations*, Oxford: Blackwell.

12
The mutual elimination of dualism in Vygotsky and Gibson*

Arthur Still and Alan Costall

Editors' introduction

The last two chapters have been about the ecological approach to the 'higher thought processes'. Reed makes it clear that although Gibson's theory does not appeal to internal cognitive processes to explain perception, it certainly does not neglect cognition. Meaning is perceived directly in an act that includes perception and cognition as inseparable parts. In addition, representational systems make possible the indirect knowledge of the world conveyed in the processes of human communication. William Noble argues that Gibson's theory needs supplementation by a more adequate account of the role of language. In the present chapter we try to extend ecological theory in these directions by incorporating the work of Vygotsky.

Gibson recognized that it was in relation to the 'social' that his theory needed to be developed. He emphasized the importance of the social in his chapter on affordances (Gibson, 1979), and it was an issue that concerned him throughout his career (see Reed, 1988). But it is a preoccupation that appears in his notebooks rather than in publications, and there is no fully worked out theory of the relationship between individual knowledge and its social origins in development and through the mediation of representational systems. To develop the theory in this direction requires more than supplementation. The problem of the 'social' cannot be addressed while leaving the rest unchanged. Knowledge is social through and through, as Bartlett seems to recognize in his early work (see Chapter 4). In our interpretation of Vygotsky's theory, intellectual development is a social matter from the beginning of an infant's life, and 'the higher mental functions constitutive of human consciousness are . . . embodied in the child's community' (Bakhurst,

---
* An earlier version of this chapter appeared in The Quarterly News letter of the Laboratory of Comparative Human Cognition, October 1989.

1990, p. 209). Thus knowledge remains social even when it becomes 'internalized'. This is the basis of our proposed extension to ecological theory, though we are aware that the proper interpretation of Vygotsky is still a matter of lively debate (see Bakhurst, 1990; Brushlinskii, 1979; and the references cited at the end of the following chapter).

References

Bakhurst, D. (1990), 'Social memory in Soviet thought', in D. Middleton and D. Edwards (eds), *Collective Remembering*, London: Sage, pp. 203–26.
Brushlinskii, A.V. (1979), 'The interrelationship of the natural and the social in human mental development', *Soviet Psychology*, 17, 34–52.
Reed, E.S. (1988), *James J. Gibson and the Psychology of Perception*, New Haven, CT: Yale University Press.

* * *

When William James wrote his *Principles of Psychology* over a hundred years ago, he unwittingly traced the subsequent history of psychology. He started off by accepting the language of mind–body dualism, because it was convenient and widely understood, and then spent a thousand pages trying to escape from it. If he seems to have been unsuccessful, perhaps it was because his gift for memorable phrases was most evident in his dualist moods – the famous 'blooming, buzzing confusion' experienced by the infant, for instance, has imposed on his successors a very dualist way of thinking about mental development. J.J. Gibson and Vygotsky are a part of this history of the struggle against dualism, but neither quite broke free. In this chapter we argue that together they, or their successors, have the means to succeed.

The ultimate aim is to rid psychological language of dualism. Nowadays mind–body dualism does not go as far as Descartes, who believed that there were two distinct substances, material and mental, which he defined in terms of their essential properties – extension and thinking respectively. All that is necessary for the modern version, cognitivism, is that the language of the mental is independent from that used to refer to the material world, and this does not entail two substances. This subtle linguistic dualism provides a justification for the study of mental structures in the laboratory, abstracted from their normal settings (Fodor, 1980). But the advantages of such dualism, if any exist, are far outweighed by the need to develop a psychology within a biological framework. This framework is not the biology of neo-Darwinism or physiological mechanisms, but an evolutionary biology which recognizes that organisms and environments evolve together. The psychological language appropriate to this biology (sometimes called 'mutualism' – Still and Costall, 1987) will incorporate in its terms their inherent interdependence.

We are motivated in this chapter by two beliefs. The first is that Cartesian dualism, especially in its modern, linguistic version, takes on many disguises, and can appear where we least expect it. And other dualisms (e.g. between sensation and perception, or organism and environment) are linked, logically and historically, to mind–body dualism.

The second belief is that although there are plenty of anti-dualist psychologies, few are radical enough to pose a serious threat to dualism. An exception is J.J. Gibson's ecological psychology, because it undermines dualist psychology at its point of origin in the traditional scheme for thinking about perception; it replaces Descartes' passive and bodiless observer (Descartes, 1985; originally published 1637) with an active creature, busily picking up information in the furtherance of its projects. From this ecological viewpoint, Cartesian perception is a kind of frozen cross-section of activity. For some purposes it may be useful to examine such cross-sections in the laboratory, by forcing the observer to suspend normal activities and report on what is seen or heard under controlled conditions. But this should not be taken as typical of the everyday interchange between an organism and its environment. This is because, according to Gibson, the structured ambient arrays contain a wealth of information that specifies their sources. This information is picked up by a suitably equipped animal in the course of its everyday activities, but is not available to a static observer. Since the information *specifies* its sources, there is no need to suppose cognitive mechanisms acting upon the sparse physical inputs available to the Cartesian observer – no need, therefore, to suppose internal representations to account for our experience and our activities.

But what about thinking? The claim has been made in a recent paper that 'the ecological approach cannot, by *definition*, offer a solution to the problem of what have traditionally been called the "higher thought processes"' (Sinha, 1984, p. 349). This is a common, and seemingly reasonable, complaint against Gibson. After all, he does not offer a solution, though he clearly believed that one can be found without going outside the framework of ecological psychology. Such faith has not convinced everybody, and even some sympathizers have concluded that thought must begin where ecological perception leaves off (Ben-Zeev, 1984; Bruce and Green, 1985).

The problem with accepting Gibson's theory of perception and then adding cognition to explain meaning and higher thought processes is that his theory of perception, in its final form (Gibson, 1979) is already also one of cognition (Reed, 1987). It is a theory of knowing which rejects the traditional separation between sensory processes and high-level, cognitive processes. The world is perceived as meaningful from the start, and there is no place at which it is possible to say the cognitive begins *here* – no modern equivalent of the Cartesian pineal gland, where the ecological language gives way to the mental.

So what account can be given of the 'higher thought processes' in ecological psychology? Gibson himself stopped short, in his published writings, at a theory of higher thought processes, which were unsystematically classified as processes of indirect perception. He also stopped short, in his published writings, of an ecological social psychology. We believe that these two stopping points are related, and that this hesitancy on Gibson's part was not merely a matter of scientific caution (Gibson was not a timid thinker) but reflects an unresolved and unacknowledged conflict in his thinking, which made him reluctant to incorporate the social, despite his repeated assertion of its overriding importance for human beings. Once the dilemma posed by this conflict is resolved (by grasping one of its horns and ignoring the other), then the way is open to an adequate theory of thinking. This, we believe, will follow from taking full account of the social in ecological psychology. Vygotsky is to be our support here, not because his theories offer neat solutions but because he asked the right questions and was faced with similar (or complementary) problems – so that his successes and possible shortcomings provide a useful map of the terrain, its pathways and its pitfalls.

This conflict in Gibson's theory is given fuller treatment elsewhere (Costall and Still, 1989) and will be summarized briefly here. It has to do with two distinctions: between direct and indirect, and social and asocial perception. In his early work Gibson equates these distinctions, so that asocial perception is also direct, social is indirect. Later they diverge, but he does not acknowledge this, or its implications for certain cherished distinctions. The following three versions of the theory correspond to Gibson's three books.

1. First version of the theory, 1950: Direct or literal perception is asocial, in contrast with indirect or schematic perception. This contrast, and the use of the terms literal and schematic perception, date from around the time of Gibson's first book (1950). They were not important to Gibson just as a means of expressing his discoveries and ideas in perception. Like many young Americans faced with the miseries of the

Depression and the rise of Fascism, Gibson was attracted by Marxism and political activism. He was therefore unhappy with the cynical implications of the moral relativism implied by the social perceptionism of the time. Direct or literal perception, open to all people independent of cultural conditioning, seemed to offer a way of avoiding these implications.

2. Second version, 1966: The social and the cultural are mediated by language, and language and perception co-operate closely, yet there is a direct perception that remains undistorted by the social. This becomes apparent when Gibson writes about language. Thus, while it is true that 'Perceiving helps talking, and talking fixes the gains of perceiving', it does not follow that 'the verbal fixing of information distorts the perception of the world . . . [for] . . . the curious observer can always observe more properties of the world than he can describe' (Gibson 1966, p. 282). It is as though there always remains an inexhaustible background of blooming, buzzing confusion waiting for classification.

3. Final version, 1979: Direct perception is of what activities the environment supports, or of what Gibson called 'affordances'; and it is clear from the examples he takes that affordances may be socially and culturally conditioned. The physical world supports activity, and activities – what we do – are culturally and socially determined. But activities are inseparable from the affordances that support them – if one is culturally determined, then so is the other. Hence affordances as well as activities must be cultural through and through. Thus affordances are both directly perceived and culturally conditioned, and direct perception can no longer be a part of experience whose importance lies in its essential freedom from social or cultural contamination. Therefore it can no longer be appealed to as a defence against social relativism.

We would go further than Gibson in socializing the human world, and fill it, as Mead did, with physical objects that have not only their special affordances (as chairs, for instance, afford sitting in) but also more general affordances shared with other objects – as detached objects, they afford being possessed, moved around, placed in position, etc. According to Mead, this world of individualized physical objects is a product of *social* development (Joas, 1985, Ch. 7), which would add another social dimension to affordances.

But even without such an extension, Gibson's final theory of direct perception is very significantly different from earlier versions. Yet he nowhere points this out, nor does he build upon the change. We surmise that this is because he is reluctant to accept the final failure of the earlier argument against relativism, and that this leads him to hold back when he writes about the social, and to ignore the problems it poses for his theory. He fails, therefore, to draw out the full implications of his theory of affordances. The concept is explained halfway through the 1979 book, but Gibson does not develop it into a new ecological theory of social psychology and thought. In fact affordances are not mentioned again, and the book returns to a language used thirty years earlier, that of direct perception of surfaces, with no explicit reference to what they afford or mean to the active observer.

There seem to be two ways forward:

1. To return to a dualism, this time of surfaces and affordances, where both may be directly perceived, but affordances are 'meaningful' and socially conditioned, surfaces 'physical' and asocial, a source of experience that is independent of culture and therefore subverts moral relativism. We do not think this would have been acceptable to Gibson. It is too reminiscent of the dualist distinction between sense-data and objects, and it conflicts with our aims laid out above.

2. To accept that human experience is social through and through, and that there is no separate pre-social realm of experience existing alongside the social. Babies live in a world that is social from the beginning; they are further socialized, but (and here we begin to draw on Vygotsky) 'Higher psychological functions are not superimposed as a second storey over the elementary processes; they represent new psychological systems' (Vygotsky, 1978, p. 124; quoted in the Afterword by John-Steiner and Souberman). It follows that experience does not contain in any form a level that remains from the phylogenetic or ontogenetic past. The biogenetic approach, with its covert dualisms contained in the continuing existence of more primitive levels, must be given up. And moral relativism must be accepted, rendered palatable, perhaps, with a more sophisticated philosophy than Gibson found in American Marxism during the 1930s.

Accepting (2) as the way forward, the higher thought processes are naturally to be thought of as arising out of social activities, rather than vice versa. Such a reversal of the traditional individualist priorities is familiar in Mead's pragmatist psychology (Mead, 1964; Joas, 1985; see this volume, Chapter 11, by Noble) and popular recently as the basis of social constructionism (Gergen, 1985; see this volume, Chapter 5, by Shotter). There are now many demonstrations of the social nature of memory and perception (Middleton and Edwards, 1990; see this volume, Chapter 10, by Reed). Also there has been a reaction against the individualism of Piaget's theories of intellectual development, and the importance of social factors in child development is now generally stressed (e.g. Olson, 1980; Wertsch, 1985a). Part of this reaction has been a revival of research into what Vygotsky called the Zone of Proximal Development (Rogoff and Wertsch, 1984; Wertsch, 1985b), since this illustrates nicely the social origins of the higher thought processes – the child's intellectual abilities are best revealed in their *normal* social setting, not in the bizarre and cramped (yet still social) setting of the psychological test.

In spite of this new interest in the social basis of cognition, we believe that it has not yet been grounded in an adequate theory of perception – Gibson's theory of affordances provides an opportunity for this. Edward Reed, in work based on a study of Gibson's unpublished notebooks, has made a start with the concept of 'representation systems' (see Chapter 10). Representation systems are systems of physical tokens, marks, etc., around which shared human activity is organized:

> In contrast to perceptual systems . . . representation or symbol systems involve *cultural* and *historical* as well as individual psychological processes. . . . As the child grows and develops in her use of language, numbers, pictures and other representations, she is more and more enabled to take advantage of explicit, socially gathered knowledge, as well as of socially developed customs. (Chapter 10, p. 189–90)

As objects become symbols in this way, so, correspondingly, their affordances (the direct perception of the activities they support) change. So also will the affordances in the world to which the developing representation systems apply – if only because applying a representation system is itself an activity.

As an illustration, Reed refers to Goody's anthropological work on 'tools of intellect' and the impact of writing. Other clear examples might have been taken from Vygotsky's work, much of which could be described as 'studies in the development of representation systems'. For instance, his investigations of the use of symbolism in play shows how the interrelatedness necessary for a representation system is revealed in social activity. Especially impressive, for our argument, is his emphasis upon gestural coherence rather than perceptual similarity. For it makes clear that what evolves during development is not a set of passive, internal perceptual structures but a system of affordances, of connected activities and the information structures that support them. Thus:

> We conducted play experiments in which, in a joking manner, we began to designate things and people involved in the play by familiar objects. For example, a book off to one side designated a house, keys meant children, a pencil meant a nursemaid, a pocket watch a drugstore, a knife a doctor, an

232 Against Cognitivism

inkwell cover a horse-drawn carriage, and so forth. Then the children were given a simple story through figurative gestures involving these objects. They could read it with great ease. For example, a doctor arrives at a house in a carriage, knocks at the door, the nursemaid opens, he examines the children, he writes a prescription and leaves, the nursemaid goes to the drugstore, comes back, and administers medicine to the children. Most three-year-olds can read this symbolic notation with great ease . . . perceptual similarity of objects plays no part in the understanding of the symbolic notation. All that matters is that the objects admit the appropriate gesture and can function as a point of application for it. Hence, things with which this gestural structure cannot be performed are absolutely rejected by children. For example, in this game, which is conducted at a table and which involves small items on the table, children will absolutely refuse to play if we take their fingers, put them on a book, and say, 'Now, as a joke, these will be children'. They object that there is no such game. (Vygotsky, 1978, p. 109)

With time, children can become skilled in the use of these symbols, 'internalise' them (according to Vygotsky) and use them to tell stories. More conventional gestures develop in a similar way, as the child's movements are assimilated to a system of social communication. Thus Vygotsky describes the development of pointing in a child:

. . . from an object-oriented movement it becomes a movement aimed at another person, a means of establishing relations. *The grasping movement changes to the act of pointing.* As a result of this change, the movement itself is then physically simplified, and what results is the form of pointing that we call a true gesture. It becomes a true gesture only after it objectively manifests all the functions of pointing for others and is understood by others as such a gesture. Its meaning and functions are created at first by an objective situation and then by people who surround the child. (Vygotsky, 1978, p.56)

This is a fine account of what we believe happens – an interpersonal process is transformed into another interpersonal process, not into the asocial intrapersonal process characteristic of dualism. Such examples, we believe, illustrate perfectly the genesis of representation systems – not least because they do not, as *descriptions*, leave behind an elementary realm of experience untouched by the development – the system is not like a second storey. Reed's account, with its suggestion of a hierarchy of systems, does not so clearly avoid this danger. He makes representation systems the basis of 'modes of indirect cognition', which leaves, by implication, a mode of direct cognition untouched by their development – a line of thought which leads back to the asocial level of experience hankered after by Gibson.

In Chapter 10 Reed does not refer to Vygotsky, but in an earlier version (1987) he likened the ecological theory of indirect cognition of the 'socialised self's use of historically developed cultural resources' to

The mutual elimination of dualism 233

'Vygotsky's (1978) account of how the child becomes socialised through cognitive means' (Reed, 1987, p. 164). However,

> Vygotsky did not have the concept of ecological information, and did not believe direct perception of the environment was possible. Like most cognitivists, he believed that the child's apprehension of the meaningful world required a process of 'internalisation' of speech, and of ideas and rules encoded in speech. (*ibid.*)

Reed went on to refer to Gibson's scepticism about the notion of internalization. Gibson wrote:

> The child who has learned to talk about things and events can, metaphorically, talk to himself silently about things and events, so it is supposed. He is said to have 'internalized' his speech, whatever that might mean. By analogy with this theory, a child who has learned to draw might be supposed to picture to himself things and events without movements of his hands, to have 'internalized' his picturemaking. A theory of internal language and internal images might be based on this theory. But it seems to me very dubious. (Gibson, 1979, p. 262)

Internalization certainly suggests the kind of dualism we, like Gibson, are trying to avoid, but how can we arrive at the higher thought processes without it? Surprisingly, in view of these strictures, Vygotsky himself shows us the way in the examples quoted above – that is, he shows how thinking could emerge out of ecologically based social activities. Like Piaget, he describes it elsewhere as a process of internalization, but does this mean for Vygotsky that thought becomes shut off in the mind and ceases to be social? Sometimes he (or his translators) writes as though this were so – for instance in his description of one of the transformations involved when internalization takes place as 'an interpersonal process . . . transformed into an intrapersonal one' (Vygotsky, 1978, p. 57). This is elaborated in the afterword to *Mind in Society* by John-Steiner and Souberman, who begin by quoting Vygotsky:

> Every function in the child's cultural development appears twice, on two levels. First, on the social, and later on the psychological level; first, *between* people as an *interpsychological* category, and then inside the child, as an *intrapsychological* category. This applies equally to voluntary attention, to logical memory and to the formation of concepts. The actual relations between human individuals underlie all the higher functions' (Chapter 4). In the buzzing confusion [Jamesian dualism again!] that surrounds the infant during the first few months of her life, parents assist her by pointing and carrying the child close to objects and places of adaptive significance (toys, refrigerator, cupboard, playpen), thus helping the child to ignore other irrelevant features of the environment (such adult objects as books, tools, and so on). This socially mediated attention develops into the child's more

independent and voluntary attention, which she will come to use to classify her surroundings. (Vygotsky, 1978, p. 128)

The fault, as we see it, lies in supposing (or at least implying) that once transformed, the process ceases to be interpersonal. But it is becoming clear that this was not Vygotsky's opinion. As more of his works become available in adequate translations, and as what Sinha (1989) calls the 'second cycle' of Vygotsky studies in the West becomes established, so it is becoming clear that for Vygotsky the higher thought processes are social through and through. The passage quoted by John-Steiner and Souberman is completed by a more recent commentator:

> All higher psychological functions are internalised relationships of the social kind, and constitute the social structure of personality. Their composition, genetic structure, ways of functioning, in one word all their nature is social. Even when they have become psychological processes, their nature remains quasi-social. The human being who is alone retains the function of interaction. (quoted in Valsiner, 1988, p. 142)

And this seems to capture well Vygotsky's mature thought on the importance of the social (Lee, 1985). Vygotsky, after all, worked within a Marxist tradition; he attempted to develop a psychology based on the theoretical structure of *Kapital* (Lee, 1987), and he remained faithful to Marx's declaration in *German Ideology* that 'Consciousness is . . . from the very beginning a social product, and remains so as long as men exist at all' (Marx, 1963, p. 86).

Thus, in learning chess, tennis or a new language, one is guided at first by a teacher into a particular set of interpersonal practices. By learning, and dispensing with further need for the teacher, one becomes a fully fledged participant – an expert, alive to the affordances provided by and shared with other experts. As Wittgenstein (1953) demonstrated in the case of private languages, nothing is gained by appealing to internal psychological processes, since they have no independent reality over and above the social interactions from which they derive their meaning. For ecological psychology, the changes that take place lie in the acquisition of representation systems and in what, as a consequence, situations afford to the participants.

This concludes our argument that the thought of Vygotsky and Gibson, each fruitful in its own right, can become even more so if they are allowed to coalesce through mutual correction. Thus Vygotsky shows the way ecological psychology might progress once it has digested its own belated discovery of the all-pervasiveness of the social. But, as Reed points out, he lacked a radical perceptual theory that would secure the inseparability of organism and environment, and guard against a drift into dualist talk. This is provided by Gibson's ecological psychology, with its concept of affordances which point 'both ways, to the environment and to the observer' (Gibson, 1979, p. 129). Each guards against the dualist backslidings of the other, and between the two, perhaps, we could arrive at an adequate mutualist account of the genesis of higher thought processes.

References

Ben-Zeev, A. (1984), 'The Kantian revolution in perception', *Journal for the Theory of Social Behaviour*, **14**, 69–84.
Bruce, V. and Green, P. (1985), *Visual Perception: Physiology, Psychology and Ecology*, London: Erlbaum.
Costall, A.P. and Still, A.W. (1989), 'Gibson's theory of direct perception and the problem of cultural relativism', *Journal for the Theory of Social Behaviour*, **19**, 433–42.
Descartes, R. (1985), 'Discourse and Essays', in *The Philosophical Writings of Descartes*, vol. 1, ed. J. Cottingham, R. Stoothoff and D. Murdoch, Cambridge: Cambridge University Press; first published 1637.
Fodor, J. (1980), 'Methodological solipsism considered as a research strategy in cognitive psychology', *Behavioral and Brain Sciences*, 3, 63–109.
Gergen, K.J. (1985), 'The social constructionist movement in modern psychology', *American Psychologist*, **40**, 463–84.
Gibson, J.J. (1950), *The Perception of the Visual World*, Boston, MA: Houghton Mifflin.
Gibson, J.J. (1966), *The Senses Considered as Perceptual Systems*, Boston, MA: Houghton Mifflin.
Gibson, J.J. (1979), *The Ecological Approach to Visual Perception*, Boston, MA: Houghton Mifflin.
James, W. (1890), *Principles of Psychology*, New York: Holt.
Joas, H. (1985), *G.H. Mead: A Contemporary Re-examination of his Thought*, Cambridge, MA: MIT.
Lee, B. (1985), 'Intellectual origins of Vygotsky's semiotic analysis', in J. Wertsch (ed.), *Culture, Communication and Cognition*, Cambridge: Cambridge University Press.
Lee, B. (1987), 'Recontextualizing Vygotsky', in M. Hickmann (ed.), *Social and Functional Approaches to Language and Thought*, New York: Academic Press.
Marx, K. (1963), *Selected Writings in Sociology and Social Philosophy*, ed. T.B. Bottomore and M. Rubel, Harmondsworth: Penguin.
Mead, G.H. (1964), *Selected Writings*, ed. A.J. Reck, Chicago: University of Chicago Press.
Middleton, D. and Edwards, D. (eds) (1990), *Collective Remembering*, London: Sage.
Noble, W. (1981), 'Gibsonian theory and the pragmatist perspective', *Journal for the Theory of Social Behaviour*, **11**, 65–85.
Olson, D.R. (ed.) (1980), *The Social Foundations of Language and Thought*, New York: Norton.
Reed, E.S. (1987), 'James Gibson's ecological approach to cognition', in A.P. Costall and A.W. Still (eds), *Cognitive Psychology in Question*, Hemel Hempstead: Harvester-Wheatsheaf.

Rogoff, B. and Wertsch, J.V. (eds) (1984), *Children's Learning in the 'Zone of Proximal Development'*, New Directions for Child Development, No. 23, San Francisco: Jossey-Bass.

Sinha, C. (1984), 'A socio-naturalistic approach to human development', In M.-W. Ho and P.T. Saunders (eds), *Beyond Neo-Darwinism*, London: Academic Press.

Sinha, C. (1989), 'Reading Vygotsky', *History of the Human Sciences*, **2**, 309–31.

Still, A.W. and Costall, A.P. (1987), 'Introduction: In place of cognitivism', in A.P. Costall and A.W. Still (eds), *Cognitive Psychology in Question*, Hemel Hempstead: Harvester Wheatsheaf.

Valsiner, J. (1988), *Developmental Psychology in the Soviet Union*, Bloomington, Ind.: Indiana University Press.

Vygotsky, L.S. (1978), *Mind in Society: The development of the higher psychological processes*, Cambridge, MA: Harvard University Press.

Wertsch, J. (1985a), *Vygotsky and the Social Formation of Mind*, Cambridge, MA: Harvard University Press.

Wertsch, J. (ed.) (1985b), *Culture, Communication and Cognition*, Cambridge: Cambridge University Press.

Wittgenstein, L. (1953), *Philosophical Investigations*, Oxford: Blackwell.

13
Alternative theoretical frameworks for psychology:
A synopsis
Benny Shanon

Editors' introduction

Although the model of human beings as 'physical symbol systems' (Norman, 1981) is perhaps still the main form of cognitive explanation, there has been an increasing diversity of theoretical approaches in the last few years. In the following chapter, Benny Shanon presents an important account of these various developments, and of the relations between them. He argues that they can all be regarded as responses to the problem of adopting a scientific approach to the 'internal domain' and to meaning, as they are traditionally conceived.

In his classification of different theories, Shanon identifies behaviourism with the mechanistic form criticized (and largely invented) by cognitive psychology (see this volume, Edward Morris, Chapter 8). Yet, as Shanon himself notes, behaviourism itself represents a wide diversity of approaches. The most fundamental differences between these approaches stems from a critical ambiguity in the term 'behaviour' itself. The term 'behaviour' originally referred to conduct as both public and in conformity with social norms, and this sense is still apparent in such usages as 'behave yourself' and in the negative form, 'misbehave'. It was initially, therefore, an essentially psychological and, indeed, moral term. Towards the end of the nineteenth century, however, the term was increasingly used to describe how an object, machine or even animal acts or reacts. When extended to objects, the term came to lose its moral significance and reference to intentionality, yet still retained the earlier connotations of observability and orderliness (Williams, 1983, p. 44).

In reacting against the mechanistic conception of behaviour, cognitive psychologists have – as in the case of S–R psychology –

retained much of the scheme they meant to replace. They have tried to understand the meaning of action as a shadowy process behind 'mere movements' rather than as an aspect of the 'structure of behaviour' itself (Merleau-Ponty, 1942/1963; see also Lee, 1988). Cognitive psychology would do much to counter 'the subjectification of meaning' (Joas, 1985, p. 45) by recovering the concept of 'behaviour' as a fundamental psychological and social category.

References

Joas, H. (1985), *G.H. Mead: A contemporary re-examination of his thought*, Cambridge: Polity Press, 1985.
Lee, V.L. (1988), *Beyond Behaviorism*, Hillsdale, NJ: Erlbaum.
Merleau-Ponty, M. (1963), *The Structure of Behaviour* (transl. A.L. Fisher), London: Methuen; (first published 1942.)
Norman, D.A. (1981), 'Twelve issues in cognitive science', in D.A. Norman (ed.), *Perspectives on Cognitive Science*, Hillsdale, NJ: Erlbaum, pp. 265–95.
Williams, R. (1983), *Keywords*, London: Fontana.

* * *

The cognitive sciences are today in the midst of a paradigm shift. Representationalism (the representational view of mind, or cognitivism) which until recently all but dominated the field, is now being subjected to increasing attack from the new paradigm of connectionism which is rapidly gaining force and influence. The present discussion sets out to place the debate between representationalism and connectionism in a larger perspective. Specifically, it is guided by the view that the debate regarding the choice of a proper conceptual framework should not be confined to the confrontation between representationalism and connectionism. While most attention is focused today on these two, competing alternatives, they are not the only options. Indeed, a perusal of the literature reveals a large variety of theoretical frameworks (or suggestions for frameworks), indicating that connectionism is not the only possible alternative to representationalism. (For further, non-connectionist criticism of the representational view see, *inter alia*, Costall and Still, 1987; Dreyfus, 1979; Haugeland, 1978; Maturana, 1978; Searle, 1980; Shanon, 1987, 1988a; Shaw and Turvey, 1980; Winograd and Flores, 1986).

In view of the large variety of alternative theoretical frameworks in psychology, the present chapter attempts a comprehensive uni-

Alternative theoretical frameworks 239

fied account. While the various alternative frameworks have been developed independently, taken together they seem to define a coherent, structured typology. Indeed, the different frameworks may be regarded as differing profiles in a space spanned by a small number of parameters. Towards the end of this chapter it will be further suggested that the different frameworks be viewed as the different responses to one common fundamental problem that underlies psychological research.

Definitions and distinctions

A clarification of terms is essential for any analysis of representationalism and its possible alternatives. It seems to me that many confusions in the literature result from the fact that basic terms are not always defined, and the same terms are often employed by different investigators in different contexts and in different senses. This is certainly true for the key notion of the present discussion, representation. This first section of this chapter starts with the consideration of several crucial distinctions pertaining to this term (for further related discussion, see Shanon, 1990a).

Representation

The first distinction to be singled out is between two major perspectives by which representation may be both defined and investigated. On the one hand, there is the perspective taken in the philosophical literature; on the other, that assumed in the cognitive literature – i.e. cognitive psychology, linguistics and artificial intelligence. In the philosophical context, what is basically at stake is the relationship between two levels of reality or two levels of discourse: concept and world, word and object, word and concept. Historically, the philosophical sense has precedence, for, after all, philosophers were the first to make the distinctions at hand and to coin the terms associated with them. Yet within the cognitive sciences, the term, and the issues of concern associated with it, are employed in a different way. Cognitive scientists of all persuasions take the representativeness of representations for granted. What they are concerned with is not the relationship between representations and other entities (not, in other words, the question of how representations refer to something else, or are endowed with semanticity) but rather the particular formal structure of representations, the relations between representational structures, and the processes by which they are manipulated and operated upon.

This is no accident. As noted by Fodor (1980), Searle (1980) and Winograd (1978), representations in cognitive models do not and cannot account for the relationship of representation (or, in other words, for the semanticity of representation) itself. Psychologists simply assume that the structures they study do, in fact, exhibit this property, and then go on from there. By way of capturing the difference between these two perspectives, one may refer to the philosophical one as *vertical* (for it is concerned with a relationship between two domains or levels of reality) and to the cognitive one as *horizontal* (for it is concerned with relationships within one domain).[1] Furthermore, even when one stays within the horizontal perspective one should distinguish between a weak and a strong sense of 'representation'. The weak sense refers to the locus which serves as the substrate for mental activity, the strong sense refers to a particular model in cognitive science postulated as a specific account of such activity. This model is defined by a profile of specific structural characteristics. Specifically, mental representations consist of abstract symbolic structures; the elementary constituent symbols are well defined and compose large structures in accordance with rules of well-formedness; together, the representational structures comprise a canonical code by means of which all knowledge can be fully characterized in a unified fashion. From the present perspective, any critique against representations is concerned with the strong, not the weak, sense.

Representationalism is the theoretical framework which bases the modelling of mind in terms of representational structures of the type just defined. This framework may be defined by the following three tenets:

1. Human beings behave by virtue of the possession of knowledge.
2. Knowledge is constituted of mental semantic representations.
3. Behaviour is executed through the manipulation of these representations, i.e. through the application of computational operations.

In the foregoing characterization, the term 'representation' should be read in the strong, horizontal sense defined above; similarly, the term 'computation' should be understood in a strong sense to be defined in the next sub-section.

Finally, the term *representational* will be noted. This term will characterize entities that exhibit the properties specified above in conjunction with semantic representations. Unlike the nominal term (representation), however, the adjectival one (representational) can be attributed not only to entities; in fact, it need not be confined to the realm of the mental. It can be applied to modes of thinking, lines of interpretation, patterns of behaviour, and even to artistic styles and cultural orientations. Moreover, the adjectival term affords flexibility in that it does not have to be attributed in an all-or-none fashion but, rather, allows a graded attribution. Specifically, patterns may be more or less representational according to the degree to which they exhibit the profile of the properties noted above. Following Langer (1942), I contrast the representational with the *presentational* and regard the two as poles along which the entire range of cognitive phenomenology may be described. In essence, the presentational profile is defined by the *absence* of all the properties I have identified with the strong sense of representation.

Computation and procedural explanation
The concept of computation is intimately related to the notion of representation. After all, there is no psychological realization for representations which does not involve their being manipulated by computations. Conversely, computations necessitate a substrate of representation for their very application. Thus, parallel to the ambiguity of the notion of representation there is an ambiguity in the notion of computation. In particular, a strong and a weak sense of computation need to be distinguished. The strong sense corresponds to the strong sense of representation employed in the representational framework, where computations are functions that map between representations (i.e. representations in the strong, horizontal sense; cf. Fodor, 1975). In contrast, computation in the weak sense denotes what in general scientific language is usually referred to as computations – namely, mathematical-like or formal-like operations that involve what may be regarded as the evaluation of values.[2] Such operations need not be applied to symbols; in connectionism, for instance, computational operations are applied to neural-like networks. From the definitions given, it should be clear that all computations in the strong sense are also computations in the weak sense, but the converse is not the case.

Related to the notion of computation is that of procedural explanation. A procedural explanation is one that sets out to explain phenomena by means of a specification of the underlying mechanisms that lead to the production or generation of phenomena. In cognition, computations applied to symbolic representations have been introduced precisely in order to provide such a procedural explanation. Thus, the paradigmatic mode of explanation in the cognitive sciences today consists of the modelling of the underlying mechanisms of mind. This characterization is true of both representationalism and connectionism. However, in the course of the discussion below other, non-procedural kinds of explanation will also be identified.

I might add that the sense of the term 'procedural' should not be confused with another sense, one standardly contrasted with the term 'declarative' (cf. Winograd, 1975). As employed in the representational literature, the terms declarative and procedural characterize two kinds of format for the representation of knowledge. In contrast, in the present context, the term procedural specifies a style of explanation. It is to be contrasted not with the term declarative but rather with terms such as non-procedural, structural or phenomenological. As will be seen, procedural *explanation* makes appeal both to declarative and to procedural knowledge.

Intention and intension
The terms intention and intentionality and terms related to them are even more problematic. The differentiation between the various senses of these terms calls for an extensive analysis that would require a separate treatment. Yet, since these terms will play a central role later in the discussion, some basic clarification is appropriate here.

In the context of everyday language, intention is that which specifies the reason for the deliberate activities of a free agent. In the classical-philosophical context, by contrast, the term intentionality has a central role, and refers to the property of relating to something other and outside, i.e. the property of aboutness. Brentano (1874/1973) was the first to single out this property as the key characteristic of mental states. In the technical semantic context, the term intension has been introduced; this is defined by contrast to extension (see Carnap, 1947). Whereas extension defines the meaning of a term or an expression by specifying the entities or states of affairs to which it applies, intension is a semantic object not defined in this fashion. Intensional is the adjective pertaining to such entities.

In the paradigm of Montague grammar, the term intension is further used to refer to semantic entities as distinct from entities in the real world (see Thomason, 1974). Lastly, in the semantic-linguistic context the term extensional specifies a particular sentential configuration, one which is associated with statements of belief and manifests opacity. Extensionality in language is a manifestation of extensionality in logic; but, given the distinct specific concerns of the two disciplines, the corresponding phenomena investigated in the two are not necessarily coextensive.

And then, what about the cognitive-psychological context? Although in this context terms are seldom, if ever, defined explicitly, it seems that two main senses are usually intended (for discussion see Boden, 1975; Johnson-Laird, 1983; Searle, 1983). The first is a general sense by which intentionality specifies goal-directed behaviour. The second is a more theoretical sense by which intention and intentionality characterize that which pertains to meaning. While pertaining to meaning, or being invested with meaning, usually denotes entities that manifest aboutness, the epithets are not synonymous. In the present discussion, it is this sense of being invested with meaning that is indicated, and this sense of the term is distinct from both goal-directedness and aboutness. Following the practice employed in logic (cf. Montague grammars) and for lack of more options in the available vocabulary, I have chosen to refer to this sense with the term intension (with an 's') and its derivatives. Thus intensions in the present psychological sense are entities which are intrinsically semantic and, similarly, theoretical frameworks characterized as intensional are ones whose basic terms are of this kind. This sense of intension is distinct from that in the semantic-linguistic sense, for it need not be restricted to the domain of language. More important, the present terms with an 's' are distinct from the other senses usually employed in the psychological literature, which are indicated with a 't'. That such a distinction is indeed required is suggested by Searle's statement: 'What we want from the social sciences and what we get from the social sciences at their best are theories of pure and applied intentionality' (Searle, 1984, p. 85). Clearly, what Searle has in mind here is neither goal-directedness nor aboutness *per se*, but rather semanticity. Being in total accord with this statement, I would propose only that the final word should preferably be spelt as 'intensionality' to indicate the special, psychological sense I have outlined.

The critique of the representational view of mind

All the clarifications made above were positive in the sense that they specified the meanings of given terms. A negative clarification, however, is also in place. In arguing against the representational view of mind (or the postulation of representational structures) I am not denying the *existence* of cognitive structures and patterns of activity that exhibit some or all the characteristics listed above in conjunction with representations. Rather, what I am arguing is that representations cannot serve as the *basis* of cognitive modelling. Representations are not conceptually primary, they do not characterize what is generally the case, and they have neither procedural nor developmental primacy. Representational structures, if and when they exist, are thus the products of cognitive activity, not the basis for it (for further discussion see Shanon, 1988a).

The basic parameters
Lastly, let me define two terms pertaining to the typology to be

introduced in the next section. The typology is characterized as a space spanned by two parameters. The first parameter is locus: it specifies the domain to which psychological phenomenology is assumed to pertain. Classically, psychological phenomena are taken to be those that pertain to the internal domain. This domain pertains to individual agents; it is covert and is not amenable to direct public observation. Non-classical approaches, however, may discard this basic assumption. In such approaches, psychological phenomenology need not be confined to the hidden, inner states of individual agents. Rather, this phenomenology may pertain either to the external domain of the observable environment or to the interface between the behaving agent and that environment. In the typology to be presented here, these two loci will be referred to as *internal* and *external* respectively. It should be noted that the term locus need not necessarily specify a geometrically defined locale in which psychological activity takes places. Rather, the term specifies a domain with particular characteristics. The locus is internal when it exhibits the characteristics specified above;[3] it is external when it does not. In other words, the term 'external' is used here in a weak sense. Essentially, this term serves to mark a contrast with the internal, and should thus be interpreted as 'non-internal'.

The second parameter specifies what, according to the given conceptual frameworks, are the basic objects of psychology. *Ipso facto*, this parameter also concerns the basic terms of the conceptual framework in question. Since the two perspectives – that of level of discourse and that of domain of reality – are intertwined, the expressions 'basic terms' and 'basic objects' will both be used in the following discussion.

The next section presents the different conceptual frameworks in psychology. These are defined as the different pairings of a locus and one of four types of basic objects.

The typology of conceptual frameworks

The following survey starts with the presentation of frameworks whose locus is internal. The first to be considered will be representationalism, followed by four of its alternatives. Like representationalism, these alternative frameworks define the locus of psychology as internal. They differ from representationalism, however, and from each other, in terms of what they take as the basic objects of psychology. Later, four parallel external frameworks will be presented. The survey ends with a consideration of the paradigm representationalism had originally sought to replace – namely, behaviourism.

Internal frameworks

In terms of the parameters introduced above, *representationalism* is a framework whose locus is internal and whose basic terms or objects are symbolic representations in the strong sense defined above. It will be noted that in bringing about the cognitive revolution, both parameters were crucial. On the one hand, the cognitive approach advocates the modelling of psychological processes by means of symbolic representations and computational operations that apply on them. On the other, this approach stipulates that between the phenomenological level of folk psychology and that of the underlying neurophysiological substrate, there is another, autonomous level – the cognitive level. The main characteristic of this level is that it is both internal and mental. (For further theoretical discussion, see Chomsky, 1959; Fodor, 1968, 1975; Pylyshyn, 1984; for paradigmatic representational models, see Anderson and Bower, 1973; Newell, 1979; Newell and Simon, 1972; Schank, 1975).[4]

The first non-representational framework to be noted is *connectionism* (see Hinton and Anderson, 1981; McClelland and Rumelhart, 1986; Rumelhart and McClelland, 1986). The framework is non-representational in that it does not stipulate the existence of underlying symbolic representations. Rather, it assumes that the substrate of cognitive activity is a large neural-like associative network. Likewise, the operations employed in connectionist models are not ones of symbol manipulation, but rather parallel, distributed patterns of activation in the network.

The objection may be made that connectionist models are representational, for, in fact, some of their proponents characterize their own models as such (e.g. Smolensky, 1988; Rumelhart and McClelland, 1986; McClelland, 1988; see also Fodor and Pylyshyn, 1988). What is at stake, I think, is a confusion between the weak and strong senses of the term 'representational'. Connectionist models are representational only in the weak sense, not in the strong sense which is the focus of discussion here.

Next to be noted are *action models*. This term denotes a rather heterogeneous class of models independently proposed in different quarters and for different reasons. What is common to all of them, however, is the view that cognition is rooted in action. According to this view, mental activity should be characterized in terms akin to those employed in the analysis of actual performance in the world. Rather than characterizing cognition as the manipulation of the symbols of the language of thought, the actional perspective characterizes cognition in terms of object manipulation, activities or skills.

Perhaps the best-known action model is Johnson-Laird's (1983) theory of mental models. Other such models include the programme proposed by Kolers and his associates (Kolers and Roediger, 1984; Kolers and Smythe, 1984), McNeill's framework for the study of language and gesture (McNeill, 1984; McNeill and Levy, 1982) and the non-standard genre of artificial intelligence suggested by Winograd and Flores (1986). An illuminating case study drawn along similar lines is presented by Sudnow (1979) for the description of creative typewriting and piano-playing. Phenomenological data which suggest that mentation is, at least at times, the acting out of behaviour in the theatre of one's mind are also noted in my own research on thought sequences, i.e. trains of verbal-like expressions that spontaneously pass through people's heads (see Shanon, 1988b, 1989a).

A third psychological perspective is the *intensional*. The epithet is employed here in the cognitive sense proposed in the first section of the discussion. At the heart of the intensional perspective is the view that the basic terms of psychology are – to use a phrase coined by Heidegger – laden with meaning. They are not contentless, formal structures. In essence, then, psychological research is the study of meanings, the forms in which they are expressed, their development and progress, their function and use. The statement I quoted in the previous section from Searle (1984) in conjunction with the definition of intention and intension summarizes this position. As noted, while I am in total agreement with the view presented by this statement, I would replace the term 'intentionality' with the term 'intensionality' in line with the definition of intension I introduced in the previous section.

At first glance, the attempt to set the intensional perspective apart as a distinctive framework may seem curious. Isn't meaning, by any account, the essence of cognition? After all, contemporary cognitive science of all persuasions is primarily concerned with semantic phenomena, semantic processing and structures and operations associated with them. Yet, in an essential sense, cognitive scientists generally shy away from the basic phenomenon of meaning: indeed, this, of course, is the *raison d'être* for the distinction between the vertical and horizontal perspectives introduced at the outset of the present discussion. Contemporary cognitive scientists study how meaning is represented, how meaning is processed, but not the matrix of meaning itself. As Searle pointed out (1980), meaning is universally taken for granted, but it is not accounted for. In principle, the representational-computational view of mind cannot account for reference, a notion that from its very own perspective is perhaps the most basic of all. With this inability to escape the confines of its own domain and reach the world, cognitive psychology assumes a principled 'methodological solipsism' (cf. Fodor, 1980; see also Putnam, 1981; Winograd, 1978). But representational psychology also avoids the phenomenon of meaning in yet another respect: its modelling of cognition is syntactic. In other words, it assumes that the processing of information is conducted by virtue of the formal-structural properties of the information in question, not its content. Such an approach to semantic phenomena is essentially non-semantic (for criticism see Searle, 1983; cf. Stich, 1983).

The paradigmatic intensional models (as this perspective is defined here) are some of the major works of phenomenological philosophy. The conviction that psychological investigation cannot divorce itself from meaning and that psychological terms are – as indicated by Heidegger (1962) – laden with meaning is fundamental in the existential philosophy and the phenomenology of Merleau-Ponty (1962).[5] Specifically, it is observed that the world that human beings perceive and in which they live and act is not constituted by naked sense-data or things. Rather, it is a world invested with meaning. How this meaning comes into being, the nature of the patterns by which it is realized, how it governs one's being and acting in the world – these are some of the key issues of the philosophical studies in question.

Lastly, one may follow a *phenomenological* approach. While in the philosophical literature this term normally denotes investigations of the type here referred to as intensional, I am using the term in a stricter, rather radical sense. The approach presently labelled phenomenological focuses not on the substrate of behaviour but on its manifest expressions. My usage of the term 'phenomenological' is consistent with the following definition presented by the *Encyclopaedia Britannica*:

> 'Phenomenology' is, in the 20th century, mainly the name for a philosophical movement whose primary objective is the direct investigation and description of phenomena as consciously experienced, without theories about their causal explanation and as free as possible from unexamined preconceptions and presuppositions. (Spiegelberg, 1975 p. 3)

The phenomenological approach is radical because it is not representational, computational or procedural. In other words, it focuses not on the substrate of behaviour but on its manifest expressions. Because of this, the phenomenological approach relinquishes the goal of specifying underlying structures and the behaviour-generation mechanisms associated with them. At first sight, this might seem to be tantamount to the total abandonment of the quest for theory. I think not. Not to pursue a procedural theory does not mean to pursue no theory at all. What is entailed, however, is the need for the definition of entirely new questions for psychological research as well as a new methodological basis for psychological investigation and analysis. I shall return to this point towards the end of this chapter.

External frameworks

A procedural, weakly computational, external non-representational framework is presented by the *ecological school of Gibson* (1966, 1979) and his followers (see, for example, Turvey and Shaw, 1979; Turvey, Shaw, Reed and Mace, 1981). As will be noted below, this particular facet of ecological psychology needs to be contrasted with another facet of that school. While in the writings of Gibson and his followers the two facets are presented together and no explicit distinction is made between them, it seems to me that the two are distinct (for a recent, independent discussion that can be read as sharing the same view, see Heft, 1989). I would like to suggest that they occupy two markedly different slots in the present typology. The variant constituting the external procedural type is that which sets out to define visual perception as the detection of invariants in the optical array. The locus of perception is not within the mind but in the outside world. All relevant information is assumed to be out there, and the organism has to pick it up, not to detect it and then process and interpret it. In this particular variant of ecological psychology, the modelling is highly mathematical: the environment is defined in terms of gradients of flow, and the behaviour of the organism is analogous to that of moving bodies as characterized in fluid dynamics (cf. Carello, Turvey, Kugler and Shaw, 1984). Like the neo-connectionist models, models of this kind are neither symbolic (the substrates to which they apply are not symbols) nor computational (in the weak non-representational sense). Like the neo-connectionist models, these models employ tools that are unusual for the standard psychologist, and their terminology and means of analysis are often not psychological.

As their name indicates, *external action models* stipulate, on the one hand, that cognition is rooted in action and, on the other, that its locus is in the external environment, be it biological or social-cultural. The clearest example of the external actional perspective is the Marxist-based work of Vygotsky (1978, 1986) and his followers in the Soviet school of activity theory (Kozulin, 1986; Leontiev, 1978; Wertsch, 1981; see also Scribner, 1986). In the English-speaking world the external actional perspective may be traced to the work of George Herbert Mead (1938). Contemporary followers of this perspective are students of social cognition (Forgas, 1982, 1983). Unlike cognitive social psychologists who have attempted to extend the information-processing paradigm from the realm of individual, mental behaviour to the realm of interpersonal, social behaviour, the followers of this approach take the converse perspective and regard cognition as an extension of one's behaviour in the public, social domain. An example is Harré's (*et al.*, 1985, 1987) characterization of memory as a collective process whose locus is the interpersonal interaction between people engaging in recollection. Indeed, as pointed out by Casey (1987), some acts of memory, such as reminiscing, take place only in the course of a social interaction.

There are also developmental models that follow the external actional perspective, and treat cognitive development as rooted in the child's activity in the world and his/her interpersonal interaction (see Bruner, 1977; Snow, 1979). Applied to language acquisition, this approach characterizes development as a progression from the pragmatic to the semantic, one which is achieved by a process of decontextualization (Bates, 1976, 1979; see also Bickhard, 1979).

Intensional models of the external type are encountered in the second variant of Gibsonian psychology. It is this facet of the theory that defines perception (and, by extension, other aspects of cognition) in terms of affordances, i.e. by the patterns of activity that an environment enables the agent to perform (Gibson, 1979; see also Shaw and Bransford, 1977; Shaw and McIntyre, 1974; Shaw, Turvey and Mace, 1982). Affordances such as 'edible', 'transversable', 'flyable', are neither properties of the behaving agent as such nor properties of the environment alone; rather, they are properties of the couplings of agent and environment (for a review, see Michaels and Carello, 1981). It is in this sense that I characterize them as external. The characterization of behaviour by reference to affordances is labelled intensional because its basic terms are patterns bestowed with meaning.

As indicated by the examples above, affordances couch meaning in action: the organism perceives and conceives the environment in terms of the activities that can potentially be accomplished in it. This actional aspect of affordances is neither accidental nor particular. External intensional models are prone to couch the basic meaningfulness of psychological terms in the interaction of the organism with the world. As such, these models would count as action models as well. On the other hand, action models – be they internal or external – need not necessarily be intentional. Likewise, internal intensional models need not be action models either.

Perhaps the clearest examples of intensional models in psychology are explanations based on narration (see Bruner, 1986; Gergen and Gergen,

250 Against Cognitivism

1983). Psychoanalytic models concerned with the dynamics of meanings may also be viewed as intensional (in particular, see Lacan, 1977). Other such models are encountered in the paradigm of ethnomethodology in sociology (Garfinkel, 1967) and in the interpretive study of culture (as in Geertz, 1973).[6] An extension of the intensional approach to the non-psychological domain can also be found in the paradigm of autopoiesis developed by Maturana and Varela (Maturana, 1978; Maturana and Varela, 1980; Varela, 1979). In this paradigm, life forms are defined not by their internal structure but by their dialectic interaction with the environment. Recently, philosophical analyses of meaning have been proposed which may be characterized as external and intensional; these include the works of Putnam (1975, 1988), situational semantics as developed by Barwise and Perry (1983), and hermeneutical investigations (e.g. Gadamer, 1976).

With regard to the phenomenological perspective, the difference between the internal and external domains is not of great importance. Since analyses pertaining to this perspective focus on the 'surface', it is not a critical issue whether the expressions under investigation are internal or external. Thought sequences, which have been mentioned above, are internal, and so are dreams. External expressions that may be investigated in the same manner include sequences of verbal discourse, spontaneous singing as well as artistic creations in word, visual form and sound. Currently, I am conducting research in which the method detailed above in conjunction with thought sequences is applied to such other domains (for some suggestions in this regard, see Shanon, 1989b).

Lastly, *behaviourism* is an external non-representational framework with a rather special stance regarding the choice of the basic objects of psychology. Specifically, behaviourism sets itself to construct a psychological theory whose basic entities are not psychological. This goal is based on the assumption that in order to be scientific, psychology has to be fully incorporated within the unified family of sciences. For this, behaviourism attempts to analyze behaviour in terms of entities that are directly observed in the external world (cf. Keller and Schoenfeld, 1950). While there are behaviouristic models incorporating seemingly internal mechanisms (e.g. mediating stimuli and responses), the difference between these models and the more radical behaviouristic ones is not critical. As Fodor (1965) has indicated, the former essentially converge to the latter. In effect, then, the behaviouristic framework is in essence external.[7]

From the point of view of the typology drawn here, behaviourism is special: it breaks a symmetry. All non-representational frameworks considered so far came in pairs: for according to the choice of basic

Alternative theoretical frameworks 251

objects for psychological research (or basic terms for psychological theory) there were two corresponding frameworks – one internal, the other external. Behaviourism, by contrast, skews the picture: it has no internal counterpart.

Yet a symmetry – or, rather, an anti-symmetry – may be defined. Just as behaviourism is an external perspective without an internal counterpart, the cognitive framework is essentially an internal framework without an external counterpart. Whereas behaviourism sets itself to model behaviour without postulating any specific psychological terms, cognitivism stipulates that in order to explain behaviour one has to postulate a level of analysis (and with it, a level of reality) which is psychological proper. Indeed, in arguing against behaviourism the cognitive approach did more than call for another, representational basis for psychological analysis and explanation. In postulating the representational basis, this approach also stipulated that between the neurophysiological level on the one hand, and the level of folk psychology on the other, there is yet another autonomous level, the level of the mental. Thus, just as behaviourism is essentially non-psychological, representationalism is essentially psychological. In terms of the present typology, it is a framework that stipulates that the locus of psychology is strictly internal and its basic object is symbols.

Thus, with the breaking of symmetry, there is yet another symmetry. Behaviourism and representationalism are both frameworks that apply to one locus only. As such, the two complement each other as the two extremes of the space of psychological frameworks. All other frameworks surveyed may be regarded as intermediate cases between these two extremes.

Summary

Let me summarize. The foregoing survey presented representationalism and nine non-representational theoretical frameworks for psychology. In terms of locus, the frameworks are either internal or external. In terms of what they stipulate as the basic objects of psychology, they differ according to whether these are symbolic representations, substrates for weak computation (be they neural-like networks or field gradients), actional patterns, entities laden with meaning, and structural patterns; the basic objects may also be stipulated to be non-psychological, as in behaviourism. By way of summary, the nine non-representational frameworks, along with representationalism, are presented in Table 13.1

As they vary in terms of the parameter of basic objects, the alternatives to representationalism may be further classified as follows. First, theoretical frameworks may differ with respect to the type of explanation

252 Against Cognitivism

Table 13.1 The typology of non-representational frameworks

Type	Locus	
	Internal	External
Symbolic	representationalism	—
Weakly computational	connectionism	ecological psychology I
Actional	mental models, mental skills	activity theory, social cognition
Intensional	existential philosophy, psychoanalysis	ecological psychology II, ethnomethodology, situational semantics, hermeneutics
Phenomenological	thought sequences	structural phenomenology
Physicalist	—	behaviourism

they set themselves to offer – be it procedural or not. Representationalism, the weakly computational models and at least some of the actional models are procedural; the intensional and phenomenological models and some of the actional models are not. Behaviourism is procedural in the sense that it sets itself to explain the mechanisms that generate behaviour; given the non-psychological character of this approach, however, these mechanisms are not underlying processes but forces in the external environment (stimuli and reinforcement schedules).

The procedural frameworks can be further divided according to whether the procedures they offer are symbol-based or not. Representationalism is, of course, of the former kind; the alternative frameworks are not. Likewise, the non-procedural frameworks can be further divided according to whether their primary focus is content or form. Intensional models are of the first kind; phenomenological models of the second.

General discussion and further ramifications

The psychological predicament

Having completed the survey of the various alternative theoretical frameworks in psychology, let us take a broader, somewhat speculative perspective. The internal structure exhibited by the typology presented

Alternative theoretical frameworks 253

here suggests that the variety of theoretical frameworks is perhaps not accidental. Indeed, it might be that the different frameworks constitute different answers to one problem, a problem that functions as a fundamental driving force for all psychological research. I shall refer to this problem as the *psychological predicament*. This predicament is defined by the combination of two basic features of scientific psychology. On the one hand, psychology is supposed to be concerned with the internal domain; on the other, psychological phenomena are characterized by being imbued with meaning. The pursuit of a scientific enterprise that brings these two features together is highly problematic. On the one hand, the internal domain is not publicly observable. On the other, the study of meaning presents a host of issues standardly associated with speculative philosophical investigation. Thus, the psychological predicament presents itself: a psychology which is genuinely psychological risks the danger of not being scientific.

The various theoretical frameworks we have surveyed may be regarded as different ways by which psychologists have (by and large unbeknownst to themselves) confronted the predicament in question. Given that the problem is generated by the coupling of the internal and the intensional, any solution requires a compromise with respect to one of these two parameters. The following discussion presents a characterization of the various frameworks from this perspective.

Consider representationalism. This is the internal framework *par excellence*. The internal domain is maintained, however, at a heavy price: the abandonment of intensionality. As already noted, even though symbols and representations are assumed to be the carriers of meaning, meaning as such is not accounted for by the representational framework. Almost all the other frameworks we have considered compromise with respect to the other parameter, that pertaining to the internal domain.

The compromise may be achieved along three lines, all of which involve some sort of *externalization*. The first is that of the externalization of locus. This is the line opted for by all the models characterized here as external. The second line is to keep the locus of psychology internal but to model it in terms akin to those encountered in the external world. This is the line adopted by the various actional models. The third line is to confine the psychological domain and limit it to the surface only. This is the line adopted by the phenomenological approach. The confinement of the phenomenological approach to the surface is twofold. On the one hand, the relevant psychological phenomena are confined only to those that can either be manifestly observed or are amenable to consciousness and thus reportable (as thought sequences are). On the other hand, psychological explanation is superficial in that it ceases to be procedural. More will be said on non-procedural explanation below.

254 Against Cognitivism

Whereas the basic terms of the representational framework are formal entities to which interpretation is imputed from outside the system, the basic terms of the actional, intensional and phenomenological models are, by one means or another, imbued with meaning. The terms of the actional models are invested with meaning in that action is the primary determinant of meaning as it is realized in human behaviour. The terms of the intensional models are by their very definition laden with meaning. The terms of the phenomenological models are assumed to be meaningful by virtue of their being the constituents of manifest human behaviour which, by its very nature, is meaningful.

The three lines of externalization cover all the frameworks we have considered except three – connectionism, behaviourism and the ecological framework of the weakly computational type. Connectionism does not opt for any sort of externalization. Like representationalism, it is an internal framework. However, unlike representationalism and most other frameworks we have considered, it is non-psychological. Specifically, the basic terms it employs are devoid of meaning. Indeed, these are terms drawn from domains other than psychology – mathematics, physics, neurophysiology. Whereas representationalism takes meaning as given, connectionism starts with a meaning-free system. It is assumed that meaning emerges somehow as a property of the network as a whole, but this is far from being a clear or settled issue (cf. Pinker and Prince, 1988). Unlike connectionism, the ecological framework of the weakly computational type is external but, again, its terms are devoid of meaning. Like connectionism, it is highly non-psychological.

As for behaviourism, it is the external paradigm *par excellence*, yet it is non-intensional. If representationalism takes meaning for granted, behaviourism denies it altogether. Thus, different as representationalism and behaviourism are, they manifest a fundamental similarity: both frameworks avoid meaning. Together, these comments indicate yet another sense of externalization – namely the drawing of psychological research outside psychology.

Genuinely psychological psychology

My characterization of some theoretical frameworks as not being genuinely psychological is definitely strong, and calls for further clarification and substantiation. What can be the basis for such a verdict? How can it be evaluated and justified? What is its point, and what are its possible ramifications?

First and foremost, there are pre-theoretical considerations. Socio-

Alternative theoretical frameworks 255

logically, disciplines are associated with distinct bodies of knowledge, particular methodological practices and their own paradigms of training and exercise. Surely, the professional practices and expertise one acquires in psychology are different from those one acquires in physics? Given this state of affairs, psychologists perusing the literature pertaining to the paradigms of connectionism and the ecological psychology of the weakly computational type may find themselves rather uneasy. Much of that literature draws on domains such as spin-glass physics, thermodynamics and fluid hydrodynamics (for paradigmatic examples in the two paradigms see, for instance, Hopfield, 1982, 1984; Carello, Turvey, Kugler and Shaw, 1984, respectively). Is the moral that psychologists should abandon their standard training and instead go and study physics? At the risk of being a professional chauvinist, I would venture to say that I hope the answer is no.

But could the sociological judgement (perhaps even prejudice) be given more theoretical substance? The following tentative comments are based on the view that the psychological constitutes a genuine ontological and scientific realm, one circumscribed by the domain to which meaning can be ascribed. Specifically, a phenomenon is psychological only in so far as it pertains to meaningful behaviour. As such, the psychological realm contrasts with the physical realm, which is circumscribed by the domain to which material composition can be specified, and with the organizational realm, which is circumscribed by the attribution of organizational or functional characterizations. Given this general view, several more specific criteria for the genuinely psychological may be thought of. Here are some suggestions:

1. That which is *laden with meaning*. By this criterion, genuinely psychological terms are terms which may be regarded as meaningful in themselves. Just as patterns of overt behaviour or the words of natural language are meaningful, so the basic terms of cognitive theory are expected to be meaningful. The *loci classici* of this perspective are the works of Heidegger (1962) and Merleau-Ponty (1962).

2. That which has *intensionality*. That intensionality is the distinctive quality of the psychological has been noted by several recent theoreticians, mostly of philosophical orientation; (these include Dennett, 1981; Putnam, 1988 and Searle, 1983 see also Double, 1986, Vellmer, 1986).

3. That which may be subject to *interpretation*. This criterion is substantially weaker than the two previous ones. It should be noted that an interpreted system requires an interpreter. If the interpreter is outside the psychological domain, then the usefulness of the criterion is very much reduced.

4. That which may be attributed to the *person*. By this criterion, the terms of psychology should be those that could be attributed to people. Note that neither symbol manipulation of the representational type nor associative activation of the connectionist type are attributable in this fashion. Suggestions along this line are noted in Bechtel (1987) and Margolis (1990).

5. That which exhibits the characteristic features of *human behaviour in toto*. This criterion is proposed in the spirit of Vygotsky's metapsychology. Vygotsky suggests that psychological explanation should be based not on a reduction to elements but rather on an analysis by units. Units are distinguished from elements in that they exhibit the characteristics of the wholes which they compose (see Vygotsky, 1986; Zinchenko, 1985).

6. That which is either *conscious* or *potentially conscious*. From the perspective of contemporary cognitive science, this suggestion may seem preposterous. Presumably, it has become commonplace knowledge that most human cognitive life is not amenable to consciousness (see, for instance, Nisbett and Wilson, 1977). Yet clearly, the conscious defines a domain which is uniquely psychological. A proposal that demarcates psychology in terms of the conscious is presented in a recent paper by Searle (Searle, 1990; see also Shanon, 1990b).

Remarkably, by practically all these criteria, neither connectionism nor representationalism is genuinely psychological (for further discussion, see Shanon, 1991).

Lest I be misunderstood, let me emphasize that in characterizing models as not being psychological, I am not disparaging them or claiming that they are not true. The models in question may very well turn out to be the most adequate ones for the modelling of the workings of the mind, yet this does not imply that they are psychological. The comments made here underlie the need to try at least to develop scientific psychology on genuinely psychological foundations.

Like all the alternative options we have surveyed, the enterprise of genuine psychological research may also involve a cost. If the underlying procedures that generate behaviour are non-psychological, and if a genuine psychological perspective is to be maintained, then perhaps procedural explanation in psychology should be abandoned. This option is radical. With it, psychology departs from the standard scientific tradition, developed in the natural sciences, which is concerned with the material composition of things and its change in time. Correspondingly, scientific theories define the mechanisms that generate their composition and govern the dynamics of their change. In attempting to attain the status of a fully fledged science, psychology has adopted this goal. In point of fact, the advent of representationalism played a significant role in this respect. By analogy with the specification of material *composition*, representational models specify the underlying structures of mind; likewise, by analogy with the specification of material *mechanisms*, representational models specify the computational operations that apply to these structures. In both cases explanation consists in the specification of the procedures that make things happen – in other words, in answering the question 'How?' as it pertains to the domain of interest. Remarkably, connectionism – the framework currently presented as the main alternative to representationalism – fully shares this goal and perspective.

The adoption of the non-procedural perspective calls for the definition of new avenues of psychological research. New questions have to be defined, new methods of investigation developed, new theories and new types of explanation devised. In a nutshell, rather than studying the underlying mechanisms of mind, psychology will study the structural constraints of cognitive expression, the meta-structures they generate, the dynamics of their progression in time, the functions they perform, the contextual dependencies associated with them, the course of their ontogenesis and the history of their evolution in cultures and societies. (For a concrete example of systematic non-procedural cognitive research, the reader is referred to Shanon, 1989a). Although the consideration of such prospects will be left for another occasion, my estimate is that rather than being impoverished, psychology may be very much enriched by this change of perspective.

Notes

1. The distinction between the vertical perspective in philosophy and the horizontal perspective in the cognitive sciences applies, *mutatis mutandis*, to other key terms such as 'semantics' and 'meaning'.
2. The phrase 'what may be regarded' specifies the perspective of an observer. From the perspective of the system itself, what may be taking place need not necessarily be regarded as a computational process. For instance, what actually takes place in the brain is the spreading of activation along networks of neurons. It is from the perspective of the analyzing scientists that these may be regarded as sequences of computation. Similar – although not identical – observations may be made in conjunction with connectionist networks.
3. While the characteristics in question usually go together, this need not always be the case. Consequently, several weaker senses of the attribute 'internal' may be noted. In the present discussion, the term is taken in the sense defined here.
4. It may be objected that the version of representationalism entertained here is strictly Fodorian and that it need not be shared by all cognitive psychologists

of the representational school. Given that most practising cognitive scientists are not explicit about their theoretical assumptions and philosophical stance, the verification of this statement is not straightforward, yet I do not think that the present characterization of representationalism is improper. First, Fodor – along with Pylyshyn, who shares the very same view of representationalism – is undoubtedly the most explicit and articulate of all representationalist psychologists. Theirs is the clearest statement of the theoretical position in the literature. Second, the present characterization of representationalism defines the essence of the framework in question. Specific representational models may differ in details and application, but the basic perspective is definitely not specifically Fodorian. Indeed, all the specific models cited above abide by all the characterizations made here. Third, given that the theoretical position is usually left unstated, I will not be surprised if, when pressed to be explicit and pushed to draw their position to its ultimate logical conclusions, most representational psychologists will find themselves agreeing with Fodor and Pylyshyn. This might be the case even if, on first sight, the investigators may balk at the Fodorian position as being too extreme. After all, Fodor is the first to have admitted that his position is, indeed, such; he just does not see any other possible alternative (cf. Fodor, 1975; Fodor and Pylyshyn, 1988).

5. The fact that works defining what is, from the perspective of the present survey, the very same position are usually referred to as either existential or phenomenological is symptomatic of classical philosophical terms not being directly applied in the contemporary cognitive-psychological context. In this chapter the term 'phenomenological' will always be employed in the sense to be defined in the next section.

6. The following view by Geertz (1973) is telling: 'The analysis of [culture] is to be . . . not an experimental science in search of laws but an interpretative one in search of meaning.'

7. The present characterization of behaviourism is, I am aware, somewhat simplistic. Behaviourism is not a monolithic school, and neo-behaviourism, especially as developed since the advent of the cognitive revolution, is remarkably sophisticated and not without mentalistic components (for a review, see Zuriff, 1985). The present characterization is, however, in line with characterizations of behaviourism as it is standardly perceived in contemporary cognitive science. For better or for worse, these are taken from the perspective of the dominant representational view. Given this (conceptually unjustified) sociological state of affairs, and since the representational perspective is the starting point of the present discussion, the perhaps stereotyped characterization of behaviourism is maintained here. Even if the actual situation in the terrain is more varied and more subtle, this stereotyped profile has an essential place in the space of possibilities which is the subject matter of the present discussion.

References

Anderson, J.R. and Bower, G.H. (1973), *Human Associative Memory*, Washington, DC: Winston.
Barwise, J. and Perry, J. (1983), *Situations and Attitudes*, Cambridge, MA: Harvard University Press.
Bates, E. (1976), *Language and Context*, New York: Academic Press.

Alternative theoretical frameworks 259

Bates, E. (1979), *The Emergence of Symbols*, New York: Academic Press.
Bechtel, W. (1987), 'Connectionism and the philosophy of mind: An overview', *The Southern Journal of Philosophy (Supplement)*, 17–41.
Bickhard, H.M. (1979), 'The social nature of the functional nature of language', in M. Hickman (ed.), *Social and Functional Approaches to Language and Thought*, New York: Academic Press, pp. 39–64.
Boden, M.A. (1975), 'Intentionality and physical systems', *Philosophy of Science*, **37**, 200–14.
Brentano, F. (1874/1973), *Psychology from an Empirical Standpoint*, (transl. A.N. Rancurello, D.B. Terrell and L.L. McAlister), London: Routledge & Kegan Paul.
Bruner, J.C. (1977), 'Early social interaction and language acquisition', in H.R. Schaffer (ed.), *Studies in Mother–Infant Interaction*, New York: Academic Press, pp. 271–89.
Bruner, J.C. (1986), *Actual Minds, Possible Worlds*, Cambridge, MA: Harvard University Press.
Carello, C., Turvey, M.T., Kugler, P.N. and Shaw, R.E. (1984), 'Inadequacies of the computer metaphor', in P. Gazzaniga (ed.), *Handbook of Cognitive Neuroscience*, New York: Plenum, pp. 229–48.
Carnap, R. (1947), *Meaning and Necessity*, Chicago: University of Chicago Press.
Casey, E.S. (1987), *Remembering: A phenomenological study*, Bloomington: Indiana University Press.
Chomsky, N. (1959), Review of B.F. Skinner's *Verbal Behavior*, *Language*, **35**, 26–58.
Costall, A.P. and Still, A.W. (eds) (1987), *Cognitive Psychology in Question*, Hemel Hempstead: Harvester Wheatsheaf.
Cresswell, M.J. (1973), *Logics and Languages*, London: Methuen.
Dennett, D. (1981), 'Intentional systems', ch. 1 in *Brainstorms*, Brighton: Harvester, pp. 3–22.
Double, R. (1986), 'On the very idea of eliminating the intentional', *Journal for the Theory of Social Behaviour*, **16**, 210–16.
Dreyfus, H. (1979), *What Computers Can't Do: A critique of artificial reason*, New York: Harper & Row.
Fodor, J.A. (1965), 'Could meaning be an r_m?', *Journal of Verbal Learning and Verbal Behavior*, **4**, 73–81.
Fodor, J.A. (1968), *Psychological Explanation*, Cambridge, MA: MIT.
Fodor, J.A. (1975), *The Language of Thought*, New York: Crowell.
Fodor, J.A. (1980), 'Methodological solipsism considered as a research strategy in cognitive psychology', *Behavioral and Brain Sciences*, **3**, 63–110.
Fodor, J.A. (1986), 'Information and association', in M. Brand and R.M. Harnish (eds), *The Representation of Knowledge and Belief*, Tucson, AZ: University of Arizona Press, pp. 80–100.
Fodor, J.A. and Pylyshyn, Z. (1988), 'Connectionism and cognitive architecture: A critical analysis', *Cognition*, **28**, 3–71.
Forgas, J.P. (ed.) (1982), *Social Cognition*, London: Academic Press and European Association of Experimental Psychology.
Forgas, J.P. (1983), 'What is social about social cognition?', *British Journal of Social Psychology*, **22**, 129–44.
Freud, S. (1900), *The Interpretation of Dreams*, London: George Allen & Unwin.

Gadamer, H.-G. (1975), *Truth and Method*. New York: Seabury Press.
Gadamer, H.-G. (1976), *Philosophical Hermeneutics*, Berkeley, CA: University of California Press.
Garfinkel, H. (1967), *Studies in Ethnomethodology*, Englewood Cliffs, NJ: Prentice-Hall.
Geertz, C. (1973), *The Interpretation of Cultures*, New York: Basic Books.
Gergen, K.J. and Gergen, M.M. (1983), 'Narratives of the self', in T.R. Sarbin and K.E. Scheibe (eds), *Studies in Social Identity*, New York: Praeger, pp. 254–73.
Gibson, J.J. (1966), *The Senses Considered as Perceptual Systems*, Boston, MA: Houghton Mifflin.
Gibson, J.J. (1979), *The Ecological Approach to Visual Perception*, Boston, MA: Houghton Mifflin.
Harré, R. (1987), 'Enlarging the paradigm', *New Ideas in Psychology*, **5**, 3–12.
Harré, R., Clarke, D. and De Carlo, N. (1985), *Motives and Mechanisms*, London: Methuen.
Haugeland, J. (1978), 'The nature and plausibility of representationalism', *Behavioral and Brain Sciences*, **1**, 215–60.
Heft, H. (1989), 'Affordances and the body: An intentional analysis of Gibson's ecological approach to visual perception', *Journal for the Theory of Social Behaviour*, **19**, 1–30.
Heidegger, M. (1962), *Being and Time*, New York: Harper & Row.
Hinton, G.E. and Anderson, J.A. (1981), *Parallel Models of Associative Memory*, Hillsdale, NJ: Erlbaum.
Hopfield, J.J. (1982), 'Neural networks and physical systems with emergent collective computational abilities', *Proceedings of the National Academy of Science, USA*, **79**, 2554–8.
Hopfield, J.J. (1984), 'Neurons with graded response have collective computational properties like those of two state neurons', *Proceedings of the National Academy of Sciences, USA*, **81**, 3088–92.
Johnson-Laird, P.N. (1983), *Mental Models*, Cambridge, MA: Harvard University Press.
Jung, C.G. (ed.) (1964), *Man and His Symbols*, London: Aldus Books.
Keller, F.S. and Schoenfeld, W.N. (1950), *Principles of Psychology*, New York: Appleton-Century-Crofts.
Kolers, P.A. and Roediger, H.L. (1984), 'Procedures of mind', *Journal of Verbal Learning and Verbal Behavior*, **23**, 425–49.
Kolers, P.A. and Smythe, W.E. (1984), 'Symbol manipulation: Alternatives to the computation view of mind', *Journal of Verbal Learning and Verbal Behavior*, **23**, 289–314.
Kozulin, A. (1986), 'The concept of activity in Soviet psychology', *American Psychologist*, **41**, 264–74.
Kugler, P. and Shaw, R. (1991), 'Symmetry and symmetry-breaking in thermodynamic and epistemic engines: A coupling of the first and second laws', in H. Haken (ed.), *Synergetics of Cognition*, Heidelberg: Springer Verlag.
Lacan, J. (1977), *Ecrits: A selection* (transl. Alan Sheridan), London: Tavistock.
Langer, S. (1942), *Philosophy in a New Key*, Cambridge, MA: Harvard University Press.
Leontiev, A.N. (1978), *Activity, Consciousness and Personality*, Englewood Cliffs, NJ: Prentice-Hall.
McClelland, J.L. (1988), 'Connectionist models and psychological evidence', *Journal of Memory and Language*, **27**, 107–23.

McClelland, J.L. and Rumelhart, D.E. (eds) (1986), *Parallel Distributed Processing: Explorations in the microstructure of cognition*, vol. 2, Cambridge, MA: MIT.
McNeill, D. (1987), *Psycholinguistics: A new approach*, New York: Harper & Row.
McNeill, D. and Levy, E. (1982), 'Conceptual representations in language activity and gesture', in R. Jarvella and W. Klein (eds), *Speech, Place and Action: Studies in deixis and related topics*, Chichester: Wiley, pp. 271–95.
Marcel, A.J. (1988), 'Phenomenal experience and functionalism', in A.J. Marcel and E. Bisiach (eds), *Consciousness in Contemporary Science*, Cambridge: Cambridge University Press, pp. 121–58.
Margolis, J. (1990), 'Explicating actions', in D.N. Robinson and L.P. Mos (eds), *Annals of Theoretical Psychology*, vol. 6, New York: Plenum, pp. 39–74.
Maturana, H.R. (1978), 'Biology of language: The epistemology of reality', in G.A. Miller and E. Lenneberg (eds), *Psychology and Biology of Language and Thought*, New York: Academic Press, pp. 27–64.
Maturana, H.R. and Varela, F.J. (1980), *Autopoiesis and Cognition*, Dordrecht: D. Reidel.
Mead, G.H. (1938), *The Philosophy of the Act*, Chicago: Chicago University Press.
Merleau-Ponty, M. (1962), *The Phenomenology of Perception*, London: Routledge & Kegan Paul.
Michaels, C.F. and Carello, C. (1981), *Direct Perception*, Englewood Cliffs, NJ: Prentice-Hall.
Montague, R. (1974), *Formal Philosophy*, New Haven, CT: Yale University Press.
Newell, A. (1979), 'Physical symbol systems', in D.A. Norman (ed.), *Perspectives on Cognitive Science*, Norwood, NJ: Ablex, pp. 37–86.
Newell, A. and Simon H.A. (1972), *Human Problem Solving*, Englewood Cliffs, NJ: Prentice-Hall.
Nisbett, R.E. and Wilson, T.D. (1977), 'Telling more than we can know: Verbal reports on mental processes', *Psychological Review*, **84**, 231–50.
Pinker, S. and Prince, A. (1988), 'On language and connectionism: Analysis of a parallel distributed processing model of language acquisition', *Cognition*, **28**, 73–193.
Putnam, H. (1975), 'The meaning of meaning', in *Mind, Language and Reality: Philosophical papers*, vol. 2, Cambridge: Cambridge University Press, pp. 215–71.
Putnam, H. (1981), *Reason, Truth and History*, Cambridge: Cambridge University Press.
Putnam, H. (1988), *Representation and Reality*, Cambridge, MA: MIT.
Pylyshyn, Z.W. (1984), *Computation and Cognition*, Cambridge, MA: MIT.
Reik, T. (1948), *Listening with the Third Ear*, New York: Farrar, Straus.
Rumelhart, D.E. and McClelland, J.L. (eds) (1986), *Parallel Distributed Processing: Explorations in the microstructure of cognition*, vol. 1, Cambridge, MA: MIT.
Schank, R.C. (1975), 'The role of memory in language processing', in C.N. Cofer (ed.), *The Structure of Human Memory*, San Francisco: Freeman, pp. 162–89.
Scribner, S. (1986), 'Thinking in action: Some characteristics of practical thought', in R.J. Sternberg and R.C. Wagner (eds), *Practical Intelligence*, Cambridge: Cambridge University Press.

Searle, J.R. (1980), 'Minds, brains, and programs', *Behavioral and Brain Sciences*, **3**, 417–57.
Searle, J.R. (1983), *Intentionality: An essay in the philosophy of mind*, Cambridge: Cambridge University Press.
Searle, J.R. (1984), *Minds, Brains and Science*, Cambridge: Cambridge University Press.
Searle, J.R. (1990), 'Consciousness, explanatory inversion and cognitive science', *Behavioral and Brain Sciences*, **13**, 585–96.
Shanon, B. (1984), 'The case for introspection', *Cognition and Brain Theory*, **7**, 167–80.
Shanon, B. (1987), 'The role of representations in cognition', in J. Bishop, J. Lockheed and D.N. Perkins (eds), *Thinking*, Hillsdale, NJ: Erlbaum, pp. 33–49.
Shanon, B. (1988a), 'Semantic representation of meaning: A critique', *Psychological Bulletin*, **104**, 70–83.
Shanon, B. (1988b), 'The channels of thought', *Discourse Processes*, **11**, 221–42.
Shanon, B. (1989a), 'Thought sequences', *The European Journal for Cognitive Psychology*, **1**, 129–59.
Shanon, B. (1989b), 'Why do we (sometimes) think in words?' in K. Gilhooly, M. Keane, R. Logie and C. Erdoc (eds), *Lines of Thought: Reflections in the psychology of thinking*, New York: Wiley, pp. 5–14.
Shanon, B. (1990a), 'Non-representational frameworks for psychology: a typology?, *European Journal of Cognitive Psychology*, **2**, 1–22.
Shanon, B. (1990b), 'What next? Ramifications for empirical psychology', unpublished manuscript, Hebrew University of Jerusalem.
Shanon, B. (1992) (forthcoming), *Representation and Presentation*.
Shanon, B. and Atlan, H. (forthcoming), 'Von Foerster's theorem or connectedness and organization: Semantic applications', *New Ideas in Psychology*.
Shaw, R.E. and Bransford, J. (1977), 'Introduction: Psychological approaches to the problem of knowledge', in R.E. Shaw and J. Bransford (eds), *Perceiving, Acting and Knowing*, Hillsdale, NJ: Erlbaum.
Shaw, R.E. and Kinchella-Shaw, J. (1989), 'Ecological mechanics: Laws scale to intentional systems', *Journal for the Study of Human Motion*, **1**, 156–200.
Shaw, R.E. and McIntyre, M. (1974), 'Algoristic foundations to cognitive psychology', in W. Weimer and D. Palermo (eds), *Cognition and the Symbolic Processes*, Hillsdale, NJ: Erlbaum, pp. 305–62.
Shaw, R.E. and Turvey, M.T. (1980), 'Methodological realism', *Behavioral and Brain Sciences*, **3**, 94–7.
Shaw, R.E., Turvey, M.T. and Mace, W. (1982), 'Ecological psychology: The consequence of a commitment to realism', in W. Weimer and D. Palermo (eds), *Cognition and the Symbolic Processes II*, Hillsdale, NJ: Erlbaum, pp. 159–226.
Smolensky, P. (1988), 'On the proper treatment of connectionism', *Behavioral and Brain Sciences*, **11**, 1–74.
Snow, C.E. (1979), 'The role of social interaction in language acquisition', in A. Collins (ed.), *Children's Language and Communication: Proceedings of the 1977 Minnesota Symposium on Child Development*, Hillsdale, NJ: Erlbaum, pp. 157–82.
Spiegelberg, H. (1975), *Doing Phenomenology: Essays on and in phenomenology*, The Hague: Martinus Nijhoff.
Stich, S.P. (1983), *From Folk Psychology to Cognitive Science*, Cambridge, MA: MIT.

Sudnow, D. (1979), *A Meditation between Two Keyboards*, New York: Knopf.
Thomason, R.H. (ed.) (1974), *Formal Philosophy: Selected papers of Richard Montague*, New Haven, CT: Yale University Press.
Turvey, M.T. and Shaw, R. (1979), 'The primacy of perceiving: An ecological reformulation of perception for understanding memory', in L.R. Nilson (ed.), *Perspectives on Memory Research: Essays in honor of Uppsala University's 500th anniversary*, Hillsdale, NJ: Erlbaum, pp. 185–210.
Turvey, M.T., Shaw, R.E., Reed, E.S. and Mace, W.M. (1981), 'Ecological laws of perceiving and acting: In reply to Fodor and Pylyshyn', *Cognition*, 3, 237–304.
Varela, F.J. (1979), *Principles of Biological Autonomy*, New York: North-Holland.
Vellmer, F. (1986), 'Intentional explanation and its place in psychology', *Journal for the Theory of Social Behaviour*, 16, 285–98.
Vygotsky, L.S. (1978), *Mind in Society*, Cambridge, MA: Harvard University Press.
Vygotsky, L. (1986), *Thought and Language*, Cambridge, MA: MIT.
Wertsch, J. (1981), *The Concept of Activity in Soviet Psychology*, New York: Sharpe.
Winograd, T. (1975), 'Frame representations and the declarative/procedural controversy', in D. Bobrow and A. Collins (eds), *Representations and Understanding: Studies in Cognitive Science*, New York: Academic Press.
Winograd, T. (1978), 'On primitive prototypes, and other semantic anomalies', in T. Winograd (ed.), *TINLAP-2: Theoretical issues in natural language understanding*, Ill: University of Illinois Press.
Winograd, T. and Flores, C.F. (1986), *Understanding Computers and Cognition*, Norwood, NJ: Ablex.
Wittgenstein, L. (1922), *Tractatus Logico-Philosophicus*, London: Routledge & Kegan Paul.
Zinchencko, V.P. (1985), 'Vygotsky's ideas about units for the analysis of mind', in J.V. Wertsch (ed.), *Culture, Communication and Cognition*, Cambridge: Cambridge University Press, pp. 94–118.
Zuriff, G.E. (1985), *Behaviorism: A conceptual reconstruction*, New York: Columbia University Press.

Index

abstraction, 8, 91, 103–4, 109, 112, 119
action, 57, 134–5
 vs. behaviour, 132–3
 external action models, 248–9
 internal action models, 245–6
 rule-based explanation of, 174
 situated action, 69
affordances, 171–2, 188–9, 204–10, 215–18, 230, 249
 social 207–10, 216–17
agency *see* action
Alexander, F.M., 30, 35–6
anthropology, 40, 45–7, 52
applied research, 44, 113, 115
Aristotle, 127
associationism, 14–15, 19, 128, 176

Baars, B.J., 3
Bartlett, F.C., 39–52, 152
 effort after meaning, 51 n4
behaviour,
 as action, not 'response', 132–3
 basic principles, 139
 direct behaviour, 138
 radical ambiguity of the term, 31, 237–8
behaviour analysis, 124–43
behaviourism, 49, 52 n7, 105, 126–31, 152, 175, 237, 250, 254, 258 n7
 as contextualism, 126
 and control, 130–1
 history of, 127–31
 subjective behaviourism, 152
 and subjectivity, 130
Ben-Zeev, A., 201, 227
Bickhard, M.H., 2, 156, 249
Billig, M., 56–9, 68, 72
Boden, M., 61, 106, 242
Bolton, N., 103–20
Brentano, F., 242
Broadbent, D.E., 45, 117, 154
Bruner, J., 2, 86, 249

Cartesian dualism *see* Descartes, R.; dualism
Casey, E.S., 39, 249
causation, 136
Chomsky, N., 83, 85, 96–7, 164 n2, 174, 183, 245

265

cognition
  direct and indirect, 177–87
  distributed, 140–1, 163
  a problem, not a solution,
    140–1, 154
  process vs. content, 139–41
  as social, 44–51, 57
cognitive development, 89–90, 91
cognitive revolution, 3, 42, 57, 61,
  75, 152, 173–5
cognitive science, 153
cognitivism, 2, 4, 7–8, 29, 32,
  34–5, 57, 151
  an abstraction, 104, 109
  vs. cognitive psychology, 4–5,
    192–3
  as false phenomenology, 105,
    107–6
  industrial and military funding,
    56, 163–4
  scope, 1, 104, 159
  as stimulus-response
    psychology, 128, 142, 151–2,
    162–3, 174–5
Coleridge, S.T., 7, 13–15, 23 n14
Collingwood, R.G., 49
computer models, 45, 58, 105–6,
  119–20, 123, 151
  analogy with bureacracies, 67
  as metaphors, 152–163
  information flow, 153–4
  rule-governed trans-
    formations, 154–6
  software vs. hardware
  unconscious inference, 156–7
  see also parallel distributed
    processing
concepts, 85, 90–1, 96–8
  acquisition, 91
  and pre-reflective intelligence,
    109
  primitive concepts, 85, 88

connectionism *see* parallel
  distributed processing
consciousness, 1, 107, 256
contextualism, 124–6
Costall, A.P., 1–6, 39–51, 138,
  151–65, 201, 225–35
Coulter, J., 2, 55, 57
cultural psychology, 44–5
culture
  vs. nature, 192, 230–4

Darwinism, 16
  vs. Neo-Darwinism, 82, 94–6
  see also evolutionism
Day, W.F., 125–31
Dennett, D., 61–6, 155–6, 255
Descartes, R., 7, 10–15, 82, 84,
  109, 127, 171, 227
development, 2, 83, 88–9, 162
Dewey, J., 27–30, 129–30, 134,
  142, 201, 210–12
  on the reflex arc, 27, 211
direct perception *see* ecological
  psychology; Gibson, J.J.;
  perception
Dreyfus, H., 2, 68, 164 n4, 238
dualism, 7–8, 27, 109, 118, 201,
  226
  of software and hardware, 157–8,
  162

ecological optics, 202–3, 205
ecological psychology, 21, 171–93,
  199–219, 248
  see also cognition; perception
ecological validity, 44
Edwards, D., 39, 44–5, 50, 230
empirical psychology, 119
environment *see* mutualism
evolutionary epistemology, 94
evolutionism, 90
  see also Darwinism

first-person status, 72
Fodor, J.A., 2, 61, 83, 85, 157, 172, 182, 192, 226, 240–1, 245, 247, 250–1, 256 n4
frame problem, 2
functionalism *see* Dewey J.; James, W.; structuralism

Gardner, H., 1, 3, 43, 151
Gergen, K.J., 9, 55, 75, 230, 249
Gibson, J.J., 2, 133, 136, 138, 171–93, 199–219, 227–35, 248–9
Giorgi, A., 107, 130
Goody, J., 190, 231

Habermas, J., 114–15
habit, 31–6
Hamlyn, D.W., 2, 204, 214
Harré, R., 57, 249
Haugeland, J., 2, 126, 238
Heft, H., 215, 248
Hegel, G., 81, 90–6
Heidegger, M., 12, 108, 118, 247, 255
higher mental processes, 43, 182
Hume's problem, 61–3, 75 n6
Husserl, E., 103, 107–8, 110, 113

imagination, 112
information processing, 58, 109, 153–4
intellectualism, 19, 111, 118
intensionality, 242–3, 253, 255
 intensional models of the internal type, 246–7
 intensional models of the external type, 249–50
intentionality, 75–6, 107–9, 127–8, 155–6, 242–3
 and care, 111
 type intentionalism, 65
internalization, 190, 232–3

James, W., 7, 16–21, 226
 and functionalism, 127, 129
 knowledge by acquaintance, 22 n6
 stream of thought and 'the vague', 17–21
Johnson-Laird, P.N., 2, 13, 61, 157, 174, 242, 246

Kant, I., 14, 187
Kantor, J.R., 127, 138, 141–2
Katz, S., 125, 199
Kelly, G.
 on human beings as scientists, 116
knowledge *see* cognition; perception
knowledge engineering, 65
tacit knowledge, 179

language, 7, 85, 161, 208–9
 acquisition, 183–6
 evolution, 188–9
 'ordinary' language, 134, 139
 predication, 186
 referential theory of, 9–10, 20, 55, 70, 75, 200
 and self-consciousness, 217–19
 see also Wittgenstein, L.
Lave, J., 21 n1, 51
Lee, V., 125–6, 128, 132, 139, 238
learning, 111, 162
linguistic relativity, 209
literacy, 190–2
Locke, J., 13–14, 86, 127–8

McClelland, J.L. 160–2, 245
MacMurray, J., 116
manipulation, 215
Marková, I., 81–99
Marxism, 229, 234
Mead, G.H., 130, 200–1, 206, 212–19, 230, 248

see also symbolic interactionism
meaning, 2, 43, 62, 156, 240, 246–7, 253
psychology as a science of meaning, 255–6
reduction to shape, 62
mechanism, 9, 19, 22, 56, 119, 126–7, 131, 142
mediated awareness see cognition
memory, 39, 43–4, 51, 125, 249
mental illness, 115
mentalism, 106, 124, 200
Merleau-Ponty, M., 103, 107–9, 117–18, 119, 238, 247, 255
metaphor, 120, 151–2
Middleton, D., 39, 44–5, 50, 230
Miller, G.A., 1, 154, 162, 164 n1
Mill, J.S., 15, 23 n14, 127
Mills, C.W., 69–70, 72
Mixon, D., 27–37
Morris, E.K., 123–43
mutualism, 28, 94–6, 98, 133–6, 163, 206, 213–15, 227, 235
  in Bartlett's early work, 49
  in behaviour analysis, 128
  and dialectical approach, 82
  in ecological psychology, 199, 202,
  in Skinner's psychology, 123

Neisser, U., 1, 43–4, 153, 200
neural networks see parallel distributed processing
Newell, A., 2, 153, 245
Noble, W., 199–219, 225
Norman, D.A., 1, 237

objectification, 200, 204, 212–16
organicism, 141–3

Palmer, A., 75 n6, 156
parallel distributed processing,
49–50, 151, 159–64, 238, 245, 254
graceful degradation, 162
Peirce, C.S., 130, 210
perception
  and cognition, 171, 173, 177, 225, 228
  as a constructive process, 107
  development, 175
  direct perception, 125, 177–9
  public, not private, 178, 219
  as social, 181, 209, 217, 228–32
phenomenology, 103, 105–20, 247–8, 253–4
  as absolute empiricism, 112
  descriptive phenomenology, 103, 105
  vs. empirical psychology, 119
  non-procedural explanation, 247
  as therapy, 113
Piaget, J., 94, 106, 109, 152, 212, 231, 233
Plato, 81
  theory of forms, 83
play, 118
Polanyi, M., 108, 201, 204
positivism, 129–30
pragmatism, 21, 130–1, 201
pre-reflective intelligence, 109
psychoanalysis, 114, 250
psychological predicament, 252–4
psychologism, 110, 118
Pylyshyn, Z., 155, 172, 245

Reed, E.S., 21, 157, 171–93, 209–10, 228, 231–3
representation systems, 172–3, 187–93, 231
representational theory of mind, 2, 61, 151, 163, 239–40, 243
  presupposes an interpreter, 62–3 75 n6, 155–6, 246–7

symbol-based accounts, 154, 160, 237–8, 245, 253
rhetoric, 55, 60, 67–9
Romanticism, 7, 13–21
Rommetveit, R., 92, 95–6
Rorty, R., 10
rules
   rule following, 27, 31–2, 34–5, 68–9, 161, 174
   rule-governed behaviour, 124
Rumelhart, D.E., 49–50, 160, 245
Runeson, S., 157
Russell, J., 157–8
Ryle, G., 27, 29, 125, 140

Sampson, E.E., 2, 59, 61
schema concept, 39, 45, 49, 161
   individual vs. group, 46–7
Searle, J., 2, 238, 240, 242–3, 246, 255–6
self
   co-perception of self and environment, 216
   self-consciousness, 72–3, 200
   see also social constructionism
semanticity *see* meaning; intensionality; intentionality
sensationalism, 19
Shanon, B., 2, 158, 237–57
Shotter, J., 22, 55–76, 156
skill, 29–37, 64
Skinner, B.F., 2, 123–5, 128, 130, 132, 137–8, 163, 174, 219 n1
social constructionism, 21, 55, 57, 81, 124, 230
   and the self, 72–3
   social accountability thesis, 58–9, 67, 69–74
social psychology, 10, 13, 29, 46, 50
   and the ecological approach, 228

sociology, 9, 13
   relation to psychology, 48
solipsism, 2, 247
Spencer, H., 15–17, 19, 91
stereotyping, 181
Still, A.W., 1–26, 225–35
stimulus-response psychology, 27–8, 52 n7, 109, 123, 128, 142, 151–2, 162–3, 173, 176, 210–12
structuralism
   vs. functionalism, 128–9
subjectivism, 109–11
subjectivity, 72–3, 130, 200
symbolic interactionism, 200
symbolism, 114, 218–9

Taylorism, 63–6
transactionalism, 134, 212–3
Turing A., 156
   Turing test, 158–9
thinking, 1, 57, 152, 227, 250

unconscious processing, 156–7, 164 n4, 172
universals, 55, 81–99, 199
   ambiguity of the term, 86–90

Valsiner, J., 136, 234
Vico, G., 13
Vygotsky, L.S., 76, 91, 95–6, 114, 219, 225–6, 230–4, 248, 256
   see also internalization; zone of proximal development

Watson, J.B., 130
Weber, M., 66–7
Winograd, T., 2, 240, 242, 246–7
Wittgenstein, L., 12, 19–20, 55, 74–5, 125, 130, 139, 219, 234
Woolgar, S., 2, 163

zone of proximal development, 231